DESIGN-DRIVEN
INNOVATION

Changing the Rules of Competition by Radically Innovating What Things Mean

ROBERTO VERGANTI

Harvard Business Press | Boston, Massachusetts

Printed in the United States of America
13 12 11 10 09   5 4 3 2 1

All chapter-opening illustrations by Daniele Barillari.

Library of Congress Cataloging-in-Publication Data

Verganti, Roberto.
   Design-driven innovation : changing the rules of competition by radically innovating what things mean / Roberto Verganti.
      p. cm.
   ISBN 978-1-4221-2482-6 (hardcover : alk. paper)
   1. Technological innovations. 2. Industrial management. I. Title.
HC79.T4.V465 2009
658.5'14—dc22

                                                              2008051751

To Francesca,
the meaning of my life

[Contents]

Part Two

The Process of Design-Driven Innovation

Part Three

Building Design-Driven Capabilities

A marketing manager for Apple described its market research as consisting of "Steve looking in the mirror every morning and asking himself what he wanted." That is the mirror of an executive's *personal culture*. Culture is one of the most precious gifts of humanity. Everyone has it. You should be not afraid of that mirror but, rather, leverage it, and see there things that others do not. [IN THE ILLUSTRATION Apple's MacBook Air.]

This is not a book on design, at least not in the way many people think of design: it is not about styling, or about creativity, or about scrutinizing users.

This is a book on management. It's about how to manage innovations that customers do not expect but that they eventually love. It shows how executives can realize an innovation strategy that leads to products and services that have a radical new meaning: those that convey a completely new reason for customers to buy them. Their meanings are so distinct from those that dominate the market that they might take people by surprise, but they are so inevitable that they convert people and make them passionate.

This strategy is called *design-driven innovation* because design, in its etymological essence, means "making sense of things."[1] And design-driven innovation is the R&D process for meanings. This book shows how companies can manage this process to radically overturn dominant meanings in an industry before their competitors do and therefore rule the competition.

The framework illustrated in the following chapters comes from ten years of research. There you will find the practical content and the evidence. Here, however, I want to step outside the flow of the argument, just for a moment, and talk more intimately about what I feel my findings imply for you as a person and as an executive (or a designer). This is my personal letter to the reader.

Managers Are People Before Being Managers

A marketing manager for Apple described its market research as consisting of "Steve looking in the mirror every morning and asking himself what he wanted."[2] This claim seems preposterous and illogical—almost blasphemous. It contradicts popular theories of user-centered innovation. We have been bombarded by analysts saying that companies should get a big lens and peruse customers to understand their needs.

The framework provided in this book shows that even if a company does not get close to users, even if it apparently does not look at the market, it can be much more insightful about what people *could* want. That mirror in which Steve Jobs metaphorically looks at himself is not a magic gizmo that delivers soothsayings: it is the mirror of an executive's *personal culture*. It reflects his own vision about why people do things, about how values, norms, beliefs, and aspirations could evolve, and also about how they *should* evolve. It is a culture built from years of immersion in social explorations, experiments, and relationships in both private and corporate settings.

Every executive has her own personal culture, her own vision of the evolution of the context of life in which her products and services will be used. Every person relentlessly builds her culture, often implicitly, by simply being immersed in society and through the individual explorations of life. Executives do not need to be experts in cultural anthropology or pretend to be like gurus or evangelists. Culture is one of the most precious gifts of humanity. Everyone has it.

Often, however, this gift remains unharnessed. Management theories do not help us unleash it. Rather, they often suggest that people hide it. The innovation tools, analytical screening models, and codified processes that experts recommend are typically culturally neutral or even culture averse. When innovation is purely technical (such as when it optimizes an existing feature), these methods may work well. However, when a firm wants to radically innovate the meaning of products and propose new reasons why people could buy things, these culturally neutral methods fail miserably.

In this book you will see how companies have transformed breakthrough ideas into acclaimed business successes right after other firms dropped them as uninteresting or outlandish. My question is, Why do some executives recognize the stunning business value of breakthrough proposals better than others? How can you prepare yourself to create and recognize these opportunities?

The answer, in terms of management practice, is in the following chapters. However, a more subtle notion underlies these accounts. Many of the executives you will meet reveal an interesting combination of two personal characteristics: a belief that culture is an essential part of everyday life (and therefore of business) and a significant unawareness of established management theories.

That is definitely true of, for example, Steve Jobs. But it is also true of the Italian entrepreneurs I discuss. In Italy, primary and secondary education have been sharply focused on the humanities, making culture an essential part of the personality of entrepreneurs. Management sciences, in contrast, have developed much more slowly in Italy than in other countries (almost none of these entrepreneurs has an MBA). These managers somehow did not come in contact with what prevented other executives from leveraging their cultural assets. This does not mean that these leaders did not fulfill their role as executives. Simply, their management practice was completely different from existing theories.

This book shows that you can direct your personal culture—your treasure, and the treasure of colleagues both inside and outside your firm—toward the creation of economic value. If properly nurtured and shared, this asset can become an integral part of your being a business leader. I hope this book will help you to be unafraid of looking into the mirror to leverage your personal culture, seeing there things that others do not. Not because you are creative. Not because you are a guru. Because you are a business*person*.

Designers Are People Before Being Designers

This is not a book on design. But I hope designers will appreciate it, because it unveils one of the forgotten angles of their contribution to business and society.

When executives think about design and designers, they usually have two perspectives. The first—the traditional—one is styling: they ask designers to make products look beautiful. The second—more recent—one is user-centered design. Designers have an amazing capacity to get close to users, understand their needs, and then creatively generate countless ideas. First styling and then user-centered design have been portrayed as vehicles by which companies differentiate themselves from the competition. Design, many analysts say, makes a difference.

And indeed this message has hit the target. No company would dare release a product without caring about its style and attentively analyzing user needs. Design is in its heyday, even more in this period of economic turmoil.

Yet, as always, success brings greater challenges. As these practices diffuse to every company, they are losing their power to differentiate. They are mandatory and not distinctive. Curiously, the same argument that has been used to promote design is now turning against it.

This phenomenon in business is not novel. It happened twenty years ago with total quality management. In the late 1980s, firms considered quality a top priority: the highest-quality performers were succeeding, and every company adopted TQM principles, each had a manager responsible for quality, each had six sigma or control charts. Two decades later, quality is no longer among the top corporate priorities. It is mandatory, of course, and each firm still has quality managers, but quality is not considered a strategic differentiator.

However, designers sometimes forget, or have been told to forget, a third angle involved in innovation. Some firms—although they use styling and user-centered design for incremental projects—look for a different type of expertise when it comes to radical projects: *radical researchers*. These are experts who envision and investigate new product meanings through a broader, in-depth exploration of the evolution of society, culture, and technology. These experts, who pursue R&D on meanings, may be managers of other companies, scholars, technology suppliers, scientists, artists, and, of course, designers. Curiously, however, designers have recently been moving in a different direction.

In presenting design as a codified, predictable, and mandatory process—making it more digestible for executives educated in traditional management theories—designers risk losing their ability to do such forward-looking research. They have enjoyed being epitomized as the quintessential creative people. But creativity has little in common with research. Creativity entails the fast generation of numerous ideas (the more, the better); research requires relentless exploration of one vision (the deeper and more robust, the better). Creativity often values a neophyte perspective; research values knowledge and scholarship. Creativity builds variety and divergence; research challenges an existing paradigm with a specific vision around which to converge. Creativity is culturally neutral, as long as it helps solve problems; research on meanings is intrinsically visionary and built on the researcher's personal culture. In attempting to mimic the language of business, design seems to have followed the pattern noted among executives: it values methods more than designers' personal culture, thus losing the capability to harness this precious asset.

This book does not question the essential value of user-centered design, styling, and creativity, which are relevant for incremental innovation. However, people need different attitudes and skills when it comes to breakthrough innovations—and those attributes are scarce.

When more than 30 percent of the population belongs to the creative class, as Richard Florida has suggested, creativity is not in short supply: it is abundant.[3] What is in short supply, I'm afraid, are circles of forward-looking researchers whom firms involve in breakthrough projects because of their culture and vision, and because they have something to say. Now that designers have become highly effective at being creative and user centered, they can pursue an exciting new challenge that taps their unique cultural background: that of being radical researchers.

. . . And Scholars Are People Before Being Scholars

A book is a collective effort, although it may list only one author. This is especially true for this book, which is based on a decade of empirical analyses, discussions, and pioneering implementations conducted through a number of academic research projects and consulting assignments to my firm PROject Science. I am profoundly indebted to all those insightful and exceptional people who have supported me in this journey.

First of all, this work would not have been possible without the contribution of many colleagues at the School of Management of the Politecnico di Milano. My research draws in many ways on the work of Tommaso Buganza, Alessio Marchesi, and, especially, Claudio Dell'Era. I cannot find words to describe how important Claudio's contribution has been. I hope he has the good fortune to meet, in his career, as outstanding and committed a colleague as he has been to me.

Many other colleagues at the School of Management also provided invaluable support: Adriano De Maio and Emilio Bartezzaghi, who have introduced me to the values of scholarship, in addition to its methods and processes; Gianluca Spina, who has shared with me the turbulence of academic life; and Camilla Fecchio and the team at the MaDe In Lab laboratory for Advanced Education on Management of Design and Innovation. Other colleagues at the School of Design of Politecnico di Milano—Ezio Manzini, Anna Meroni, Giuliano Simonelli, and Francesco Zurlo—introduced me to the theories, processes, and dilemmas of design and helped immerse me in the local and international design community. Ezio deserves much credit. He opened my eyes to the deep dynamics of design-driven innovation and its differences from user-centered approaches. He is the quintessential radical researcher. If one wants to envision how research on innovation will look tomorrow, she need only read what Ezio wrote yesterday.

I'm also indebted to colleagues at Harvard Business School, where I wrote this book. Alan MacCormack was among the first to encourage me in this research and value its potential, even introducing a pioneering class on design-driven innovation in his course on the management of innovation and product development. Marco Iansiti—whose early investigations on the power of networks and ecosystems in technological innovation anticipate much of the framework I introduce here for design—provided ideas, insights, and resources. Alan and Marco are also great friends and musicians; our band sessions during the year I spent writing this book added the unpredictable touch of inspiration to long days of sitting. They have been my own "elite circle" and have confirmed the theories of Michael Farrell on the importance of friendship dynamics for moving outside dominant paradigms.[4]

Also at HBS, Gary Pisano helped position my work within the realm of studies of collaborative innovation, and this enabled me to focus on its peculiarities and find new directions to explore. Rob Austin, Lee Fleming, and Karim Lakhani helped me uncover connections and analogies between my findings and recent theories on creativity and technology management.

Several other scholars contributed their ideas, comments, and constructive critiques: Bengt-Arne Vedin, Eduardo Alvarez, Sten Ekman, Susan Sanderson, Jim Utterback, and Bruce Tether, of the project Design Firms in Product Innovation; Martti Lindman of Vaasa University; John Christiansen of Copenhagen Business School; and Marco Steinberg of the Harvard Graduate School of Design.

I'm grateful to all the institutions and corporations that, through a series of projects spanning ten years, provided funding and empirical ground for analysis, exploration, and implementation: the Politecnico di Milano, the Italian Ministry of University and Research (for the projects Sistema Design Italia, and the three FIRB—Fondo per gli Investimenti della Ricerca di Base—projects: ArtDeco, MATT, and IRIS), the European Commission (for the projects HICS, EVAN, and

FIRST), the Regione Lombardia, its research institute IReR (Istituto Regionale di Ricerca della Lombardia) and its financial institution Finlombarda, the Chamber of Commerce of Milan, the Associazione Torino Internazionale, Barilla, Filati Maclodio, Indesit Company, Snaidero, and Zucchi Group.

I discussed and implemented design-driven innovation with a number of executives and interpreters whose insights were extraordinarily valuable. Although it is impossible to mention all of them, I owe them much, especially those I have disturbed more: Alberto Alessi, Gloria Barcellini, Mauro Belussi, Paolo Benedetti, Scott Cook, Silvio Corrias, Lucia Chrometzka, Carlotta de Bevilaqua, Marco Del Barba, Ernesto Gismondi, Lee Green, Tom Lockwood, Tiziano Longhi, Francesco Morace, Marco Nicolai, Flemming Møller Pedersen, Mino Politi, Renzo Rizzo, Aldo Romano, Mark Smith, Edi Snaidero, Benedetto Vigna, Brad Weed, Gianfranco Zaccai, and Matteo Zucchi. A special thanks to Francois Jegou, with whom my colleagues and I have pioneered and perfected many of the methodologies we have then applied with the clients of my consulting firm PROject Science, especially concerning the Design Direction Workshops.

The editorial process of this book has benefited from the contribution of many minds and hands. From Jeff Kehoe, the developmental editor at HBS Press who helped frame the overwhelming material from my research and focus it in the right direction; to Sandra Hackman, the editor who patiently and thoroughly honed and streamlined this manuscript; to Daniele Barillari, the talented illustrator who made this book the first-ever design book without a single photo. This approach is, in itself, a radical innovation of meanings. And, indeed, I came across Daniele by pursuing the same design-driven process I describe in this book: through interpreters and mediators. I'm especially grateful to Stefano Boeri for having introduced me to Daniele. Jeff, Sandra, and Daniele have worked on this book with dedication, competence, and something more: passion and enthusiasm. This has given me the courage to pursue editorial experiments that I hope the reader will enjoy.

My family's contribution to this book comes from afar. It is not only the practical and emotional support that has been enormous. It is something more profound: the qualities of scholarship that one cannot learn in doctoral programs but can only tacitly assimilate and then, one day, uncover—the love of knowledge, the passion for endless inquiry, and the pleasure of comprehending the perspectives of others. I'm grateful to my father, Mario, and my mother, Marisa, for infusing in me those qualities.

For years I did not realize the potential of those qualities. Francesca, my wife, saw them in me better than I did. She took me by the hand to uncover those quiescent qualities and led me to believe in my real nature when the context was adverse. This is the most precious gift a person can give another. She has been my personal epiphany. Everyone has his own quiescent meaning, his own personal culture, to uncover. It's only a matter of research. I hope I will be able to help my children, Alessandro, Matilde, and Agnese—who have lovingly endowed me with their flood of life—in their own search, as Francesca has done with me.

—Roberto Verganti
Boston, May 2008

1
DESIGN-DRIVEN INNOVATION

[An Introduction]

With Metamorfosi, Artemide had completely overturned the reason why people would buy a lamp. Not another beautiful lamp, but a light that makes you feel better. It had radically changed its meaning. [IN THE ILLUSTRATION On the table: Artemide's Yang lamp (of the Metamorfosi family); in the painting: Artemide's Tizio "task luminaire."]

M ARKET? WHAT MARKET! We do not look at market needs. We make proposals to people."

Without another word, Ernesto Gismondi, chairman of Artemide, stared at the professor to see his reaction. A strong personality and a brilliant mind, Gismondi was not the kind of person to be in awe of a major scholar, even one from a well-respected U.S. business school. We were enjoying a steamy risotto alla milanese at the restaurant Da Bice right in the center of Milan. The dinner followed a late afternoon visit to Artemide, a leading manufacturer of lamps, where I had taken a group of professors interested in the innovation process of design-intensive Italian manufacturers. Gismondi, who had a bad case of flu, had invited us to continue the discussion over dinner. At a certain moment one of the professors, a leading scholar in the management of innovation, asked him how the company had analyzed market needs to come up with a product we had seen earlier during the visit: Metamorfosi.

Metamorfosi, released in 1998, was a unique product that one would hardly call a lamp. The lighting industry typically conceives of lamps as modern sculptures. People usually choose them according to how beautiful they are and how well they fit into their living rooms. Taking for granted that lamps illuminate, competition concentrates on style. And Artemide had been a main protagonist, having created beautiful icons, such as Tizio in 1972.

Metamorfosi, however, was completely different. It was a sophisticated system that emitted an atmosphere created by colored light, which could be controlled and adapted according to the owner's mood and need. Artemide's vision was that ambient light—especially its color and nuances—has a significant influence on people's psychological state and social interaction. The company therefore created a system that could emit a "human" light, a light that made people feel better and socialize better. The object itself was not even meant to be seen. Artemide had overturned the reason people bought a lamp. It had radically changed its meaning.

The interest of the American professor in this unique product was therefore legitimate, and the way he framed his question inevitable. In the business community worldwide, and especially in the United States, the imperative for success is user-driven or user-centered innovation. According to these approaches, companies should begin an innovation project by analyzing market needs, looking closely at users. Executives, MBA students, and designers are told repeatedly that the first thing they must do is take photos of how customers use products, to understand their unsatisfied needs. No one would dare question user-centered innovation.

Ernesto Gismondi's answer, hence, was unexpected. It did not fall within the spectrum of answers the professor was contemplating (such as "Yes, we did some ethnographic analysis of people using lamps in their apartments and changing bulbs . . ."). It was so startling that the professor thought he had misunderstood because of the noise in the restaurant. Luckily, he did not ask the second question in his quiver ("Did you use brainstorming or other creativity-enhancing techniques?"), which would have provoked a similar answer. Instead he turned to another topic. Perhaps he thought Gismondi's temperature was getting too high.

Gismondi, however, was of sound mind and his answer was loud and clear. And it could not have been different, because it perfectly suited the innovation strategy he was pursuing with Metamorfosi: a radical innovation of meaning.

The Strategy of Design-Driven Innovation

Two major findings have characterized management literature in the past decades.

The first is that radical innovation, albeit risky, is one of the major sources of long-term competitive advantage. For many authors, however, the phrase *radical innovation* is an ellipsis for a longer construction that spells radical *technological* innovation. Indeed, investigators of innovation have focused mainly on the disruptive effect of novel technologies on industries.

The second finding is that people do not buy products but *meanings*. People use things for profound emotional, psychological, and sociocultural reasons as well as utilitarian ones. Analysts have shown that every product and service in consumer as well as industrial markets has a meaning. Firms should therefore look beyond features, functions, and performance and understand the real meanings users give to things.

The common assumption, however, is that meanings are not a subject for innovation: they are a given. One must understand them but cannot innovate them. Meanings have indeed intensively populated the literature on marketing and branding. And user-centered perspectives have recently provided powerful methods for understanding how users (currently) give meaning to (existing) things. But in studies on radical innovation, an examination of meanings has been largely absent. They are not considered a subject of R&D.

Innovation has therefore focused on two strategies: quantum leaps in product performance enabled by breakthrough technologies, and improved product solutions enabled by better analysis of users' needs. The former is the domain of radical innovation pushed by technology, and the latter of incremental innovation pulled by the market (see figure 1-1).

Artemide has followed a third strategy: *design-driven innovation*—that is, radical innovation of meaning. It has not provided people with an improved interpretation of what they already mean by, and expect from, a lamp: a more beautiful object. Rather, the company has proposed a different and unexpected meaning: a light that makes you feel better. This meaning, unsolicited, was what people were actually waiting for.

Competing Through Radical Innovation of Meanings

Artemide is by no means alone in this strategy. Design-driven innovation is at the heart of numerous success stories of products and firms.

In November 2006, Nintendo launched the Wii, a game console with motion-sensitive controllers that allows people to play games by moving their bodies. For example, they might serve tennis balls by

FIGURE 1-1

The strategy of design-driven innovation as the radical change of meanings

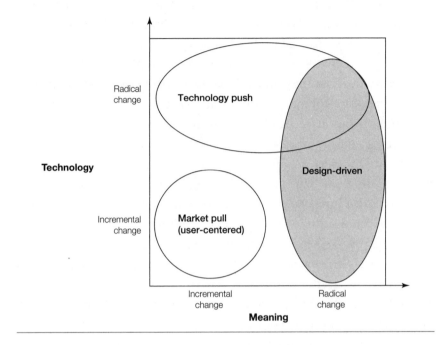

circling their arms overhead or play golf by swinging their arms. Up to the moment the Wii was introduced, game consoles were considered entertainment gadgets for children who were great at moving their thumbs; they offered a passive immersion in a virtual world. And indeed, Sony and Microsoft further reinforced this meaning by developing the PlayStation 3 and the Xbox 360, consoles with more-powerful graphics and performance. The Wii overturned this meaning: it stimulated active physical entertainment, in the real world, through socialization. The intuitiveness of its controllers made it easy for everyone to play. The Wii transformed consoles from an immersion in a virtual world approachable only by niche experts into an active workout for everyone. People did not ask for that meaning, but they loved it once they saw it. Six months after the Wii's release, sales in the U.S. market were double those of the Xbox 360 and quadruple those of the

PlayStation 3. And even though the Wii was much cheaper than its competitors, its profitability was much higher.

The late 1990s witnessed the birth of the first MP3 players: MPMan and Rio PMP300. They were meant as portable music players: more-powerful substitutes for the popular Walkman, which used old technology—cassettes and CDs—to carry tunes. These MP3 players changed the technology but left its meaning untouched: listening to songs away from home. Market response was lukewarm. Apple, in contrast, proposed a completely different vision: enabling people to produce their own music. Between 2001 and 2003 it released a *system* of products, applications, and services that supported a seamless experience of discovering, tasting, and buying music (through the iTunes Store); storing and organizing music collections in personal playlists (through the iTunes software); and listening to it through the iPod (which became simply *the* player, even in homes). The business that Apple built on this proposal was stunning.

In 1980 a team of visionary lovers of good-tasting, healthy food opened a store destined to change the future of food retailing: Whole Foods Market. These visionaries focused on organic and natural food. When you entered other organic food stores, you felt as though you were an ascetic in a small sect doing penance, but Whole Foods Market celebrated pleasure. Not only did labels and posters educate consumers about the virtues of natural and organic foods, health, nutrition, and sustainable agriculture, but also produce was arranged as if on a stage: an irresistible party of colors and smells. Whole Foods Market has radically changed the meaning of healthy nutrition from a severe, self-denying choice to a hedonic one, and shopping from a chore to a reinvigorating experience. (New services even allow people to get a massage while a grocery valet takes care of the shopping list.) Whole Foods Market is the fastest-growing company in the competitive grocery business.

Everyone knows that corkscrews are meant to pull corks and that citrus squeezers are meant to squeeze lemons. These are tools; thus innovation has always aimed at making them more functional or more beautiful. In 1993 Alessi, a manufacturer of household items, released a new family of products that were not necessarily more functional and did not comply with existing standards of beauty. This family included a series of playful plastic objects, most with an anthropomorphic or metaphoric shape, such as Mandarin, a citrus squeezer stylized as a Chinese mandarin in a conical hat, and Nutty the Cracker, a nutcracker in the shape of a squirrel whose teeth crack the shells. Shallow observers labeled the family a fanciful, crazy idea—the output of extemporaneous and useless creativity. But that wasn't the case. The product line was the result of years of serious research aimed at proposing a radical new meaning: household items as objects of affection, as substitutes for teddy bears for adults. Rather than talk to the little engineer or the little stylist inside each of us, Alessi was talking to our inner child. This unsolicited meaning turned out to be exactly what people were looking for. During the past fifteen years this vision has inspired many companies beyond the kitchenware industry to pursue now-popular *emotional design*. Meanwhile Alessi has enjoyed double-digit annual growth.

Companies such as Artemide, Nintendo, Apple, Whole Foods Market, Alessi, and many others I discuss in this book show that meanings do change—and that they can change radically. The design-driven innovations introduced by these firms have not come from the market but have created huge markets. They have generated products, services, and systems with long lives, significant and sustainable profit margins, and brand value, and they have spurred company growth.

An Unexplored Conundrum

The reason Gismondi's "proposals to people" assertion sounds surprising to many practitioners and scholars is simply that we know little about how design-driven innovation occurs. Years of research have yielded several compelling explanations for technological breakthroughs, but no theory about how to manage radical innovation when it comes to meanings. It's a conundrum enshrouded in mystery.

In 1998, returning to Politecnico di Milano after a period at Harvard Business School investigating the management of breakthrough innovations in Internet software, I had the chance to become involved in two major projects. One was Sistema Design Italia (Italian Design System), a first-ever research project on the economics and organization of design processes in Italy.[1] The other project was the creation, at Politecnico di Milano, of a graduate school of industrial design, the first ever in Italy. I seized both opportunities enthusiastically. Italy was quite weak in software but an acknowledged worldwide leader in design, especially in industries such as furniture, lighting, and food.

I was especially attracted by the fact that the success of Italian design is rooted in manufacturers rather than designers. (Indeed, foreign designers actually perform much of so-called Italian design: innovative Italian furniture manufacturers hire about 50 percent of their designers from abroad.) The secret of Italian design was concealed in the hands of entrepreneurs and executives, making this empirical ground particularly interesting for management studies.

The most distinctive and advanced firms in this regard are concentrated in northern Italy, in industries that deal with domestic lifestyle. Many of these companies, such as Artemide, Alessi, Kartell, B&B Italia, Cassina, Flos, and Snaidero, are industry leaders despite their small size (only the latter has more than five hundred employees). They have built their leadership on innovation, and not on complementary assets such as distribution, market penetration, and low labor costs. Between 1994 and 2003, in an industry where other Western companies considered themselves lucky if they had any growth (EU furniture manufacturers grew 11 percent over that decade), the revenues of these companies grew between 54 percent (B&B Italia) and 211 percent (Kartell).

Even more interesting, these firms had a unique innovation strategy. Contrary to common wisdom, their success was not related simply to their capacity to create beautiful objects. Rather, they often moved against the dominant aesthetic standards, as the Artemide and Alessi examples clearly show. What made these firms different from many others that use design for styling or user-centered innovation was that they were leaders in the radical innovation of meanings.

The Italian design system therefore proved to be a unique empirical setting for investigating the management of design-driven innovation. I was lucky. However, the research proved much more painful than I had expected, revealing why design-driven innovation had remained unexplored.

First, companies that are very successful at design-driven innovation are not really open to someone who wants to investigate their process, especially if he is a management scholar. As you will see, their model is based on elite circles, which admit novices only if they bring interesting knowledge. Unfortunately, existing management theories are so far removed from the strategies of these firms that they see almost no utility in them. It took me literally years to gain their trust, to be admitted into the circle and gain access to their processes. Luckily, the two projects in which I was initially involved provided a wealth of contacts and networking.

Second, once I got there, I found it a major challenge to understand what was going on. The innovation process of these firms was tacit, invisible—no methods, no tools, no steps. Instead, it was based mainly on networks of uncodified interactions among various agents of innovation and was directly led by top executives. The only pursuable empirical method was immersion and close contact with these participants.

This effort eventually paid off. This book opens a window to a unique set of firms that provides valuable insights on how radical innovation of meanings occurs.

In ten years of research I progressively enlarged the sample to include firms of various sizes in various industries, countries, and markets (consumer and industrial, niche and high volume), in products and in services.[2] (Appendix A provides a glimpse of the variety of companies discussed in this book.) Given that one of the major benefits of design-driven innovation is the development of products having long lives, in many cases I focused on projects conducted a number of years earlier. But these are not old examples. Most of these products are still successful in the market and appear to be younger than their recent counterparts.

The final step was to move from exploration to implementation. With a team of colleagues at my consulting firm, PROject Science, I worked with companies to enable them to realize radical innovation of meanings by establishing the process and building the related capabilities. This even deeper immersion provided further insight into the dynamics of design-driven innovation, especially in large corporations.

Proposals

Apple is building a scenario of life in which people rent or buy movies at the iTunes stores, download songs from this online store and listen to them through the iPod, and back up data and upload applications wirelessly. In this scenario there is no room for CDs and DVDs. Apple has therefore released its newest notebook, the MacBook Air, without an optical drive—a surprising and unsolicited bold move. Apple's approach to innovation shines through the words of Steve Jobs at the 2008 Macworld Conference in San Francisco: "You know what? *We* do not think most users will miss the optical drive. *We* do not think they will need an optical drive."[3]

This statement perfectly mirrors Ernesto Gismondi's. Jobs is telling people what he believes they will need and won't miss. Both statements are in contrast to a huge array of studies on innovation that piled on our desks in the past decade.

And indeed, the first finding from my investigation is that radical innovation of meanings doesn't come from user-centered approaches. If Nintendo had closely observed teenagers using existing game consoles, it probably would have improved traditional game controllers, enabling users to better immerse themselves in a virtual world, rather than redefining what a game console is. If Alessi had visited users in their homes to scrutinize how they pulled corks from a bottle, it would have created more-efficient tools, not objects of affection that a person buys twice—once for herself and once for her best friend. User-centered innovation does not question existing meanings but rather reinforces them, thanks to its powerful methods.

These companies are instead making *proposals*, putting forward a vision. That is why I call this strategy design-driven: like radical innovation of technologies, it is a push strategy. These proposals, however, are not dreams without a foundation. They end up being what people were waiting for, once they see them. They often love them much more than products that companies have developed by scrutinizing users' needs. These proposals are wellsprings for the creation of sustainable profit.

How do you develop a successful design-driven innovation? How do you propose a vision that people have not solicited—one that perhaps initially confounds them but that eventually converts them into enthusiastic users?

When a company proposes a radical change in meaning, analysts often reject it as crazy or outlandish. That is not a surprise. A design-driven innovation, by definition, differs substantially from the dominant meaning in the industry. When analysts eventually acknowledge that a proposal has become a success, they call it a fluke. Or they think that the executive or designer who proposed it had a sudden spark of creativity or has some magical capability. I described this conundrum to a professor during the centennial celebrations of Harvard Business School in April 2008, and he told me, "There should be some kind of 'guru' process." My ten years of research shows instead that these radical proposals come from a very precise process and concrete capabilities.

Interpreters

Firms that develop design-driven innovations step back from users and take a broader perspective. They explore how the context in which people live is evolving, both in sociocultural terms (how the reason people buy things is changing) and in technical terms (how technologies, products, and services are shaping that context). Most of all, these firms envision how this context of life could change for the better. The word *could* is not incidental. These firms are not simply following existing trends. They are making proposals with which they will modify the context. They are building scenarios that would perhaps never occur (or that would occur more slowly) if the firms did not deliver their unsolicited proposals. Their question, therefore, is, "How could people give meaning to things in this evolving life context?"

When a company takes this broader perspective, it discovers that it is not alone in asking that question. Every company is surrounded by several agents (firms in other industries that target the same users, suppliers of new technologies, researchers, designers, and artists) who share its interests. Consider, for example, a food company that, instead of closely looking with a magnifying lens at how a person cuts cheese, asks, "What meanings could family members search for when they are home and are going to have dinner?" Other actors are investigating this same question: kitchen manufacturers, manufacturers of white goods, TV broadcasters, architects who design home interiors, food journalists, and food retailers. All are looking at the same people in the same life context: dinner with family at home at night. And all are conducting research on how those people could give meaning to things. They are, in other words, *interpreters*.

Companies that produce design-driven innovations highly value their interactions with these interpreters. With them they exchange information on scenarios, test the robustness of their assumptions, and discuss their own visions. These companies understand that knowledge about meanings is diffused throughout their external environment; that they are immersed in a collective research laboratory where interpreters pursue their own investigations and are engaged in a continuous mutual dialogue (see figure 1-2).

FIGURE 1-2

Interpreters in a collective research laboratory

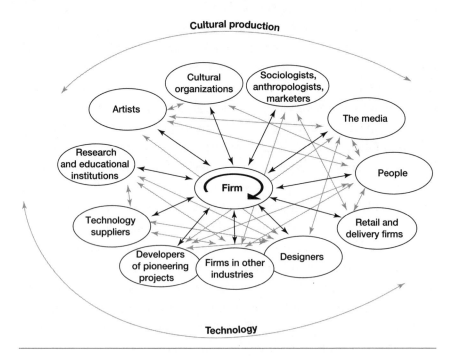

The process of design-driven innovation therefore entails getting close to interpreters. It leverages their ability to understand and influence how people could give meaning to things. This process, described in detail in this book, consists of three actions.

The first one is *listening*. It is the action of gaining access to knowledge about possible new product meanings by interacting with interpreters. Firms that listen better are those that develop privileged relationships with a distinguished group of key interpreters. These are not necessarily the most famous in the industry. Rather, successful firms first identify overlooked interpreters, usually in fields where competitors are not searching. Key interpreters are forward-looking researchers who are developing, often for their own purposes, unique visions about how meanings could evolve in the life context we want to investigate. Firms that realize design-driven innovations are better than their competitors at detecting, attracting, and interacting with key interpreters.

The second action is *interpreting*. Its purpose is to allow a company to develop its unique proposal. It is the internal process through which the firm assesses the knowledge it gains by interacting with interpreters and then recombines and integrates this knowledge with its own proprietary insights, technologies, and assets. This process reflects the profound and precise dynamics of research rather than the speed of brainstorming. It implies sharing knowledge through exploratory experiments rather than extemporaneous creativity. It resembles the process of science and engineering (although it targets meanings rather than technologies) more than that of a creative agency. Its outcome is the development of a breakthrough meaning for a product family.

The third action is *addressing*. Radical innovations of meanings, being unexpected, sometimes initially confuse people. To prepare the ground for groundbreaking proposals, firms leverage the seductive power of interpreters. By discussing and internalizing a firm's novel vision, these interpreters inevitably change the life context (through the technologies they develop, the products and services they design, the artworks they create) in a way that makes the company's proposal more meaningful and attractive when people see it.

The Unharnessed Power of Relational Assets

Managers are attracted by codified approaches to innovation. They love methods, tools, step-by-step processes. They hope that innovation systems can be bought and replicated immediately. Highly codified approaches, however, have a downside: competitors can easily replicate them.

The process of design-driven innovation is not codified into steps. Rather, it is interwoven into relational assets with a network of key interpreters. These relationships are an engine of innovation—a core capability—that competitors can seldom replicate.

It is crucial to notice that the firms that pursue this approach do not source thousands of ideas from hordes of anonymous inventors, as touted by popular models of open innovation. Rather, they carefully search, select, and attract the most promising interpreters and work jointly with them. Collaboration is closed and not open. Not everyone is invited, and the capability to invite the right interpreters—thereby keeping them from competitors—is what makes the difference. These firms invest in relationships. Solutions will follow.[4]

Where are these relational assets located? First, they reside in your entire organization. Often firms, especially large corporations, already have numerous interactions with potential key interpreters. However, they do not have a picture of this multitude of personal relationships, do not nurture them, and have no process for converting them into radical innovators of meanings. This book provides a framework for harnessing this often-untapped treasure.

Second, this process has, as its main protagonists, top executives. Design-driven innovation is not about being creative. Rather, it is about setting a direction and investing in relational assets. And this is definitely a job for executives.

This job is not based on codified techniques but on two capabilities that are typical of management: judgment and the ability to build social capital. That is why the process of design-driven innovation seems invisible and magical. However, notwithstanding its apparent impalpability, it is based on a clear set of principles and practices. They are different from typical innovation processes—less visible, perhaps, but not less systematic. This book makes those principles and practices accessible.

The Plan of This Book

This book is organized into three parts. Part 1, The Strategy of Design-Driven Innovation, elaborates on the concept of design-driven innovation. It explains its specific nature and, most of all, its crucial role in a firm's overall innovation strategy. It clarifies this strategy's value in creating a sustainable competitive advantage—and its challenges. It focuses especially on the interplay between radical innovation of meanings and radical innovation of technologies: the domain where technology-push and design-driven innovation overlap (the upper-right corner of figure 1-1). Contrary to the common assumption that meanings and design become relevant only when an industry matures, I show instead that design-driven innovation may overturn industries in the emerging phases of breakthrough technologies.

Part 2, The Process of Design-Driven Innovation, shows how companies can realize successful radical innovations of meanings: how they can make unsolicited proposals that turn out to be what people love. Chapter 6 discusses the basic principle underlying the process: leveraging the knowledge of key interpreters to envision and influence how people could give meaning to things. Chapters 7 through 9 dig into the three main actions of design-driven innovation: listening, interpreting, and addressing.

Part 3, Building Design-Driven Capabilities, shows how to start. It explains how to activate a dynamic that can allow a company to become a leader in design-driven innovation. It shows how to recognize and value the relational assets that a company already has, and how to nurture and expand them. In particular, it shows the key role that top executives play in this process.

You will not find photos of products in this book. In fact, this is everything but a book on the form of products. Rather, it is about meanings and management. Given, however, that many of the cases, especially those of the Italian manufacturers, are less well known than those typically presented by the business press, I asked a young architect-artist, Daniele Barillari, to help me visualize some of the proposals—focusing, of course, on their meanings rather than their forms.

A related Web site (www.designdriveninnovation.com) has links to company pages where you can find photos of the examples I discuss here.

The site also has colored versions of Daniele's wonderful illustrations (and I must say that it is definitely worth a visit). The site acts as a supporting platform for this book, where readers can, among other things, suggest and upload more examples of radical innovation of meanings.

The variety of cases and examples discussed in this book is in any event so broad as to show that design-driven innovation is a suitable strategy for every firm, whether large or small, and whether it offers products or services, addresses consumer or business markets, and makes durable or fast-moving goods (see the list in appendix A). Although I base a number of my cases on Italian manufacturers, that is simply because they have pioneered this approach intensively for decades, and it has remained largely undiscovered. However, firms in every country and industry have applied this strategy.

Even more important, the discussion shows that design-driven innovation is not simply an option. It happens always and everywhere. Like technologies, which evolve through periods of incremental and radical change, product meanings also alternate between marginal and radical transitions. Sooner or later a radical change in meanings inevitably occurs. And when it does, it is because a firm has introduced it. Do you want to master the process for giving birth to a radical change, or witness a competitor proposing such a change and leading the market?

In the mid-1980s, with the invention of quartz movements, incumbents in the watch industry such as Seiko and Casio believed that people viewed watches as technical instruments, and therefore they focused on how to add new features. What happened, however, was that people started to see watches as fashion accessories: regardless of their features and precision, people were more interested in collecting several watches, matching them to various clothing styles, and changing them every other season, just like shoes and hats. An innovative product triggered this radical market shift: a watch introduced by Swatch, a Swiss company, in 1986. Seiko and Casio were closely observing users and existing meanings, and they observed Swatch creating new ones.

Part One

THE STRATEGY OF
DESIGN-DRIVEN
INNOVATION

DESIGN AND MEANINGS

[Innovating by Making Sense of Things]

Every product has a meaning. Yet many companies do not care about how to innovate meanings. They strive to understand how people currently give meaning to things—only to discover that this meaning has been suggested by an innovation designed by a competitor. [IN THE ILLUSTRATION   On the wall: Kartell's Bookworm bookshelf. The computer on the small table runs Intuit QuickBooks.]

ANY COMPANIES ACKNOWLEDGE that market competition is driven by products' meanings—by "why" people need a product more than by "what" they need in a product. People buy and use products for deep reasons, often not manifest, that include both functional utility and intangible psychological satisfaction. Consumers, managers, and engineers buy food, consultant services, and software for cultural and emotional as well as practical reasons.

This is perfectly natural. We are humans, and when we use products, however utilitarian, we search for personal fulfillment—for meaning. Studies in various scientific disciplines, from psychology to sociology, from cultural anthropology to semiotics (the study of signs and symbols), have provided so many insights into consumption behaviors that few people would challenge the statement that "every product has a meaning."

Yet many companies do not care about how the meanings of products change or about how to innovate them. They believe that meanings are a matter of marketing and communication, and not of R&D. Through user analysis they strive to understand how people give meaning to things, only to discover that this meaning has been suggested by a new product introduced by a competitor.

But like technologies, meanings may be subject to an R&D process. And the process through which a company can innovate product meanings is design. This chapter illustrates the profound link between meanings, innovation, and design.

Design has become a popular topic in management literature, opening it to many ambiguous interpretations, from the immediate conception of design as styling to the broader notion that links any creative and innovative activity to design. To find a way through this confusing landscape, this chapter first guides you through well-developed notions of design theorists. It then reinterprets their contributions through the lens of management—especially management of innovation—by focusing on the essence of design: that it is "making sense of things."

This focused perspective allows you to better understand the peculiar nature of design and to see how it differs from other innovation processes such as engineering. It also reveals why design is important to creating competitive advantage: design innovates meanings, and meanings make a difference in the market.

This chapter concludes by discussing more deeply the notion that every product has a meaning. What's more, as with technological innovation, innovation in meanings occurs in every industry, from food to financial services, from cars to business software. In any industry, design is therefore crucial to competition, because innovation of meanings is critical to competition. Companies that do not innovate product meanings through design lose a core opportunity and leave it in the hands of their competitors.

Design: A Kaleidoscope of Perspectives

It's a nice sunny afternoon in central London, even though it's mid-December. The UK Design Council, in the heart of Covent Garden, is the perfect place to hold a meeting on the future of design in business, and the view of the Royal Opera House is heartening when the discussion loses steam. A group of experts is talking animatedly about how to convince companies to invest more in design. On the table, amid a jumble of teacups, biscuits, and notebooks, are scattered the business cards of the participants: design thinkers, professors of design and management, consultants, and business leaders from various parts of the world. At a certain moment, a gentleman on the other side of the table raises his hand and asks the fateful question: "Yes, but . . . what is design?"

This question might seem odd amid a meeting of experts. Who would dare or even think to ask, "What is management?" at a meeting of business school faculty? However, I am used to it. Since I began investigating design, someone at every meeting, conference, or debate—regardless of the credentials of the participants—inevitably asks, "What do we mean by 'design'?"

The definition of design is fluid and slippery. That is not because people do not consider and debate the meaning of design—actually, they do, a lot. The problem is a lack of convergence. Thomas Kuhn, in his groundbreaking study of the sociology of science, shows how new disciplines and theories eventually coalesce around shared principles and norms—what he calls *paradigms*. But before this convergence occurs, disciplines are in a preparadigmatic phase. Well, it is as if the field of design perpetually remains in a preparadigmatic phase—as if scholars were afraid of converging on shared definitions and boundaries, fearing that doing so would limit their investigations. As Peter Butenschøn, former president of the International Council of Societies of Industrial Design, noted in a keynote speech at Brunel University, "Discussing design has become an increasingly complex affair, since the agenda seems to be shifting all the time."[1]

Indeed, the debate is so open-ended that when I asked Ezio Manzini, a respected design theorist and colleague at the Faculty of Design of Politecnico di Milano, whether he could help me understand the definition of design, he suggested that I read a book on the history of design.[2] Although that may seem like odd advice to give a management scholar—after all, business schools seldom study the history of management—it was very wise, because it encouraged me to avoid the shortcut of simple answers and allowed me to grasp the multifaceted nature of design.

Yet to understand the unique contribution of design to companies' innovation strategy, we need a sharp definition. Given that scholars have debated the concept at length, I will not invent a new definition but rather choose the one that highlights the unique contribution of design to innovation: design as making sense of things. Before elaborating on this definition and its implications, however, I first provide a brief overview of other interpretations of design to clarify what I *do not* mean by design.[3]

Design as the Form of Products

In a 1999 broadcast of ABC's *Nightline*, anchor Ted Koppel was about to present a video illustrating how influential design firm IDEO realizes innovations. To introduce the topic, he provided probably the most popular and diffuse definition of design: "Everything we use was designed to create some sort of marriage between form and function. Does it work? And can we make it look interesting or attractive?"[4] Design has often been seen as the form of products—often in juxtaposition to their function. Indeed, many people believe that design basically deals with form. If engineers use technology to make products function, then designers use form to make things beautiful.

Of course, modernists questioned the predominance of form—from the claim of American architect Louis Sullivan that "form follows function" at the dawn of the twentieth century, to the aphorism "less is more" of Ludwig Mies van der Rohe, one of the directors of the Bauhaus art and architecture school active in Germany between 1919 and 1933. Yet if we look at the most frequent applications of design in business over the past century, they have paid prevailing attention to form and have complied with the dogma that "ugliness does not sell" coined by Raymond Loewy, the French-American designer who is a founding father of "styling." And most businesspeople still associate product design with beauty.

Unfortunately, this concept has little in common with innovation. Indeed, beauty and innovation sometimes even compete. People associate beauty with aesthetic standards they already have in mind. However, novel products—especially those that are radically innovative—do not conform to existing standards: they try to impose new ones.[5] Lorenzo Ramacciotti—a past vice president of Pininfarina, a car design firm, and today head of design at FIAT—told me, "When I was at Pininfarina, often our clients came to us asking for a very innovative concept for a car. Then, when we presented the innovative ideas we had devised, their reaction was, 'Couldn't we have something more beautiful?'"

Design as Innovation and Creativity at Large

If the notion of design as form is too narrow, many experts have reacted by expanding the concept to embrace any innovative activity. Their first step has been to link design to product innovation in general. Indeed, people have often used the term *engineering design* or *software design* to describe innovation that focuses mainly on technology, and many books on design are handbooks of product development. By using the word "design" instead of "development" these books denote a greater focus on the generation of new ideas rather than pure technical implementation, and more conscious attention to user needs.[6]

Perhaps the best-known definition of design in this regard is that proposed by Thomas Maldonado and adopted by the International Council of Societies of Industrial Design (ICSID) in 1969: "Industrial design is a creative activity whose aim is to determine the formal qualities of objects produced by industry. These formal qualities are not only the external features but are principally those structural and functional relationships which convert a system to a coherent unity both from the point of view of the producer and the user. Industrial design extends to embrace all the aspects of human environment, which are conditioned by industrial production."[7]

The council has since broadened this definition by adding the design of services, processes, and systems: "Design is a creative activity whose aim is to establish the multi-faceted qualities of objects, processes, services and their systems in whole life cycles. Therefore, design is the central factor of innovative humanisation of technologies and the crucial factor of cultural and economic exchange."[8]

In a progressive extension, design has also increasingly been associated with branding, the ability to understand users' needs, business strategy, organizational design, and market design.[9]

This brings us very close to the short but penetrating comment by Herbert Simon that "everyone designs who devises courses of action aimed at changing existing situations into preferred ones."[10] In this interpretation, design encompasses all creative professions that modify their environment: "Engineering, medicine, business, architecture and painting are concerned not with the necessary but with the contingent—not with how things are but with how they might be—in short, with design."[11]

This evolution has spurred a vital debate on the need for more design thinking in business.[12] As Simon notes, such thinking—the ability to envision new possibilities—is an integral part of being a manager, although business schools have often concentrated on developing students' analytical skills while overlooking their creativity.[13] Still, however interesting and intriguing this debate, I do not want to contribute to it here. We know that managers need to be creative, but this book has a different purpose: to show how managers can *leverage* design to enable their organizations to innovate.[14] Just as a good art dealer needs to have an artistic attitude but does not necessarily have to paint, we are interested here not in how to design but in *how to do business* with design. Many of the executives you will meet are not designers—although many have a design attitude—but they create competitive advantage through design. Unfortunately, the broader notions that associate design with any kind of creative activity do not help in this regard. They are so generic that if you ask a manager or a friend what design *really* is, what is unique about it, she will eventually say, lacking any other conceptual foothold, "Oh yeah! Design is what makes things beautiful—it is what adds that touch of magic to my iPod."[15]

Neither extreme—one focusing narrowly on the beauty and form of objects, the other seeing design as basically everything—had satisfied my question as a researcher of innovation management. What makes design different from other widely investigated forms of innovation such as technological advance? What makes companies that invest in design successful in global markets? As I began my search I came across a lamp . . .

Design as Making Sense of Things

Close your eyes and think of a beautiful lamp.

How do you envision it? Is it sleek? Does it have the trendy combinations of aluminum and polymeric materials? A round anthropomorphic shape? Or does it suggest new luxury, with a golden luster, precious glass decorations, and bold geometry?

Now open your eyes.

What you see is a room, and you are immersed in an intense indigo and violet atmosphere, with an array of shades and nuances from light to deep blue. The illumination is subtle, and you feel comfortable. You see no lamps. You turn toward the windows, thinking it is sunset, but outside it is night. Then you realize that the light is coming from behind a chair. You slowly move closer. Looking behind the chair, you find a strange device composed of translucent material, three bulbs, visible circuits, and a display. It is Metamorfosi, the lighting system mentioned in chapter 1. It is made by Artemide, an Italian manufacturer.[16]

Artemide is well known in the design world. Founded in Milan in 1961 by Ernesto Gismondi, an aerospace engineer who specialized in rocketry, and Sergio Mazza, an architect, the company has produced some of the most important icons of modern design. These include the Tizio, designed by Richard Sapper in 1972, the first table lamp with a halogen bulb and metallic rods carrying current without electric cables; and the Tolomeo, a lamp designed by Michele De Lucchi and Giancarlo Fassina in 1986, still a best seller more than two decades later.

Artemide's products have appeared in more than one hundred exhibitions in the world's most important museums of contemporary art and design, from the Museum of Modern Art in New York to the Victoria and Albert Museum in London. The firm has also won many design awards, including the European Design Prize, more than one Compasso d'Oro, and Red Dot. In short, Artemide is a world-renowned producer of beautiful modern lamps.

How does Metamorfosi fit into this picture, given that the device itself—as opposed to the light it emits—isn't even meant to be seen? Carlotta de Bevilacqua, managing director for brand strategy and development at product launch in 1998, provides an answer: "Nowadays every market-oriented company has understood that design is an advantage. As a result, all companies can use it. Design is not only a way to give a nice form, but it should rather anticipate a need, proposing a vision."[17]

Chairman Ernesto Gismondi provides another: "As design entered one of its most difficult phases, we decided to work not as much on the object, but more so on light, especially its color . . . As a matter of fact, we started with a research on the psychological component of light."[18]

Designing beautiful lamps was simply no longer enough. In its narrow interpretation as styling, design was becoming a commodity. The company felt the need to be radical in its innovation strategy, to differentiate itself from encroaching competitors. Although Metamorfosi did require significant research on new technologies, what Artemide did was to radically redefine the meaning of its product.[19] The company reinvented the reason people buy a lamp: not because it is beautiful, but because it makes them feel better.

Indeed, Metamorfosi is based on the concept of a human light: one that contributes to people's desire for pleasure and need for human interaction. The owner uses a remote-control device to alter the colored ambient light according to his mood and the situation. The indigo blue atmosphere, called "dream," slowly dims as the owner gets into bed. Other configurations of the light encourage relaxation, interactivity, creativity, and love. This innovation in what people mean by a lamp is radical, because it shifts people's attention not only from the object to the light (people often buy lamps simply because they will look nice in their living room, forgetting to figure out whether the illumination will be appropriate for their needs), but also from white to colored light—that is, to psychological well-being.[20]

This example clarifies that design is not solely about form and styling; after all, this lamp is not even intended to be seen. Nor does it support a generic interpretation of design as creativity at large. Instead, it is about a particular type of innovation: the innovation of meanings. Klaus Krippendorff offered a masterly definition of this unique aspect of design in *Design Issues* in 1989: "The etymology of design goes back to the latin *de + signare* and means making something, distinguishing it by a sign, giving it significance, designating its relation to other things, owners, users or gods. Based on this original meaning, one could say: *design is making sense [of things]*." He clarified that "when [ordinary people] . . . are presented with very personal items, they relate these in the following terms: who gave it to them; how it was acquired; of whom it reminds them; in which circumstances it figured prominently; how much care, service, repair, or even affection it consumed; how well it fits with other possessions; how enjoyable its presence is; how it feels; and how close it is to the user's definition of him/herself."[21]

Every Product Has a Meaning

Influential design scholars have recognized and endorsed the link between design and meanings.[22] For example, Victor Margolin and Richard Buchanan introduced *The Idea of Design* by stating that "products embody notions of identity that are socially recognized and thus become tokens in the symbolic exchange of meaning."[23] An entire section of their book explores the meanings of products.

Studies in other disciplines have also shown that every product has a meaning. By interviewing and observing individuals in their homes, for example, psychologists Mihalyi Csikszentmihalyi and Eugenie Rochberg-Halton showed how people assimilate objects into their private lives and give them symbolic meaning as expressions of their experiences. "Things embody goals, make skills manifest, and shape the identity of their users. His self is to a large extent a reflection of things with which he interacts. Thus objects also make and use their makers and users."[24]

Sociological and anthropological studies of consumption underscore the role that people and their interactions play in defining the symbolism and meaning of products.[25] And an entire branch of semiotics studies the language of products.[26]

Finally, extensive research in marketing and consumer behavior has shown that the emotional and symbolic dimensions of consumption are as important—even within industrial markets—as the utilitarian aspect emphasized in classical economic models. Sidney Levy's classic 1959 article noted that "people buy products not only for what they can do, but also for what they mean" and spawned a huge body of theoretical and empirical studies.[27] And researchers in marketing and consumer behavior have recently focused on services, where the emotional dimension is often even more important.[28]

Among scholars of innovation management, Clayton Christensen, with his framework based on the "job to be done," has further supported the importance of targeting meanings and understanding what people are really trying to achieve when they buy products.[29]

What emerges from these investigations is the twofold nature of products. The utilitarian dimension deals with function and performance, and an equally important dimension concerns symbols, identity, and emotions—in other words, meanings.[30] The dialectic therefore is not between function and form, but between function and meaning.[31]

People Have Always Given Meaning to Things

An interesting observation that emerges is that the emotional and symbolic side of products does not result from recent market evolution toward "postmodern consumption."[32] Meanings have always ruled product success.

Witness George Eastman's understanding in 1888 that people wanted to take photos of their personal lives in the simplest possible way—"you press the button, we do the rest"—in an era when innovation was aimed at producing complex cameras for elite photographers. Today Toyota's popular Prius hybrid is not as sleek and chic as an SUV, but it helps the owner save pocket money while saving the planet (which is as cool as having an SUV).

Thus, although people may have become more sensitive to the intangible, experiential side of products and services, products do not need to become *more* emotional or *more* symbolic. These studies simply tell us that every product or service has a meaning and that firms have always innovated meaning.

Even the cultural statement that form should follow function—the manifesto of modernism and rationalism—has been a radical innovation of meaning. The credo that products should be purely utilitarian assumes that a group of customers regards functionality as a core value. Says Bernhard Wild, chairman of Braun, a German manufacturer of small appliances, "Doesn't Braun stand for 'form follows function' in the purest sense of the word? Yes and no. Braun Design has strived to help free people's lives. Which is its ultimate goal and function."[33]

Yet many companies have disregarded this aspect of their products or have not seen it as subject to innovation. They have continued to improve performance within existing market concepts, leaving a few visionary companies to gain competitive advantage by proposing new meanings.

Beyond Market Segments and Particular Industries

Just as all products have meanings, those meanings are not restricted to particular market segments. For example, some managers, confusing design and luxury, think that meanings are important only in high-end market segments or in a thriving economy. If you think that meanings are not important for your company because your customers are interested only in price cuts and utility, you are saying they are subhuman. On the other hand, if you operate in a high-end market and think that creating meanings implies simply designing opulent things, you are saying your customers are stupid. They want something more meaningful.

In periods of economic downturn, product meanings become even more relevant. Firms must be able to cut costs without cutting identity and value. Products that are cleverly parsimonious and unpretentious may have indeed a strong personality. If they have been explicitly designed for that meaning, people may love them as icons of essentiality. Customers would buy them not merely because of their low price, but because they would epitomize a smart and responsible way of living. Sneakers, for example, are not cheaper versions of sophisticated and elegant leather shoes. Simply put, they have a different meaning. Although they can cost as low as one tenth of their luxury counterparts, they have no less value, to the point that people may wear them at work, at events and even at wedding ceremonies. Instead, when low price is the result of meaningless cost cutting, then customers clearly feel miserable and envious of more meaningful, and valuable, products. In this book I discuss cases of innovation of meanings for both high-end and low-end products. (For example, Chapter 5 offers the FIAT Panda as a good example of utility and essentiality as a basic value.) All these examples share a common thread: people love meaningful things. Design is completely orthogonal to price segments.[34]

Nor are meanings restricted to particular industries. Some people, for example, think that emotions and symbols are relevant only in fashion. Nothing could be more wrong. Radical innovations of meaning are rare in fashion. Of the dozens of examples in this book, not one concerns fashion.

Food has meanings; anthropologists and sociologists often investigate people's identity and culture through their gastronomy.[35] Durable goods have meanings; think of Nokia, which transformed the meaning of mobile phones from devices for businesspeople to all-purpose products for everyone. Although the function of the product—making calls away from home—remained basically unchanged, people started to see Nokia phones as personal accessories for social relationships; hence the claim "connecting people" rather than offices. Business-to-business products and instruments have meanings. Think of the euro pallet system, which has redefined logistics by giving meaning to the result—moving freight—rather than the tool (the pallet) by defining standards and protocols (while also raising trade barriers for non-EU manufacturers). And many business-to-business components eventually find their way into consumer products and allow radical change (you will see an interesting example with MEMS accelerometers used in Nintendo's Wii).

Services, too, have meaning. Think of people moving from traditional to online banking, or the new meaning of air travel provided by low-cost carriers, or the advent of car sharing as a semipublic transportation system. McDonald's changed the meaning of fast food. Before McDonald's, there were only car hops and diners. McDonald's served similar food, but the meaning was different. It became a place you could count on wherever you were: safe, clean, reliable. Similarly, Starbucks changed the meaning of a coffee shop from a place to buy coffee to a place to hang out: a home away from home. Safaricom's simple M-PESA service allows people to use mobile phones, one of the most trusted and popular devices in Kenya, to send money to relatives without opening a bank account, introducing simple telecommunications devices into the world of banking.

Even software has meanings (and what could be considered more functional and bereft of form than code?). Think, for example, of Quick-Books, which Intuit designed to address the needs of small business owners for whom accounting is often painful—in contrast to applications conceived for professional accountants. Whereas competitors created applications for people who want to do accounting, Intuit proposed applications for people who actually *do not* want to do accounting.

A significant part of our exploration focuses on products that live inside homes (furniture, lamps, kitchenware, food, and consumer electronics), simply because our inspirational sample of Italian manufacturers is well positioned in these industries. However, I hope that the diversity of my examples from several other industries and markets (see the table in appendix A), supported by findings from key studies, will leave no doubt in your mind that every product has a meaning.

After all, we are humans. We spend our entire lives looking for meaning. Who really believes that we can smile at our spouse and children or cheer our colleagues, and then, after a millisecond, switch off our limbic system and become inhuman when we drive our cars or buy the next peripheral for our offices?

Product Meanings and Languages

Our model for investigating design and innovation—illustrated in figure 2-1—shows that products appeal to people and their needs along two dimensions. The first one is familiar to anyone managing innovation: the utilitarian function, provided by product performance and based on technological development.

The second dimension concerns sense and meaning. It is the "why" of a product—the profound psychological and cultural reasons people use the product. This dimension can imply an individual or a social motivation. Individual motivation is linked to psychological and emotional meaning: I use a Metamorfosi lamp because it helps strengthen the parental bond and create poetic feelings while I'm doing infant massage on my baby. Social motivation is linked to symbolic and cultural meaning: what the product says about me and others. That is, I buy a Metamorfosi lamp because it tells visitors that I like to explore contemporary home lifestyles and philosophies.

A product's *language* is its material, texture, smell, name, and, of course, form (style is only one aspect of a product's language).[36] For

FIGURE 2-1

Innovation and people's needs

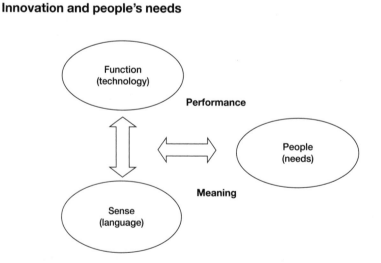

Adapted from Roberto Verganti, "Design as Brokering of Languages. The Role of Designers in the Innovation Strategy of Italian Firms," *Design Management Journal* 14, no. 3 (Summer 2003): 34–42.

example, in Metamorfosi, translucency and minimalism are the language used to express the sense that the lamp is not important, that it is the light that matters. Many other languages can also help users make sense of things. One example is sound: everyone knows that the distinctive language of a Harley-Davidson motorcycle is the roar of its engine as well as its form. I once met with Bang & Olufsen engineers while they were testing a prototype of their Serene mobile phone. The prototype had an unusual feature: a small electric motor, activated with a little nudge, that allowed the shell-shaped phone to unfold and fold slowly and gracefully. This feature, and the whir of the tiny motor, reminded me of other famous B&O products, such as the BeoSound 3200, a CD player that opens automatically as the user moves closer and that makes the same buzzing sound. "That is Bang & Olufsen!" I thought, as the sound of the little phone tickled my memory.

The product functions themselves are also fundamental in enabling us to make sense of things—thus the vertical arrow at the center of our framework. For example, an array of customizable technical features on the Metamorfosi lamp enables users to control color combinations and light intensity and thus to feel in harmony with the domestic environment. Technologies are therefore closely related to meanings, and indeed technological breakthroughs often trigger radical innovations in meanings (we explore this further in chapter 4).

Nevertheless, although the two dimensions of our model are sometimes so entangled that distinguishing performance from meaning, and technology from language, is almost impossible, the distinction between the two dimensions can have a profound impact on firms' innovation strategy and process, as you will see. Indeed, there is a profound difference between changing a product's function but leaving its meaning untouched, and changing a function in order to radically innovate what a product means. In the latter case, the ultimate purpose of innovation is to innovate meaning (hence "function follows meaning"). And the impact on business value is much more significant, as this book shows.

The Meaning of Bookcases

To become more familiar with the framework in figure 2-1, let's examine another example of radical innovation of meanings: a bookcase.

Bookcases are commodities, you may say. Indeed, the Italian market alone sells more than 240 branded bookcases, and small artisan shops provide hundreds of unbranded ones. You may add that a bookcase is a simple product with a straightforward meaning—carrying books—and that perhaps the only way to differentiate bookcases is to provide simpler ways to assemble them and affix them to a wall, or perhaps to embroider them with beautiful materials and ledges.

However, Kartell—one of the fastest-growing furniture manufacturers in the Italian design cluster—did not follow that path in creating Bookworm. The firm grew 211 percent between 1994, the year it released Bookworm, and 2003—compared with industrywide growth of 28 percent in Italy and 11 percent in Europe during that decade. Founded in 1949 by Giulio Castelli, a chemical engineer who studied at Politecnico di Milano under Giulio Natta (who won a Nobel Prize for inventing polypropylene), the company focuses on plastic furniture. Like Artemide, Kartell has created design landmarks, such as the modular container Componibili designed by Anna Castelli Ferrieri, on view at the Museum of Modern Art in New York and the Georges Pompidou Centre in Paris; the transparent chairs La Marie and Louis Ghosts, and the plastic sofa Bubble Club, both designed by Philippe Starck. I will return often to this innovative company as we explore design-driven practices, but for now, to illustrate our product framework, let's focus on Bookworm.

This unique product, depicted in the illustration at the beginning of this chapter, has contributed significantly to the company's amazing growth: Kartell has sold more than 200,000 units. What are the reasons for this success? Bookworm represents a radical innovation of meaning: it is not meant to be affixed to the wall to carry hordes of books. Instead, it has a more intimate role: to replace a painting. Let's apply our model in figure 2-1 to this product.

The Bookworm has no shape, and that makes it another good example of the idea that design is not about form. It is a long, narrow band of colored polyvinyl chloride, traditionally a semirigid material but here having the flexibility of a sheet of stainless steel. When the user opens the small cardboard package, the shelf unrolls flat on the floor. The user then bends it into a sinuous shape of her liking.

What message does Bookworm carry? What is its sense and its language? First, it tells us it is not very studious: it cannot hold as many books as its right-angled counterparts. Second, it is not shy: its bold colors and sinuous configuration attract people's attention to the few select items that the homeowner creatively places on it. Third, it is not ostentatious: its material is plastic and its price is low compared with typical bookcases; it starts at about $200. Fourth, it is personal and unique: it comes in six colors and three possible lengths and can be shaped according to its owner's imagination.

Overall, its nitty-gritty message is, "What am I? I need to be interpreted to become your personal, unique, ingenious, and shining piece of art." And indeed, the meaning of Bookworm is not to carry books (one would definitely need to buy another bookcase, perhaps using it as a background fixture in another room). If you look at how people use this product in their homes or offices, you will always find it affixed to their most visible wall, typically at the entrance to their home. Our parents used to hang their most precious painting on such a wall to welcome visitors. But young modern householders do not want to buy anonymous paintings from unknown minor artists of the twentieth century, and masterpieces of contemporary art unfortunately are not affordable to most of them. However, through travel and hobbies young people have often been exposed to a greater range of cultural opportunities than their parents. They can substitute something even more valuable—something that talks about their own knowledge, experience, creativity, and taste: a unique bookcase, one they have shaped themselves, on which to display their preferred books, souvenirs, and trophies.

Bookworm's value is thus not in the object itself (it is not ostentatious) nor in its function, but rather in the owner's personal interpretation (indeed, Bookworm demands sophisticated use, creativity, and aesthetic taste). It helps the user say, "I belong to a cultural elite," regardless of her wallet. Bookworm thus anticipates and meshes perfectly with cultural changes in our society. After all, aren't we living in a knowledge society—one that values creativity and personal experience? Knowledge, creativity, and experience are like personal art for many young households. Aren't we living in the age of individualism? Like tattoos, Bookworm expresses each person's individuality.

Suggesting, Interpreting

Meanings result from interaction between user and product. They are not an intrinsic part of a product and cannot be designed deterministically. A company may think of a product's possible meanings and design its features, technologies, and languages to act as a platform, a space where the user can provide his own interpretation. Indeed, people love a product that suggests a meaning but allows them to make it their own companion through interpretation.

The meaning of a product can change significantly over time, although the object remains unchanged. Many people now probably buy Bookworm simply because it has become trendy. Successful products often go through a fashionable phase. However, we are more interested in the original meaning that allowed it to become so successful.

People sometimes give meanings to products that differ greatly from the original purpose. When a company detects, understands, and supports such a shift, its products may benefit from a second life. Consider Skyline, a kitchen produced by Snaidero, a major Italian manufacturer. The initial aim of the project, started in 2002 under the name Skyline_lab, was to develop a kitchen for disabled people, who have trouble using standard kitchens because wheelchairs cannot fit under worktops and cabinets are inaccessible. In designing this product, Snaidero relied on intense ethnographic observation—in cooperation with local rehabilitation institutions—to thoroughly analyze how disabled people use kitchens.

The result, Skyline_lab, released to the market in 2004, won the Good Design Award. However, in addition to attracting families and institutions with disabled residents, the product drew the attention of users who did not suffer from disabilities. The rounded form of the worktop, for example—which allows people in wheelchairs to move about easily—had broader appeal, because it increases the work area and allows people to cook without turning their backs on other people. The kitchen therefore acquired the meaning of easier interaction with family and friends. The worktop carousel, which makes items more accessible to people in wheelchairs, also appeals to users who are not disabled.

Although Snaidero had assumed that Skyline_lab's features would prove meaningful for many users, the firm did not anticipate that the biggest demand would come from traditional users. In response, the company released a version of the kitchen addressed to a broader market. This version became the firm's best-selling product after only two months and today accounts for more than 20 percent of Snaidero's revenues. Many customers do not know about the product's origin.

As these examples show, what is truly unique about design—what makes it different from other types of innovation—is that it entails innovating the meaning that people inevitably give to products. This conception shines a spotlight on the cultural dimension of products and consumption, a perspective that innovation managers often overlook when they think only in terms of improving performance.

Innovating design requires managers to ask, What is the deepest reason people buy our product? Why is it meaningful to them? And most of all, How can we gratify people and make them more content by providing products that suggest new meanings? I know you can immediately provide a long list of answers to these questions. However, I would not be surprised if these are the same answers your competitors would give. Therefore, please do not answer immediately. First, take a deep breath.

RADICAL PUSHES

[Placing Design-Driven Innovation in the Strategy of a Firm]

Innovation of meanings, like innovation of technologies, may also be radical. And radical innovation of meanings is rarely pulled by users but is instead *proposed* by firms. [IN THE ILLUSTRATION   In the woman's hand: Alessi's "Anna G." corkscrew from the Family Follows Fiction product family.]

I spied "Anna G." in a shop window. She was smiling to me, her mouth expressed a childish joy. She was wearing a combed dress in pastel colors. I picked it up in my hands[, and] her head was going up and down among her shoulders, and she waved towards me with long, thin chromium-plated arms. When I left her, I felt strangely well, as if comforted. That corkscrew of Alessandro Mendini made me feel less alone . . . It brought me back to times when I was a child, when I milled during my parents parties, and I would have picked that corkscrew and would have twisted it on the tablecloth. I'm sure these associations are pretty common in all of us, but these experiences are hardly discussed. These are things that happen, but that usually remain confined in the privacy of our imagination.[1]

In 1991 Alessi, an Italian manufacturer of household items, started a project that would revolutionize consumer goods well beyond its own industry while propelling the company to double-digit annual growth. The project, Family Follows Fiction, resulted in an entirely new family of playful plastic objects, most with an anthropomorphic or metaphoric shape. These objects included Alessandro Mendini's "dancing" Anna G. corkscrew, with its twisting head and armlike levers; Stefano Giovannoni's plastic citrus squeezer, a stylized depiction of a Chinese Mandarin in a conical hat; his nutcracker in the shape of a squirrel whose teeth crack the shells; and Mattia Di Rosa's pressure plastic bottle cap, whose name says everything: "Egidio. The little man has lost something."

People often think such products result from a sudden spark of creativity. Perhaps a designer was taking a shower, and suddenly she saw the image of a Chinese Mandarin with an orange on his head working as a squeezer. Nothing could be more wrong.

No one, before 1991, would have dared to think that a corkscrew could be "dancing" or that people could crack nuts by twisting the head of a squirrel. That kind of design does not happen by chance, and, if it does, managers usually reject it as a crazy idea, if not an insult. Family Follows Fiction is instead the result of a long research process, promoted by CEO Alberto Alessi to pursue radical innovation in what household objects (and other products) could mean to people.

Most analysts hold that the innovation strategy of firms consists of two domains: incremental and radical. According to these theories, radical innovation is the realm of technological breakthroughs. Meanings are supposed to be part of the first domain: companies can understand them better only by scrutinizing user behavior and using the resulting insights to improve their products.

However, this chapter shows that innovation of meanings, like innovation of technologies, may also be radical. And radical innovation of meanings is rarely pulled by users but is instead proposed by firms. Thus there is a third—and largely unexplored—domain in the innovation strategy of firms. This is the domain of design-driven innovation.

Radical Innovation of Meaning

Alessi's research took its inspiration from Donald Winnicott, a pediatrician and psychoanalyst who noticed how children associate everyday objects with feelings and meanings. He focused in particular on the role of *transitional objects:* those things, such as toys, teddy bears, and safety blankets, that represent the happy world when children were still united with their mothers. These objects help children move from intimate dependence on their mothers to a more autonomous psychological status, and thus these objects become almost indispensable regardless of their actual function.[2] Winnicott showed that adults also have transitional objects—although not blankets or teddy bears!

Alessi gleaned further insights from the theory of affective codes developed by Italian neuropsychiatrist and psychoanalyst Franco Fornari. This theory implies that all objects communicate a message to people through five possible codes: paternal, maternal, childish, erotic, and birth/death.[3] We can recognize many of these codes in the Alessi product family. Indeed, according to Alberto Alessi,

> Thanks to this epistemological contribution I was more comfortable when at the beginning of the '90s I started to work on our meta-project called "Family Follows Fiction." Its aim was precisely to explore in depth the Affective Structure of objects . . . There is no difference, at heart, between a coffee pot or a kettle and a teddy bear . . . We know very well that our activity has not as much the purpose to satisfy a primary need: we know that one can light up a burner, boil water, make a coffee or serve tea, dose salt and pepper, crack nuts and clean toilets also with tools that are more "normal" than those created by us. What we do is to try to answer to a desire of happiness of people.[4]

To explore these insights, Alessi assembled a research team that included Laura Polinoro, then coordinator of Centro Studio Alessi, dedicated to advanced design research; and several external advisers, such as Luca Vercelloni, an expert in consumer food culture; and Marco Migliari, an architect. This team's research suggested that the company focus its product family on the object-toy. To express this concept in specific objects that spoke a radically fresh language, the company then carefully selected a team of designers, architects, and artists, most in their thirties, with whom the company had not traditionally collaborated. This team succeeded in transforming what competitors viewed as mundane tools into transitional objects that people were waiting for.

Thus what a novice might have seen as a brainstorm stemming from a quick and spontaneous creative process was instead the fruit of a long research endeavor spurred by an explicit strategy: to radically innovate the meaning of products.

The market welcomed Family Follows Fiction with warmth. In an industry where competitors consider themselves fortunate if they keep sales stable, Alessi's revenues doubled within three years after it released Anna G. and other products. The Alessi brand was already well known among lovers of innovative objects: founded in 1921, the company had created icons of design such as the Graves kettle (see chapter 8). Now, however, the company's name became popular among everyday consumers around the world. And although Alessi occasionally enriches the family with new releases, many Family Follows Fiction products launched in 1993 and 1994 are still best-sellers.

Once the company paved the way, competitors followed. Family Follows Fiction has often been imitated—not only among household objects but also in other settings. Alessi had shown the importance of products' affective dimension, and a stream of objects inspired by "emotional design" flew into our lives.

Despite competition, imitators did not impair the brand recognition of Alessi, the radical innovator of meaning, and people still pay a premium price for its products. Indeed, while many competitors are still indulging themselves by replicating the object-toy formula, Alessi has launched other research designed to foster radical innovation. The most recent project, Tea and Coffee Towers, which ran from 2001 to 2003, is now in product development.

Radical Innovation of Meaning Always Occurs

Family Follows Fiction is one of many examples showing that companies can innovate meanings—and that they can do so radically. This book explores radical innovation of meaning in a variety of industries, from computers to food, from software to cars, from communication services to consumer electronics.

We have already encountered some of these examples. Artemide's Metamorfosi system, which shifted people's attention from a fixture to the light it creates, overturned the reason people buy lamps. Similarly, Kartell's Bookworm produced a radical change in the meaning of a bookcase. I discuss other examples, such as the Nintendo Wii, the Swatch, and the Apple iPod, in depth in the coming chapters.

Radical innovation of meaning can occur in any industry, even broadcasting. Think of the turmoil created by the reality show, invented in the late 1980s, which reached its peak in 1999 with *Big Brother*, launched by the Dutch production company Endemol. This breakthrough in the meaning of TV shows also suggests that, unfortunately, not all radical innovations of meaning contribute to human happiness, fulfillment, and growth.

Like technological change (and often because of technological change), meanings evolve through cycles of radical and incremental transitions. Think, for example, of audio players. In the 1960s and 1970s, hi-fi meant electronic systems organized in racks, with dimensions and user interfaces typical of telecommunications and laboratory equipment.

Bang & Olufsen understood that people used hi-fis not in laboratories but in homes. The company therefore asked its designers to consider how people live in these spaces and what languages modern furniture was speaking—and then had engineers adapt its products to that context. In so doing B&O turned hi-fis from pieces of electronic equipment into pieces of furniture. This overturning of meaning was so radical that not even General Electric grasped it when Jacob Jensen, a Danish designer, presented a prototype to GE before moving on to work with Bang & Olufsen.[5] This meaning dominated the market for almost three decades.

The discussion about what audio players really meant for people languished until the advent of the MP3 audio standard. Now people listen to music in their homes through computers and portable devices such as the iPod. Audio players have been dematerialized, metamorphosing from furniture sculptures into experiential systems that allow people to produce, select, buy, and share music. As with many radical technological transitions, new entrants (such as Apple) have sustained this radical transition in meaning, and that poses major challenges to incumbent firms (especially B&O).

Software applications for personal finance and small business accounting provide another example of transition cycles. As chapter 2 notes, in the late 1980s Intuit led a transformation from complete but complex applications toward simplification. Social networking is leading a new transition. Web communities such as www.wesabe.com are sources of insights on how people can increase their savings and make sensible investments. Intuit itself is exploring this emerging meaning, in which people rely on other unknown lay people, rather than only on an application or a company's experts, to deal with personal finance and accounting. Who would have imagined that people would openly share information on such a sensitive subject as taxation?

Meanings and the Innovation Strategy

We can use these lessons to expand the innovation framework introduced in chapter 2. That framework highlights two dimensions of product-user interaction: performance (functionality and technology) and meaning (product sense and language). Because companies can innovate in both dimensions, their strategy—usually described as concerned only with technologies, and thus one-dimensional—is better conceived as two dimensional. Most important, innovation can be either incremental or radical in both dimensions (see figure 3-1).

On the vertical axis, technological innovation may drive incremental improvements (such as longer life for batteries used in mobile phones) or quantum leaps in performance or breakthrough functions (such as mobile phones themselves). On the horizontal axis, innovation in product meanings can also be incremental or radical—if the new meanings differ significantly from those of products that dominate the market.

FIGURE 3-1

Framework for innovation strategy

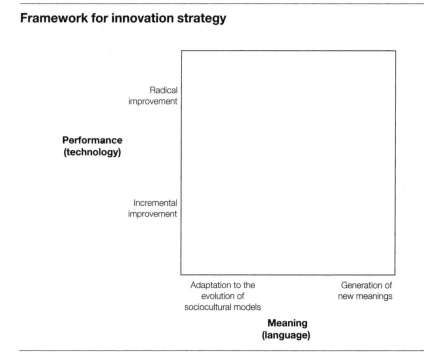

Examples include Alessi's Family Follows Fiction and Artemide's Metamorfosi system.

A Clarification: Beauty, Style, and the Incremental Innovation of Meaning

Incremental innovation in meanings occurs much more often than breakthroughs. Companies often update and adapt the language of their products to suit gradual changes in taste in the dominant meaning in the market. This is typical of fashion, for example: companies adapt the style, color, and length of clothes frequently and rapidly without questioning the basic meaning of a shirt or a pair of pants. That is why this book has little connection with the fashion industry.

Of course, incremental innovation in meanings is not limited to fashion; it occurs in any industry. Think of how the language of automotive styles gradually changed from the boxy vehicles of the 1970s and 1980s to the curvy, flowing shapes of the 1990s (some of which were so rounded that we seemed to be driving Mickey Mouse cars), to today's complex, prismatic, edgy shapes.

Or think of trends in materials and colors across industries, such as the diffusion of different hues of translucent plastic in the 1990s after the release of the Apple iMac, and the use of chrome-plated materials in cars, bikes, mobile phones, and computers today. All these examples represent incremental adaptations of product languages to evolution in societies and markets. These innovations do not question dominant meanings but simply refresh and further reinforce them. This is the domain of style.

Chapter 2 shows how beauty and innovation are often in tension. Now we can be more precise. Aesthetics and beauty—when they are the sole drivers used to design a product—are in the domain of the incremental innovation of meanings.

Look at a product that is sitting near you at this moment. Do you find it cool, sleek, and stylish? If so, you are acknowledging the ability of its manufacturer to interpret the trendiest standards of beauty in the market. Do you have the clear feeling that a designer has devised its shape, or that a manufacturer asked a design firm to create the product's user interface or style? That is a clear sign that designers have completed their exercise—that the product is stylish, in line with the dominant language of the market—but that they have also been very conservative. This is simultaneously both the success and the failure of design as styling.

It is successful because people are increasingly asking for updated and yet correct product language: they are asking for "design." Consumers have become very literate in reading the language of products, and companies hardly dare to release a product whose language is not trendy. But this is also the failure of styling from a strategic perspective. If all companies invest in incremental design and if all do it the same way using the same languages, design loses its power to differentiate one firm from another. Like total quality management, this type of approach to design is mandatory—nothing more.

That is the reason, when I listen to professors and managers say that design is a source of differentiation in mature industries, I think they are ten years behind. It used to be that way, but no longer. In 1996 Carlotta de Bevilacqua of Artemide explained that "nowadays every market-oriented company has understood that design is an advantage. As a result, all companies can use it."[6] Alberto Alessi reinforces her point:

> This interpretation of design [is] in my opinion a "gastronomic" vision of design, which acts as a more or less rare spice, as a superficial seasoning to make the industrial preparation more palatable, that is to make products more interesting . . . One can simply look around to see the results of this reductive vision of design: we are surrounded by a world of anonymous products, of boring objects, most often lacking any emotion and poesy. A classical example comes from the automotive industry, where all cars seem to look alike, rarely transmit emotions and often are totally lacking any aesthetical characteristic that is really innovative.[7]

This is not to say that companies that introduce radical innovations of meaning, such as Alessi and Artemide, do not also create incremental improvements. Alessi's catalog includes more than two thousand products, and the company releases about forty new models each year, many of them creative reinterpretations of the central theme of Family Follows Fiction. Artemide releases dozens of new lighting fixtures every year, some of them adaptations of the Metamorfosi concept of human light and others reinterpretations of the more traditional meaning of lamps as beautiful objects.

The difference between these firms and their competitors is not in whether they pursue incremental innovation but in whether they invest in radical innovation: these firms periodically search for dramatically new meanings, but their competitors do not. The radical innovators know that meanings in the market alternate between periods of incremental change and periods of rapid and disruptive transition. They aim to ensure that they will lead these transitions and let their competitors suffer the consequences.

Want to Be Radical? Forget User-Centered Innovation

How does radical innovation of meanings occur? As you saw in chapter 1, Ernesto Gismondi has been clear: "Market? What market! We do not look at market needs. We make proposals to people." Gismondi is saying that radical innovation does not occur when companies get closer to users and understand what they currently need.

He is not alone. Executives who have invested in radical innovation of meaning acknowledge that rather than start with user needs, the process goes in the opposite direction: the company *proposes* a breakthrough vision. Stunningly, Alberto Alessi uses almost the same words as Ernesto Gismondi to illustrate this concept: "Working within the meta-project transcends the creation of an object purely to satisfy a function and necessity. Each object represents . . . a *proposal*."[8]

To reinforce this idea, Alessi often refers not to users but to the "audience": "There is a way of doing design that is giving people what they ask, which is never something innovative. And there is a way of doing design that is more artistic and poetic. It is like commercial art ('commercial' because it needs to be approved by the audience; eventually people need to love it) . . . When Picasso painted, he never thought about a target audience. He didn't have a target segment of users in mind. But eventually he was not only a great artist. Those who discovered him made also a great business. There is an enormous (and unexploited) business potential also in this type of innovation."[9]

Flemming Møller Pedersen, director of design and concepts at Bang & Olufsen, uses similar language: "In our firm developing a product is like conducting an orchestra: the customers are the *audience*."[10]

The Risk of Relying on Users

Traditional market-pull methods of innovation—which scrutinize customer acceptance before releasing a product to the market—sometimes even restrict radical innovation of meaning. That is because radical innovation assumes a different context and user approach than those of products already on the market. If a company tests a breakthrough change in meaning by relying on a typical focus group, people will search for what they already know. And they will not find it in a product that is radically innovative, unless they encounter it in the right scenario.

That is why companies such as Alessi and Artemide rarely use traditional market-testing techniques. If in 1991 you had shown prospective users five nutcrackers—four traditional ones and Stefano Giovannoni's squirrel—people would have simply thought you were showing them four nutcrackers and a toy. Indeed, many accounts of radical innovation in meaning reveal that companies would never have released them to market if they had relied on market tests.

Consider, for example, Speak & Spell, the first portable electronic toy to include a low-cost single-chip voice synthesizer. Texas Instruments released Speak & Spell in 1978 at a price of $50. This product featured five educational games that helped children learn the alphabet and spell words while having fun. The meaning that Texas Instruments introduced with this object was so radical that it escaped traditional market segmentation: not a toy, not an educational tool, not a consumer electronic product, but all of them simultaneously: it was one of the first concepts of a robotic interactive *friend*, popular now, that was not meant to precisely emulate a human teacher but with whom to play, learn, and get acquainted with electronics.

Many people remember how children loved to play with this electronic friend once it was on the market. Few, however, know that early market tests of the concept were disappointing and that the company almost killed the project: focus-group leaders reported that parents thought it was only another noisy toy and that the synthesized voice was cold and dull. Only the vision and drive of four engineers (Larry Brantingham, Paul Breedlove, Gene Frantz, and Richard Wiggins) convinced the company to move the product into the market.[11]

The same thing happened when Herman Miller created the Aeron chair. Conceived as a seating machine rather than a stylish and beautiful chair, the product represented a breakthrough in meaning. The chair's most notable characteristic is that it is not upholstered nor padded. Its back and seat are instead made of a semitransparent pellicle (a synthetic material) that conforms to each person's shape, minimizes pressure, and maximizes aeration of the back. The material's transparency makes the structure and mechanisms of the chair even more visible—hence the meaning of "a seating machine."

"When we showed an early prototype to customers," says Bob Wood, vice president for research, design, and development at Herman Miller, "they asked if they could see a finished upholstered model instead of a semifinished prototype. They could not believe that was the final version." Of course, once the Aeron was on the market people loved it, and it remains one of the most coveted office chairs more than ten years after market launch.

I once asked Poul Ulrik Skifter, who was CFO of Bang & Olusfen when the company radically overturned the meaning of hi-fis, "How did you analyze user needs?" He answered, "The only time we did market research was with Beogram 4000 [a unique turntable record player whose arm does not pivot but instead moves horizontally along a radius of the disc, for greater precision]. Marketing people said it would sell fifteen units in Denmark and fifty in the world. It turned out to be one of our most successful products."

Nintendo faced similar challenges when it created the breakthrough game console Wii (see chapter 4). The Japanese company did not ask users their opinion when developing this radically innovative product. According to Shigeru Miyamoto, senior marketing director and general manager of entertainment analysis and development, "We don't use consumer focus groups. We got a lot of feedback from developers in the industry." Satoru Iwata, president and CEO, attested, "When we showed a glimpse of it at the Tokyo Game Show in September 2005, there was a stunned silence. It was as though the audience didn't know how to react."[12]

Pushing Innovation

Many observers cite Apple as a user-centered company. However, Apple actually pursues innovation by making proposals to people. In 1997 it proposed that people use the Internet to exchange electronic files. Its new desktop, the Apple iMac G3, would have been the first without a floppy-disk drive.

"Look," CEO Steve Jobs explained, "you've got to do the right thing. Just take the floppy: people aren't thinking clearly. Nobody's going to back up a 4-gigabyte drive onto 1-megabyte floppies. They'll use a ZIP drive if they want to do it."[13] He outlined the firm's approach to innovation: "We have a lot of customers, and we have a lot of research into our installed base. But in the end, for something this complicated, it's really hard to design products by focus groups. A lot of times, people don't know what they want until you show it to them."[14]

What these executives are telling us is that radical innovation of meanings does not occur when companies get closer to users. It goes in exactly the opposite direction: a company pushes a breakthrough vision into the market by making a proposal to people. When this proposal is successful and people love it, the company gains significant long-term competitive advantage.

This may sound blasphemous to many managers and scholars. We have experienced years of hype about user-centered design—theories that innovation occurs when companies get closer to users, books and stories holding that the first thing companies should do is get out there and take pictures of people using products. User-centered innovation has been the dominant paradigm of the past decade, in books and universities alike.

But we already know that radical technological innovation seldom emerges by chasing users. Mobile communication reflected decades of research on electromagnetic radio waves that targeted a basic human need: to communicate away from home. The need itself did not require much user analysis. Instead, companies made huge investments in technological research to create a device that they then pushed into the market in the early 1980s. A flow of incremental improvements supported by user-centered processes later helped produce better interfaces.

Technological breakthroughs result from the dynamics of science and engineering. And we know, thanks to studies by Clayton Christensen, a professor at Harvard Business School, why incumbent companies are incapable of creating disruptive technological innovation: they are so focused on chasing the needs of their clients that they lose sight of the big picture.[15]

The same is true of radical innovation of meaning. It does not occur when companies get closer to users with a huge lens and scrutinize how they behave in the current context. If Ernesto Gismondi and his Artemide team had gone into people's homes to take pictures of how they use lamps, change bulbs, and turn lights on and off, they would have found better ways of changing bulbs and switching lights on and off. That is useful, but not when companies are investing in radical innovation of meaning.

No one can seriously think that people were asking for "a light that makes me feel better" before Artemide created Metamorfosi. Nor can one seriously think that it is possible to create a dancing corkscrew that substitutes for a teddy bear simply by looking at how people pull corks from a bottle. That was outside the spectrum of possibilities of what people knew and did. But it was not outside what they could dream of and love, if only someone could propose it to them. And after Artemide and Alessi launched their products, people did indeed love them.

New Meanings, New Culture

Hence, although these executives may seem like crazy or old-style managers who have not read the latest best sellers on user-centered innovation, they know what they are doing. They are persistent radical innovators who actually make people happier than many of their incremental and user-centered competitors do.

Simply put, their innovation process is different. And that is reasonable, if we think about how meanings evolve. Meanings reflect the psychological and cultural dimensions of being human. The way we give meaning to things depends strongly on our values, beliefs, norms, and traditions. In other words, they reflect our cultural model. And that, in turn, reflects what occurs in our personal lives and our society.[16]

For example, if a person thinks that owning and driving an SUV is cool, that is because in her social world, products that are big, powerful, and expensive are valuable. And if someone likes the complex leverage of a corkscrew when she pulls a cork from a bottle, perhaps that is because it tickles the little engineer inside each of us and gives us a sense of mastery over the wine bottle.

But if society changes and fuel consumption becomes a great concern in our social world, then the meaning of an SUV also changes, and a Toyota Prius, a hybrid previously considered a little goofy, becomes the object of our interest. Similarly, when we see an anthropomorphic corkscrew smiling at us from a shop window, we suddenly discover a new dimension of childhood we did not think of before when using a corkscrew. A radical innovation of meaning therefore reflects a radical change in sociocultural models.

And sociocultural models do change. They often change incrementally. But, periodically, they undergo major transitions. That may occur for several reasons: rapid changes in the economy, public policies, art, demographics, lifestyles, and, last but not least, science and technology.

Companies that propose products with new meanings may enhance, support, or even trigger these transitions. The products we see and use shape our culture. If we like to spend more time in our kitchens and even connect them to other rooms, it is because companies such as Alessi transformed a closed-off area dedicated exclusively to the functional aspects of preparing food and washing dishes into a space that is open, hospitable, and enjoyable.

Or if we think a watch can be a fashion accessory rather than a jewel or a timekeeping tool, it is because Swatch launched its watch in 1983. The company changed the way we see things. The seed of this new meaning was probably already there, hidden within sociocultural changes during the early 1980s. But the seed did not sprout and blossom until a company spotted it and transformed those changes into a product and made it real. If Swatch had not done so, perhaps a competitor would have found the seed later. Or maybe not. Who knows? It is like technologies: who knows whether and when lightbulbs would have been invented if Thomas Edison had not created them in 1879.

Maybe it was only a matter of time, or maybe technological trajectories would have followed a different path as new opportunities emerged.

Searching for New Cultural Paradigms

To better illustrate the link between sociocultural models and radical innovation of meanings, we can borrow the concept of *regimes* or *paradigms* from studies of technological innovation. A technological regime dominates an industry: it is the set of research routines shared by engineers in the field and their beliefs about what is feasible, or at least worth attempting. Technological regimes signal the boundary between incremental and radical innovation. Incremental innovation occurs within a technological regime, whereas radical technological innovation is associated with a change of the dominant regime.

Analogously, we can talk of a sociocultural regime or paradigm: the dominant sociocultural model in a social world. Innovation of meanings can occur within the current sociocultural regime, in which case it is incremental, or it may create a completely new regime, in which case it is radical.[17]

A company looking for radical innovation of meaning does not get too close to users, because the meaning users give to things is bounded by the existing sociocultural regime. Instead, when investing in radical innovation of meaning, companies such as Artemide and Alessi take a step back and investigate the evolution of society, economy, culture, art, science, and technology.

This is not to say that they analyze trends: those are visible because they are already happening. These companies instead search for new possibilities that are consistent with the evolution of sociocultural phenomena but that are not there until a company transforms them into products and proposes them to people. They look for the seeds that they can cultivate into blossoms. They have a superior ability to understand, create, and influence new product meanings.

This does not mean that they do not care about people's needs. Rather, they carefully investigate how people give meaning to things. First, Ernesto Gismondi says, the company looks at *people*, not users. When a company gets very close to a user, it sees him changing a lightbulb and loses the cognitive and sociocultural context—the fact that he has children, a job, and, most of all, aspirations and dreams.

Second, the company looks at people within a changing sociocultural context. To understand possible new meanings, the company steps back and looks at the big picture to see what people *could* love in a yet-to-exist scenario and how they might receive new proposals.

Three Innovation Strategies

These insights enable us to identify three innovation strategies (see figure 3-2).

Market-pull innovation starts with an analysis of user needs and then searches for technologies that can better satisfy them, or updates product

FIGURE 3-2

The three innovation strategies

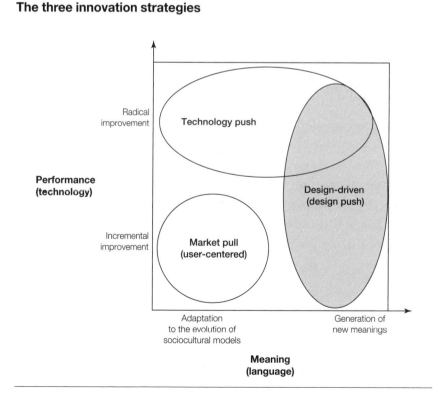

languages to respond to existing trends.[18] User-centered innovation (or user-centered design) can be considered a type of market-pull innovation. It aims not to question and redefine dominant meanings but rather to better understand and satisfy them. Because user-centered innovation is more effective than traditional market-pull approaches, it reinforces the existing sociocultural regime even more powerfully. It therefore falls within the domain of incremental innovation.

Radical innovation of technologies—or *technology-push innovation*—reflects the dynamics of advanced technological research. Light-emitting diodes (LEDs), which are now diffusing throughout the lighting industry, stem from research in the 1920s on the ability of semiconductor diodes to emit electroluminescent light. This research followed the typical pattern of scientific discovery and technological development: it was punctuated by breakthroughs (the discovery of red, green, and then blue LEDs), followed by incremental improvements pushed into the market to answer a need for smaller and more efficient ways of creating light.

Technology-push innovation has been the focus of voluminous studies for a simple reason: technological breakthroughs have a disruptive impact on industries and are often the source of long-term competitive advantage.[19] Such innovation has been called *radical, disruptive, discontinuous, competence-destroying, new paradigms, new cycles,* and *new trajectories,* among other names.

We call the radical innovation of meanings *design-driven innovation,* or *design push,* because it is propelled by a firm's vision about possible breakthrough meanings and product languages that people could love (retrospectively, people often seem to have been simply waiting for them). Design-driven innovation resembles the process of technology push more than that of market pull.

Balancing the Innovation Portfolio

Companies can use the diagram in figure 3-2 to analyze their innovation strategy. Many projects fall within the domain of market pull. These include modifications and expansions of existing product lines, adaptations of product languages and styles to new market trends, and new models with improved performance or new functions that satisfy existing needs. All these can be the source of short-term profit. However, sustained competitive advantage and long-term profit come from projects that embody radical innovation in technology or meaning. Here is where companies build their future.

Studies have shown that firms that create successful breakthrough technologies become industry leaders, often replacing incumbents that focus on existing technologies. Design-driven innovation can be similarly disruptive and essential. It is essential simply because sooner or later, a radical transition in dominant meanings in the market will occur. Just as with technologies, which evolve through alternating periods of incremental and radical change, sociocultural models inevitably alternate between marginal and radical transitions. Explains Brian Walker, CEO of Herman Miller, "Every few years we do global-scale scenario planning, where we look out a number of years and create multiple visions of how we think the world may change. We ask ourselves, if the world did evolve along one of those paths, how would that affect the way people work, live and feel?"[20]

Analogously, Alessi has launched four major research projects in the past twenty-five years aimed at design-driven innovation. These projects include Tea and Coffee Piazza (1979–1983), which focused on the new languages of postmodernism (see chapter 5); Memory Containers (1990–1994), which focused on creatively and spontaneously mixing cultures; Family Follows Fiction (1991–1993), described earlier in this chapter; and Tea and Coffee Towers (2001–2003), which focused on finding new design codes in the language of digital architecture and the new poetic languages of Asian designers. These projects have given birth to entirely new product families (followed by several incremental reinterpretations) that have changed the industry's sociocultural regime, built the Alessi brand, and sustained the firm's growth for three decades.

A company whose innovation portfolio has no projects in the domain of design-driven innovation can be confident of one thing: it will soon witness a competitor introducing a radical change of meaning and therefore leading the market.

4

TECHNOLOGY
EPIPHANIES

[The Interplay Between Technology-Push
and Design-Driven Innovation]

Radical innovation of technologies and radical innovation of meanings are closely entangled. Every technology embeds many meanings, some of which are potentially disruptive, although they are not visible at first. [IN THE ILLUSTRATION Nintendo Wii.]

An article in the July 2007 issue of *Sports Illustrated* included the following passage:

> It wasn't exactly Bjorn Borg shrieking at the sky after winning Wimbledon, but there was a certain drama to Russ Yagoda's celebration at the Brooklyn tavern Barcade last Saturday. The 23-year-old advertising account executive fell to his knees on a patch of AstroTurf, exultant at having won the first Wiimbledon championship. That's no typo—Yagoda was competing in Wii Tennis, which is played on the popular Nintendo video-game console with motion sensor controllers that players swing like a real racket . . . "I feel like a champion," said Yagoda, who won a Wii console. "Somebody asked me if I'd rather win Wiimbledon or Wimbledon. I said, 'What's Wimbledon?'"[1]

With the Wii, Nintendo overturned the electronic entertainment industry. The game console is now the most popular on the market, having overtaken its competitors, the PlayStation 3 and the Microsoft Xbox. The Wii effectively combines a radical innovation of meaning with a radical innovation of technology. On the one hand, it has redefined what playing with a game console means: not passive immersion in a virtual world targeted to young adepts, but active entertainment, even a workout, in the real world for people of all ages and demographics. On the other hand, the company has achieved this result thanks to the use of a breakthrough technology: MEMS (microelectromechanical systems) accelerometers, which allow the console to sense the speed and orientation of the controller.

This chapter focuses on the interplay between radical innovation of meanings and radical innovation of technologies—an interplay that can reconfigure competition in an industry. In other words, the chapter focuses on the upper-right corner of our map of innovation strategy, where technology-push and design-driven innovation overlap (see figure 4-1).

FIGURE 4-1

The interplay between technology-push and design-driven innovation

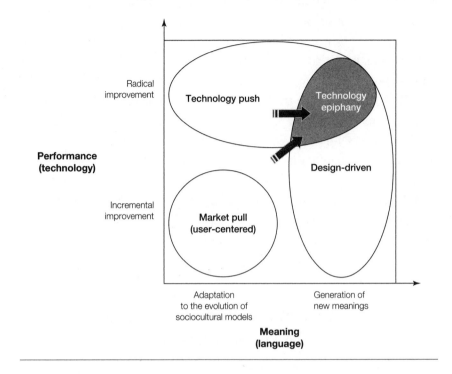

Although these two strategies do not conflict, some companies tend to focus on only one aspect. Microsoft, for example, has mastered technological transitions while often allowing competitors to define breakthrough meanings.[2] Alessi, in contrast, has mastered radical innovation of meanings but is a follower in technological breakthroughs. Despite these examples, the two strategies can significantly complement each other. The reason is that technological and sociocultural models are tightly entangled. They *coevolve* through both small (incremental) and large (radical) innovation cycles.[3]

This interplay between design-driven and technology-push innovation is at the heart of some of the most successful products in varied industries. This chapter considers three cases: the Nintendo Wii, the Swatch, and the Apple iPod. These examples show that when a novel technology emerges, shortsighted companies simply substitute it for an old one, leaving existing meanings untouched. But a new technology often hides a more powerful meaning. Eventually a company discovers and reveals that quiescent meaning—celebrating what I call a *technology epiphany*—and in so doing becomes the market leader.

High-tech companies, especially their R&D managers, and technology suppliers often see design as marginal in their context. This chapter is especially for them. High-tech firms (such as Nintendo) will see how technology epiphanies—the discovery of quiescent meanings—can allow them to seize the full potential of their research and investments. Technology suppliers (such as the producers of MEMS accelerometers for the Wii) will see how to leverage design-driven innovation to search for disruptive commercial applications of new components.

This chapter is also for scholars of technology management who think that design has no role in the early, turbulent phases of an industry, and that it may become relevant only (if ever) in mature phases as a differentiator. Enjoy your reading.

Overthrowing Competition: The Wii and the Resurrection of Nintendo

Nintendo is one of three major players, with Sony and Microsoft, in the $30 billion video game market.[4] The company was the leader in game consoles in the late 1980s and early 1990s, when it refueled a collapsed industry with new approaches to game design, better graphics, and new titles.

But with the launch of the Sony PlayStation (1995), the PlayStation 2 (2000), and the Microsoft Xbox (2001), Nintendo lost its leadership and fell on hard times. The market did not welcome its new consoles with warmth: the Nintendo 64, released in 1996 as the first 64-bit console, and the GameCube, released in 2001 as a 128-bit console. The company sold 21.6 million units of the GameCube, compared with 24 million Xboxes and 120 million PlayStation 2s. Even companies designing the actual games were laying Nintendo aside: they created only 271 titles for GameCube versus 1,467 for PlayStation 2.

Microsoft and Sony pushed even harder with their latest consoles, the Xbox 360 (May 2005) and the PlayStation 3 (November 2006). Both were more powerful than their predecessors, offering high-definition images and more-complex games and graphics.[5] Nintendo instead decided to play a completely different game. "We started work on the project Revolution [the internal code name for the Wii] around the time the GameCube went on sale in 2001," says Shigeru Miyamoto, senior marketing director at Nintendo and general manager of Nintendo Entertainment Analysis and Development. "The consensus was that power isn't everything for a console. Too many powerful consoles can't coexist. It's like having only ferocious dinosaurs. They might fight and hasten their own extinction."[6]

The Wii, released in November 2006, offered a radical change in meaning compared with its competitors. It was a physical experience to be played not with thumbs but with the entire body, using natural movements common to sports and vigorous games. Thanks to its innovative motion-sensitive controllers, people could serve tennis balls by circling their arms overhead, play golf by swinging, run an automotive grand prix by turning a steering wheel, engage in combat by thrusting swords, and shoot by pointing at targets as if they were holding a gun. These were not simple changes in features. The Wii transformed what a console meant: from an immersion in a virtual world approachable only by niche experts into an active workout, in the real world, for everyone.

The product's language thoroughly reflects this radical change in meaning. The graphics are simplified. The style of the console is not cool and futuristic, as with the PlayStation and Xbox, but rather simple and reassuring. The motion-sensitive controller is straightforward. Even the name Wii (pronounced "we") talks about the people who are using the device rather than about playing or mystery. To clarify that this was not a traditional device for gamers, Nintendo did not even put its brand name on the console. And TV commercials for the Wii reinforced the overturning of meaning. Instead of showing virtual images, the ads turned the camera 180 degrees toward the people who were playing—typically representing many ages—as they moved and enjoyed themselves.

At the heart of the Wii and its motion-sensitive controllers is a breakthrough technology: MEMS accelerometers. These small semiconductor components sense movement and inclination along three physical dimensions (x, y, and z) by measuring changes in capacitance between moving and fixed structures. This allows the device to sense how people are holding the controller and how fast they are moving it.

The automotive industry had used MEMS accelerometers, especially in air bags, to detect whether a vehicle was undergoing a serious accident. The PC industry had also used MEMS to detect when a laptop is falling—such an event triggers a lock that secures the hard disk to protect it from damage—and to detect when handheld devices are horizontal or vertical, which triggers the device to rotate the image on the screen.

MEMS were not even new at Nintendo. The company had used a previous generation of these components, sensitive to only two dimensions (x and y), in its Game Boy portable console, allowing the user to move a ball-shaped character around a maze. However, the market reacted coldly to this product, because the meaning of the game remained the same: movement was virtual, occurring inside the game and not in the player. The Wii does not merely add a new *functionality* (being sensitive to movements of the controller) to a traditional game console, but creates a radically different *meaning* that is conveyed by all aspects of the product, including the brand, the product name, and the commercials.

The physically active experience is really at the core of the product concept. One MEMS component is in the main controller, and the other is in the Nunchuk controller, attached to the main one by a cord. This combination—along with an infrared sensor bar on the TV that detects the position of the controller—allows the device to fully sense the player's physical movements and thereby to redefine the playing experience.

Figure 4-2 illustrates the innovation strategies of the three competitors. Both Microsoft and Sony moved vertically: they invested in technological development while leaving the meaning of the product unchanged. Their investments reinforced the concept of a game console as physically inactive virtual entertainment for passionate young adepts. The Wii, in contrast, represents a radical innovation in both technology and meaning. Nintendo brought a new technology into the industry (MEMS) to transform a game console into a physically active experience for everyone.

FIGURE 4-2

Comparison of the innovation strategies of Nintendo, Sony, and Microsoft in the game console industry

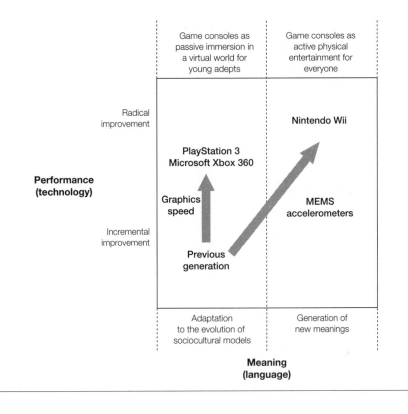

This strategy is especially interesting in the early stages of technological development. When a component such as a MEMS accelerometer is invented, its range of potential applications is huge. But for these applications to become reality, companies must consider which markets to apply them to and what possible new meanings they can drive in these markets. It is as if a breakthrough technology also embeds a set of disruptive new meanings that are waiting to be uncovered. As mentioned earlier, I call this manifestation of hidden meanings a technology epiphany. It allows companies to tap a technology's full value.

Unfortunately, theories on radical innovation often overlook the dynamics of this strategy, focusing instead on the search for new markets for a technology without questioning its meanings. The effect is that when looking for potential applications, companies focus on technological substitutions: they use a new technology to supplant an old one, thus reinforcing the existing meaning. And if the technology cannot support the existing meaning, companies simply disregard it. Indeed, Microsoft and Sony did not search for how to apply MEMS because it was useless to passive players who use only thumbs. Nintendo invested in three-dimensional accelerometers because it wanted to overturn a meaning.

This strategy of combining a breakthrough in technology with a breakthrough in meaning has proven extremely profitable for Nintendo. In the first two months after its release, the Wii sold 1 million units. In April 2007, six months after its release, the Wii's sales in the U.S. market were twice those of the Xbox 360 and four times those of the PlayStation 3. The Wii sold at an even faster rate than the most successful console ever created, the PlayStation 2. During summer 2007, cumulative worldwide sales of the Wii surpassed those of the Xbox, released a year and a half earlier—10.57 million units to 10.51—with the PlayStation 3 lagging behind at 4.3 million units.

In response, Sony announced a $100 price cut (from $599 to $499) for the most expensive version of its console. Microsoft followed with a $50 price cut on the Xbox (priced from $300 to $500, depending on the version). Sony and Microsoft ended up competing on price within the same meaning. Analysts estimated that Sony lost $200 to $300 on each PlayStation 3 console (production costs were around $800, and the multicore cell chip alone cost about $90).

It should be noted that the Wii was less expensive than its competitors (about $250). Even more important, Nintendo made a significant profit (about $50) on each console, because the Wii was equipped with less-powerful components than its rivals and therefore cost less to make.

The impact of the Wii on the Nintendo brand was also remarkable, considering that the company did not tag the device with its name. Nintendo surged seven places in the 2007 *BusinessWeek*/Interbrand annual ranking of the 100 Best Global Brands, compared with the 2006 ranking. The firm's stock price rose by 165 percent during the year after the Wii's release. On a Monday in July 2007, Nintendo's market capitalization topped $53 billion—higher than Sony's, even though that giant is ten times as large as Nintendo and also operates in the movie, music, and consumer electronics industries.

Nintendo's innovation had implications for the entire industry ecosystem. The Wii attracted game developers, allowing the company to overcome its previous weakness in game titles. Because the Wii's graphics were much less complex than those of its rivals, developers could create new games much more quickly and cheaply. Experts estimated that the average cost of developing a game for the Wii was $5 million, compared with $10 million to $20 million for PlayStation 3 and Xbox 360 (Grand Theft Auto IV required as much as $50 million). Developing a game for the Wii took only about a year, compared with two to three years for its competitors. In June 2007 the Wii counted fifty-eight titles, surpassing the forty-six titles of PlayStation 3.

The Wii's impact on society and culture also surpassed any forecast. The most popular games for the Wii were about sport: that is, they required physical movement. (A lot of movement and sweat: a high-level Norwegian official told me, in an undertone, that he had to rearrange the furnishings in his living room to use the Wii without hurting himself and damaging ornaments.)

In November 2007, Nintendo released a new breed of motion-sensitive devices (such as the Balance Board) that, with a set of Wii Fit titles, allow the user to perform various balance games (such as spinning a Hula Hoop or skateboarding) and exercises (such as yoga poses). This shifted the meaning of the Wii even further—from a traditional game console toward a tool for fitness and even physical therapy. A Canadian chain of health clubs announced plans to use the console as part of its exercise equipment. And the Sister Kenny Rehabilitation Institute at the Abbott Northwestern Hospital in Minneapolis began using the Wii to help stroke victims recover. "Doing your physical therapy is pretty boring," attested a therapist. "If you can make it into an enjoyable activity where you're moving physically and going through motions that are helping you recover, and as a part of that you're playing games that are fun, it's just a great, creative use of the technology."[7]

The Wii has also become a means of socialization. The controller's simplicity and ease of use simplify learning, allowing cruises and retirement communities to use the console. What a distance from the image of a solitary boy playing in the basement with a traditional console!

Exploiting the Potential of Quartz Technology:
The Swatch as Fashion Accessory

Swatch is a triumph of engineering. But it is really a triumph
of imagination. If you combine powerful technology with
fantasy, you create something very distinct.

—Nicolas G. Hayek, Chairman and CEO, The Swatch Group[8]

In the early 1980s, the Swiss watch industry was on the verge of extinction.[9] With a share of more than 40 percent of the world market, Swiss companies had led the watch industry until the mid-1970s. But things changed dramatically with the advent of quartz movements and digital displays.

Swiss manufacturers invented quartz movement but did not grasp its potential—shunning it instead as a technology unsuited to their core competence in precision mechanics and assembly. Japanese and Hong Kong manufacturers, however, exploited quartz, combining it with cheap labor to conquer the low end of the market.

Japanese company Hattori Seiko was the first to develop and commercialize a quartz watch with an LED (light-emitting diode) display in 1970, and the first to introduce a watch with an LCD (liquid crystal display) in 1973. As a countermove, the Swiss raised their prices to focus on the luxury market—further opening the door to the Asians, who then moved upmarket and conquered the middle segments.

By the end of the 1970s the Swiss had pulled ahead in the tiny high-end segment of watches priced at more than $400, which sold 8 million units per year worldwide: the Swiss held 97 percent of that market. But their share of watches selling for $75 to $400—42 million units sold worldwide each year—dropped to 3 percent. And their share of the 450 million-unit low-end market disappeared completely. The result was dramatic: almost 1,000 of 1,600 Swiss watch companies closed within about ten years, and employment fell from ninety thousand in 1970 to about thirty thousand in 1983. Seiko, the largest Japanese manufacturer, produced as many units as the entire Swiss industry.

In the early 1980s Nicolas Hayek was a consultant for Swiss banks that had stumbled on the crisis enveloping two major Swiss watch manufacturers: SSIH and ASUAG. These firms were considering selling some of their major brands to the Japanese. After studying the watch industry, Hayek suggested that the two manufacturers merge and compete directly with the Asians in the low-end market by offering a cheap plastic product—the Swatch.

"The banks studied our report and got nervous," says Hayek, "especially about the Swatch: 'This is not what consumers think of when they think of Switzerland. What the hell are you going to do with this piece of plastic against Japan and Hong Kong?'" But that cheap watch was not simply a piece of plastic: Hayek intended to change completely what people meant by a watch and what "consumers thought of when they thought of Switzerland."[10]

Simply put, the Swatch was not about timekeeping—although from a functional perspective it still provided this feature—but about fashion. It was priced at $40 and came in "collections" of witty and outlandish designs created by designers, architects, and artists. As in fashion, the company released two collections each year, tying dozens of models into the language of popular youth culture and current events. Given the low price of the Swatch, people could own more than one, just as with fashion accessories. When asked by a journalist how many Swatches someone could own, a Swatch manager replied, "How many ties hang in your closet? Do you stop buying new ones just because you already have 100 of them?"[11]

Nicolas Hayek explained:

> I understood that we were not just selling a consumer product, or even a branded product. We were selling an emotional product. You wear a watch on your wrist, right against your skin. You have it there for 12 hours a day, maybe 24 hours a day. It can be an important part of your self-image. It doesn't have to be a commodity. It shouldn't be a commodity. I knew that if we could add genuine emotion to the product, and attack the low end with a strong message, we could succeed . . . We are not just offering people a style. We are offering them a message.

> This is an absolutely critical point. There are many elements that make up the Swatch message. High quality. Low cost. Provocative. Joy of life. But the most important is the hardest to copy. Ultimately we are offering our personal culture.[12]

Price is an important part of the language of the Swatch. To be an accessory, the Swatch had to be cheap enough to spur an impulsive purchase. Franco Bosisio, head of the Swatch Design Lab, Milan, explained:

> Few people appreciate how and why price has been so important. Everywhere in the world. Swatch is sold at an affordable price. But it's also a simple price, a clean price. In the U.S., $40. In Switzerland, SFr50. In Germany DM60, in Japan ¥7,000. It has also been, in the first 10 years, an unchanging price . . . A Swatch is not only affordable, it's approachable. Buying a Swatch is an easy decision to make, an easy decision to live with. It's provocative. But it doesn't make you think too much.[13]

Of course, as is often the case with radical innovations of meaning, neither analysts nor consumers initially grasped what was happening. Banks were reluctant to invest and were convinced only after Hayek himself took the challenge, buying 51 percent of the new merged company, SMH (later renamed The Swatch Group), with a pool of other investors. Early market tests, especially those in Dallas, Salt Lake City, and San Diego, were disappointing. But in March 1983 Hayek launched the product anyway. "We kill too many ideas by laughing at them without thinking about them," he notes.

Although many people do not realize it, the Swatch represents a radical innovation of technologies as well as meanings. Not only did it employ the latest quartz movement (with an analog display), but also it required a breakthrough in product architecture. A watch traditionally consisted of a mechanism that was first built in its entirety and then assembled inside the case. To create the Swatch's movement, in contrast, the company bonded the components directly into the lower part of the case and sealed it with ultrasonic welding. That allowed the firm to reduce the watch's thickness from more than 4 millimeters to less than 1 millimeter, and to reduce the number of parts from about 150 (for a conventional analog watch) to 51. That, in turn, enabled the company to assemble each Swatch in a fully automated Swiss plant in a mere 67 seconds—with a labor cost of less than 10 percent of the total cost. The architecture was also modular, allowing designers to create novel collections easily and quickly, and to use computer-aided design to rapidly feed the new designs to the manufacturing plant. Without all these technological innovations, the company would never have achieved the meaning of a watch as a fashion accessory.

Uncovering a Hidden Meaning

Figure 4-3 illustrates innovation strategies in the watch industry in the early 1980s. Before the advent of quartz technology, when movements were mechanical, buying a watch meant buying a jewel. Indeed,

FIGURE 4-3

Comparison of innovation strategies in the watch industry in the early 1980s

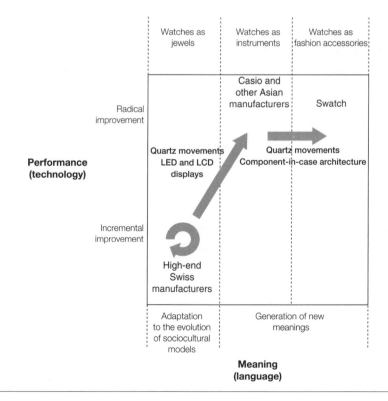

watches were usually sold in jewelry stores. I remember that in Italy, as a child, you would have received your first watch as a present for First Communion, at the age of eight. You would have kept it in a drawer: you did not expect to play soccer with a jewel on your wrist.

When quartz technology emerged, Swiss manufacturers remained static: they did not embrace it nor change the meaning of what they were proposing. By moving further upmarket, they even reinforced the traditional meaning of a watch as a luxury good. The Asians instead rode the new technological thoroughbred. By doing so, they also implicitly changed the meaning of a watch, transforming it into an instrument. Watches became tools, equipped with added functions such as timers, alarm clocks, games, and even calculators.

What Swatch did instead was to uncover the real potential of quartz movements. Before Swatch, no one had asked what radical meaning this technology could open up. A quiescent meaning was hidden behind the more obvious interpretation of digital watches as instruments: it was waiting for its epiphany—for someone to reveal it.

That the right interpreter was a forward-looking Swiss leader from outside the industry is not surprising (Hayek had a consulting company called Hayek Engineering). He was not as locked in to mechanical movements as were the Swiss incumbents and was not afraid of the new technology. But, as a Swiss, he leveraged the strength of the local manufacturing base: its legendary ability to design miniaturized watch architectures.

It was not by chance that the Swatch used analog displays instead of LEDs or LCDs. Analog movements allowed Swiss manufacturers to value their core competence by creating the component-in-case architecture. As you will see, all these characteristics—being forward-looking, seeing sociocultural phenomena from a different angle, being ready to take a risk, disregarding market tests, and leveraging a strong technological base—are key characteristics of effective design-driven innovation.

Everyone knows the outcome of the story. As with many radical innovations of meanings, sales started relatively slowly but soon soared. The company sold 1.1 million Swatches in 1983, 4 million in 1984, 8 million in 1985, and so on. The innovation produced continuous long-term growth: in 1993, ten years after product launch, the company sold

31 million watches. In 1992 the company celebrated the 100 millionth Swatch sold. In 1985, Christie's auction house sold a Swatch by Kiki Picasso, whose retail price had been SFr100, for SFr68,200. That tells us a lot about the value of the Swatch brand.

SMH, the company that launched the Swatch (and which also owns other brands, such as Omega), benefited greatly. In 1983, right after SSIH and ASUAG merged, revenues totaled SFr1.5 billion, and losses SFr173 million. Ten years later SMH generated revenues of SFr3 billion and profits of more than SFr400 million and was the world's leading manufacturer of watches, with a market share of 14 percent.

As with the Wii, the impact on profits was astonishing. Among *Fortune* 500 companies, SMH ranked 232 in revenues, 119 in market value, 70 in profits, and 22 in profits as a percentage of sales in 1994. Indeed, the entire Swiss watch industry benefited from the "Swatch effect." The world market share of Swiss manufacturers—which had been almost extinct in the early 1980s—rose to almost 60 percent in 1994, higher than in the early 1970s, before the quartz revolution.

Like the Wii, the Swatch also had an impact on culture. The meaning of a watch as a tool almost disappeared: by 1988 the market share of watches with digital displays dropped to only 12 percent. As always happens with design-driven innovation, in retrospect people seemed to have been waiting for the Swatch, although they did not think to look for it. They were waiting for the technology epiphany.

The Quiescent Meaning of Breakthrough Technologies and the Myopia of Technological Substitutions

Shortsighted companies often miss the interplay between technologies and meanings in another way: they limit their innovation strategy to *technological substitutions*. That occurs when a company simply replaces an old technology with a new one, with the goal of radically improving performance or adding functionality, leaving the existing meaning untouched. This is different from what happened in the watch industry. By investing in quartz technologies, Asian manufacturers actually transformed the meaning of watches to instruments, although another quiescent meaning (that of fashion accessory) had more powerful potential. In technological substitutions, instead, companies assume that the basic reason people buy and use a product will remain the same. Put simply, the myopic bulk of the industry embraces the new technology for utilitarian reasons—until a firm invests in design-driven innovation, unveils the hidden meaning, and realizes its full potential.

We have already seen examples of these epiphanic events. Alessi, for example, was not the first to use plastic in kitchenware. Competitors had long been substituting polymers for steel and other expensive materials for a simple reason: to cut costs. Plastic kitchenware conveyed the meaning of cheap, convenient, sometimes even disposable goods. That meaning remained unchanged until Alessi understood that the formative properties of plastic were perfectly suited to freedom of expression and playful objects that used the same materials as toys. The goal was not to reduce costs, make kitchenware disposable (one would never trash an Alessi object), or improve convenience (people often give Alessi objects as presents). Instead, it was to reveal the quiescent meaning of plastic.

The case of Kartell—the Italian manufacturer of plastic furniture such as Bookworm, as noted in chapter 2—suggests a similar revelation. Furniture manufacturers had already replaced wood with polymers because of cost and convenience. The result was that people kept such less-valuable furniture in less-noticeable areas of their homes. But who says the essential meaning of plastic is "cheap and convenient"? Kartell instead dignified plastic, exploiting its properties to create substitutes for pieces of art that everyone could afford. Similarly, in the case of Artemide's Metamorfosi, electronic and remote controls had already made their way into the lighting industry as a means to facilitate power switching and control. But such controls improved lamps as objects; they did not suggest conceiving of light as a source of well-being.

But perhaps the most famous case of a technology epiphany—of a company unveiling the hidden meaning of a technology and therefore overtaking shortsighted competitors focused on substitutions—is the Apple iPod. I will not recount the iPod story here, because business journals have already done so (even to the point of annoyance), making the iPod the archetype of successful innovation, one that challenges the lightbulb as the icon of great ideas. Instead, I will go directly to our model of innovation strategies to illustrate the myopia of technological substitutions and the power of technology epiphanies.

Figure 4-4 compares innovation strategies in the portable audio player industry, with the advent of digital audio encoding—in particular, MPEG Audio Layer 3, commonly known as MP3. Korean firm SaeHan Information Systems launched the first portable MP3 player, MPMan, in 1997. Diamond Multimedia, headquartered in California, followed with Rio PMP300 in 1998, and Compaq introduced Personal Jukebox PJB-100 in 1999. The latter had a 6-gigabyte hard drive that could store as many as one hundred CDs (about twelve hundred songs). In 2000, manufacturers launched many more MP3 players with additional features, such as Creative Worldwide's Nomad Jukebox, which had an equalizer and a sort feature.

FIGURE 4-4

Comparison of innovation strategies in the portable audio player industry in the late 1990s through the early 2000s

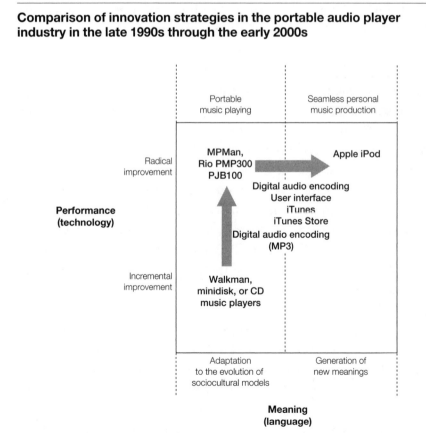

All these products shared the same vision: they were meant to substitute for existing portable cassettes or CD players. Although they offered more effective and powerful functionality, their meaning remained the same: they allowed people to listen to songs away from home. The ad for Rio PMP300 noted that "it is smaller than an audio cassette and has no moving parts, so it never skips. It's ideal for extreme sports or just walking around." The shape, size, style, and interface of these players were even exactly like those of a traditional Walkman or Discman. The names—MPMan, a substitute for the Sony Walkman; and Rio Portable Music Player300—said everything about the innovation strategy of these firms.

Instead of investing in a technological substitution, Apple seized the opportunity offered by digital audio encoding to create a radical innovation of meaning in 2001: allowing people to produce their own personal music. The iPod is not simply a portable music player. The entire system that Apple created—the iPod, the iTunes software application, the iTunes Store, the business model for selling music—offers a seamless experience: of discovering and tasting new music, buying music at an affordable $0.99 price (which meant that you were symbolically saying, "I'm not stealing music; I care for artists and I contribute to subsidize the industry. I'm a producer for new artists"), storing and organizing music collections into personal playlists, and listening to it through the iPod. (The latter became simply *the player*, and not necessarily portable: many people substitute the iPod at home for a CD player.)

Thus the iPod's success is not only due, as many claim, to its sleek style and unique functionalities such as its user interface and the number of songs it can carry (by the way, the first model, with a 5-gigabyte drive, was less powerful than the PJB-100 and the Jukebox). The main reason for its success comes from the meaning people associate with the iPod's immaterial components (iTunes, iTunes Store, and the related business model).

Not convinced? Let's look at a few hard figures. Apple launched the iPod in 2001, the iTunes Store in early 2003, and iTunes support for Windows in late 2003. Demand for the iPod started to soar in 2004, when sales were eight times as high as the cumulative sales of the first two years.[14] Similarly, Apple's stock remained at the 2001 level (less than $10) until the beginning of 2004, but it grew to almost $200 by October 2007, less than four years later. The iPod's market share among portable music players—about 75 percent in 2006—is remarkable, but that of the iTunes Store is even more outstanding: the store accounts for about 90 percent of all legal music downloads in the United States.

The iPod is therefore a perfect example of a technology epiphany: whereas other companies simply substituted a new technology for the old one but left the existing meaning intact, Apple revealed the quiescent meaning of digital audio encoding. And by integrating technology-push and design-driven innovation, the company gained extraordinary competitive advantage.

Implications for R&D and Technology Strategy

Near the Georgian border there is a spring, from which gushes a stream of oil in such abundance that a hundred ships may load there at once. This oil is not good to eat; but it is good for burning and as a salve for men and camels affected with itch or scab. Men come from a long distance to fetch this oil, and in all the neighborhood no other oil is burnt but this.

—Marco Polo[15]

The three stories I have told—of the Wii, the Swatch, and the iPod—clearly show that radical innovation of technologies and radical innovation of meanings are closely entangled. Every technology embeds many meanings, some of which are potentially disruptive, although they are not visible at first. They resemble the fountains of petroleum that Marco Polo encountered: he grasped their immediate meaning—that they can naturally produce fire and heal scabs—but no one at that time could fully envision their disruptive potential.

Few companies have understood this close link between meanings and technologies. Yet its implications are significant: first for technology-intensive firms (especially for their R&D departments), and second for technology suppliers. Let's examine why this is true.

The R&D department in any firm is the kingdom of engineers and scientists (I am telling you this as an engineer who spent his early years after graduation working for a high-tech telecom manufacturer). In R&D departments, especially in technology-intensive companies, design has a minor role, if any. High-tech companies may acknowledge that design is eventually useful for designing a proper user interface, thus making a technology more accessible, and for wrapping the technology core in a nice box, but nothing more.

Existing theories of management of innovation and technological breakthroughs corroborate this view of design. These theories usually describe industries as evolving through several stages.[16] In the early stage, one or more radically new technologies break into an industry, allowing leapfrog changes of functions and performance. This stage sees the birth of many new competitors, which struggle to find the most effective product architecture and solve technological problems. Then, when the technology has run its course, innovation becomes incremental, the product becomes a commodity, and everyone waits for another technological breakthrough.

In these theories, design plays a role only downstream (if theorists even consider it) after the technology has provided everything it can— that is, during incremental innovation, and even commoditization. Theorists see design as a *differentiator:* the last weapon companies may use to make their products look different from those of their competitors. Hence the association of design with mature products, fast creativity, user interface, and style. This interpretation is appropriate in the context of incremental innovation. But as the stories of the game consoles, watches, and digital music players reveal, it is myopic in the case of technological breakthroughs.

"Technologies offer opportunities," says semiologist Giampaolo Proni, "which are of course not infinite (quartz movements cannot be used to wash teeth), but are greater in number than those imagined by early developers. Like the petroleum wells of Marco Polo: their opportunities had not been completely envisioned."[17]

In its radical version as design-driven innovation, design may play a major role at an industry's inception, especially when a breakthrough technology arises. Figure 4-5 illustrates the lessons from our three cases. When a breakthrough technology emerges, it embeds many potential meanings. Some are immediate, usually promoted by those who have initially guided technological development. Other meanings are quiescent, but sooner or later they become manifest, like those of the Vesuvio volcano. Inhabitants of Pompeii gave that friendly peak

FIGURE 4-5

Comparison of strategies to manage breakthrough technologies: purely technology push or interwoven with design-driven innovation

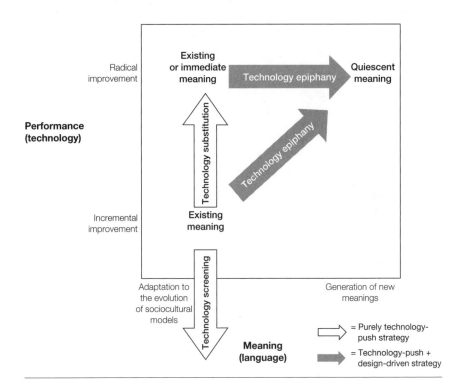

the most immediate meaning they could think of: it was a mountain. These residents populated the mountain with vineyards and farms, disregarding even strange signs such as frequent earthquakes (considered normal in that area) and the conical summit, with its large flat area surrounded by a steep and rocky rim. In 79 A.D. the mountain dramatically revealed its quiescent meaning.

A company that sees innovation strategy as monodimensional—that is, consisting only of technological innovation—will not search for the quiescent meaning. This approach leads to two myopic behaviors. On the one hand, if the most immediate meaning of a new technology does not fit with the existing meaning in the market, companies will likely screen that technology off and consider it irrelevant to competition (the down-pointing white arrow in figure 4-5). This is what happened in the game console industry, when Microsoft and Sony did not invest in MEMS accelerometers simply because physical movement in the real world was not what their adept users were searching for.

If the most immediate meaning of the new technology does fit the existing meaning, a company will invest by substituting the new technology for current technologies (the up-pointing white arrow in the diagram).

However, someone will eventually have a technology epiphany: the manifestation of the essential and more-powerful meaning of the technology.[18] The impact on competition will be disruptive. The innovator might be a competitor (such as Nintendo or Swatch), a new entrant in the industry (such as Apple), or even users themselves.[19]

A technology epiphany may occur when a company has understood that a radical new meaning can emerge in the market and therefore is open to new technologies (Nintendo and MEMS accelerometers)—usually those that competitors have screened off (the diagonal arrow in figure 4-5). Or a technology epiphany may occur when a company searches for the more-powerful meanings that a new technology embeds (Swatch and Apple), as indicated by the horizontal arrow.

What are the bottom-line implications of this analysis? First, the full potential of technological breakthroughs is achieved only when someone uncovers the more-powerful quiescent meaning of a new technology. Second, a technology epiphany is usually much more disruptive to competition than is the technological breakthrough itself.

Third, as soon as a new technology emerges, companies should rapidly look for the technology epiphany before their competitors do. They should ask, "What is the hidden meaning of this technology? What is its real interpretation? How can we exploit its full potential? What breakthrough changes in meaning (and therefore in competition) could it drive?" In other words, they should invest in both technology-push and design-driven innovation.

Fourth, given that technology-push and design-driven innovation are closely linked, design is critical for high-tech firms and their R&D departments. If investigations into radical new technologies should go hand in hand with investigations into radical new meanings, then R&D cannot be immune to design. Nicolas Hayek had studied mathematics and chemistry and created an engineering company—none of which prevented him from asking himself about the quiescent meaning of quartz technologies.

Part 2 of this book shows how this process works. In particular, chapter 8 shows how an R&D manager at Barilla, an Italian food company, has activated the search for a technology epiphany. Part 3 illustrates more deeply how pioneering companies are reorganizing R&D to leverage the interplay between technologies and meanings.

Implications for Technology Suppliers

In 2007 an organization launched a design competition called Vision-Works Award: People in Motion. The competition asked young designers to envision how people could live in cities in 2020 and to propose products accordingly. This organization is not a car manufacturer, not a transportation service company, and not a governmental institution concerned about the future of its citizens. The organization is Bayer Material Science, a German company that produces polymeric materials, part of the Bayer Group. What does Bayer have to do with design?

Companies operating upstream in the supply chain—especially those providing high-tech components and materials—often think that design is not relevant for them. They assume that it matters only in consumer products. That would be true if design dealt only with style, beauty, and ergonomics. But if we think of design as the process of innovating meanings—especially the interplay between technology-push and design-driven innovation—we can see how design could bring value to upstream technology-intensive companies.

They can leverage design in two ways. The first is the most immediate: their industrial clients look for new meanings when they buy a component, a material, or an instrument. Consider manufacturers of custom integrated circuits. Traditionally, clients asked these companies to develop a specific chip tailored to their needs. This process was largely ineffective: the client had to provide specifications, and then the manufacturer designed a prototype requiring several costly iterations. In the 1980s, LSI Logic Corporation created a do-it-yourself software application. When combined with a "gate array" chip architecture, this software allowed clients themselves to design, simulate, and test a chip according to their specific needs. The clients could then simply give LSI the file, with instructions to manufacture the component. In this way LSI changed the meaning of what chip manufacturers could offer: instead of a rigid design-manufacturing process, it empowered its clients' design abilities, stimulated their creativity and innovation, and supported them with flexible manufacturing.[20]

Technology suppliers can also leverage design and meanings because their components and materials will eventually interact, through their clients' products and services, with end consumers. Some upstream manufacturers have even made their core component a clearly visible part of an end product so that users will ask for it. Think, for example, of the Intel Inside strategy (which links purchasing a personal computer to choosing an internal microelectronic component) or of Brembo, which transformed anonymous brakes for cars and motorbikes into symbols of high performance, sometimes made in bright colors, that are visible through a vehicle's wheels.

But regardless of visibility, what is most interesting is that a supplier's technological breakthrough can radically change the meaning of an end product. In other words, the reason technology suppliers should be highly concerned with innovation of meanings and design is that their components often generate technology epiphanies. They hide a quiescent meaning that could overturn their clients' industries, as you have seen in the case of MEMS accelerometers and the Nintendo Wii.

How STMicroelectronics Leveraged the Meaning of MEMS

If a client asks for a specific feature or component, it means that someone else has already created it.

—Bruno Murari, scientific adviser for MEMS,
   STMicroelectronics

If you are a technology supplier, are you waiting for your client to understand the quiescent meaning of a novel component, or—even worse—waiting for a competitor to propose it? Or will you move first?

STMicroelectronics, a major manufacturer of MEMS components and a supplier of accelerometers for Nintendo, moved first. Research on microelectromechanical systems made its first faltering steps in the

1970s, shadowed by investments in MOS (metal oxide semiconductor), the most popular chip device. Bruno Murari led STMicroelectronics' research on MEMS for several gloomy years, gaining top management support before the first commercial applications took off in the early 2000s. Says Murari, "We were struggling to find viable applications in large markets. We tried applications in rotational and linear sensors for hard disks, but it didn't work."[21] Yet Aldo Romano, CEO of STMicroelectronics Italy, was confident of the abilities of his team: "We started to envision possible applications in different fields. The basic idea was to think more *abstractly* of what MEMS could provide in final products: information on movement and position. This can be used for automation, or, even more interestingly, for simplifying human interfaces. Then we proposed our envisioned applications directly to the most innovative engineers of potential clients in current or new markets."

The first commercial application of MEMS in 2003 was the least expected: Maytag, a white goods manufacturer that aimed to make its products more durable, used MEMS as vibration-control devices in washing machines. Significant sales came in 2005, when Toshiba used STMicroelectronics MEMS to implement the Free Fall feature, which senses when a notebook PC is falling and automatically retracts the head from the hard disk.

Finally, in 2006, Nintendo used the company's MEMS in the Wii. "We had already tried applications of MEMS in game consoles," says Benedetto Vigna, STMicroelectronics vice president and general manager of the MEMS product division:

> Our vision was to enable people to play through real and intuitive movements. In 2001 we created a prototype of a game controller for Microsoft in 11 days. It was a hand controller, to be used as a handlebar in a game of motocross competition. But the technology was still not ready. Next we simulated a Ping-Pong game with our labs in Grenoble and Milan. The device was fine, but there was no software. Finally, we proposed our technology to Nintendo in March 2005. We had three-axis accelerometers, and had created a packaging solution that cut costs significantly. Nintendo was looking for that, and was already working on the software. We were just ready.

From applications in washing machines, to game consoles, to future biomedical systems, the evolution of MEMS is one of continuous epiphanies. MEMS is now the fastest-growing market in semiconductors, expanding by 50 percent per year and expected to produce $10 billion in sales by 2010. It is also the fastest-growing business for STMicroelectronics. The company continues to envision new meaningful applications by investigating final consumer markets with its clients. For example, it has conducted a joint investigation with a leading manufacturer of mobile phones. A team of eight engineers and business development managers from both firms held a three-day workshop to explore new interactive scenarios using mobile phones enabled by MEMS.

Bayer Material Science also heavily invests in understanding sociocultural changes so that it can propose new materials and uses to its clients before its competitors do. The Creative Center—within the upstream technology supplier's New Business division—systematically analyzes and simulates changes in society and culture that could affect the markets of its current and prospective clients and lead to new applications of polymers. In other words, the Creative Center is the company's research lab for technology epiphanies.

In 2005, for example, the center launched Future Living 2020, with thirteen research institutions, universities, and clients, to investigate how trends such as dramatic urbanization and nomadism among workers will affect people's lives in the long term. The project produced two scenarios envisioning what life in cities, homes, and workplaces will look like. Says engineer Eckard Foltin, who heads the Creative Center,

> It is important to identify the development needs and market opportunities for new plastics applications as early as possible. The Creative Center develops new solutions for growth markets that focus on a timeframe of more than 10 years. Our sister group, New Technologies, concentrates on finding new developments and processes for materials. Industry Innovations then uses its practical experience to convert our project ideas—which we depict via feasibility studies—into initial applications with key customers. By building a picture of how the future might

look, we can make the development paths for our materials more transparent, and shape them accordingly. This approach enables us to tap into new business opportunities in both existing and completely new markets.[22]

The project has since focused on specific sociocultural scenarios to better understand how to showcase the full potential of new polymers. These efforts include Future Construction, with companies from the construction and housing industry, which investigates potential applications in homes; Future Logistics, which focuses on delivering goods; and People in Motion, which examines how people will move around in cities. The latter project, for example, is developing new materials such as smart luminous surfaces for car interiors, which aims to change how people feel about spending time in a car.

Bayer couples these long-range scenarios with shorter-term explorations of potential applications, often cooperating with students and professors at design schools. For example, in 2007 the company launched a competition focusing on urban mobility among five European design schools. Bayer provided the schools with the sociocultural scenarios from the Future Living 2020 project, know-how in materials and technology, and support for creating prototypes. Students proposed some one hundred concepts, judged by an independent jury, which awarded prizes. Through such strategies clients have come to rely on Bayer to suggest opportunities they have not yet envisioned.

Note that Bayer's strategy is to search for *meanings* rather than only market applications. And the company investigates sociocultural scenarios with design schools—not marketing schools and MBAs. It does not look for linear projections and figures on potential markets but for meaningful new proposals. This approach is crucial. In the case of the Wii, a technology supplier focusing only on markets and not on meanings would have screened off several disruptive applications simply because they did not fit the dominant meanings in the market. No one would have thought of using MEMS accelerometers in game consoles if the meaning had been that of virtual entertainment, implying only movement of thumbs. But once a company questioned the dominant meaning and explored new possibilities in culture and society, fresh applications became visible.

Unfortunately, this forward-looking approach to meanings and search for epiphanies is uncommon among upstream technology suppliers. Those companies often wait and see. Most do not focus on the final market, or they mistakenly believe that their clients can better understand the evolution of society and culture.

Consider Corning, a well-known manufacturer of glass and related components. Corning relies on its clients—such as Luxottica, an eyeglass manufacturer, and Samsung, which makes LCDs for cell phones and flat-screen monitors—to provide specifications for glass substrates. Corning's scientists think that because these clients are closer to end users, they are better positioned to understand future meanings and translate them into technical requirements. Investigating how people could use screens differently in their homes, or how they could use eyeglasses, is deemed not of Corning's concern. It would rather play the role of solving the problems of immediate clients by providing better functionality. A Corning scientist justified the company's minor interest in meanings and epiphanies by saying that the company "makes flat screens, and they are flat." But the risk is that the company will act too late when its clients ask for completely new developments, or that the clients will turn to other suppliers that have actively searched for technology epiphanies—or simply that Corning will lose market opportunities in new businesses.[23]

This chapter has challenged the common assumption that design is irrelevant in turbulent high-tech industries and that it simply acts as a differentiator in mature consumer markets. On the contrary, in its radical form as design-driven innovation, design may be as disruptive as a breakthrough technology. Even better, it can be the weapon that allows a breakthrough technology to disrupt an industry.

Design therefore plays a much more critical role in the early phases of technological development than in mature markets (where, as earlier chapters note, it no longer acts even as a differentiator). The real impact occurs when design enters the agenda of high-tech firms and their technology suppliers.

Car manufacturers are struggling to replace internal combustion engines with more-sustainable technologies, such as fuel cells. These technologies, however, will not leave the meaning of cars unchanged. For example, they will overturn a car's architecture, changing it into a large skateboard (with a flat, thick base filled with batteries and other propelling components), with the body easily assembled on top of it. This architectural change will likely unleash new, radical meanings and a redefinition of business models in the industry; the first company to grasp it, by combining investments in technology with design-driven innovation, will eventually lead the competition.

THE VALUE AND THE CHALLENGES

[Why Companies Do or Do Not Invest in Design-Driven Innovation]

It was a "car in sneakers." You buy sneakers not because they are cheaper, but because you want them. [IN THE ILLUSTRATION Fiat's Panda.]

K ARL, I'M HAPPY you like our design for the new printer. Our guys will appreciate knowing that," said Susan to her CEO. Susan was the director of industrial design and human interface in a well-known company in the office equipment business. She had heard, through colleagues, about the CEO's blessing of the printer design. Their fortuitous encounter in one of the long, impersonal corridors of company headquarters was the opportunity she had been waiting for. She continued, "Karl, I think . . . our team thinks we might have the potential to provide a more substantial contribution. I mean, more than designing the body and user interface of our products."

The CEO, who was rushing into a board meeting, smiled at Susan as if she were his teenage daughter asking for permission to go to a concert. "Are you saying we should invest more in design? Susan, you know I'm always open. But we need to gauge the return on the investment. Could you provide me with a financial analysis of the value of design?"

I was witnessing the scene. Karl turned to me and winked. He knew that questions fall into three categories: those for which there is an answer, those for which there is no answer but that are worth investigating, and those that have no answer. His was of the latter species. It was a clever way to politely say no.

Indeed, I had heard Karl's question, in one form or other, several times, and I had read articles and reports trying to assess the value of design—some methodologically quirky, others patently flawed. Three weeks later Susan contacted me, asking for help. "I'm sorry, Susan," I responded. "Executives like Ernesto Gismondi, Alberto Alessi, and Steve Jobs did not invest in design on the basis of a financial analysis." A comment by Jacob Jensen, a Danish designer who had designed many top sellers for Bang & Olufsen, came to mind:

> If the idea is so exciting and sustainable, [then] the manufacturers don't care if it's difficult. They will spend the money when

and if they can see that the idea is so obviously right. There's no excuse, no "Sorry, I can't afford that" . . . If you bring your idea to your friends, which the people you work with or for should preferably be, and if when you put your idea on the table in front of them, you have to explain the idea, then you can just forget it. On the other hand, if you bring your idea and people say, "I'll be damned! How can we make this?" then you are already rolling. The process grabs itself, steers itself, and one is almost shoved aside in the beginning, because the technicians have a problem to solve . . . a solution to find.[1]

My experience with top executives is that if they ask for a financial analysis *before* they decide something, it is because they are not convinced. Moreover, no financial analysis, even when it is produced, will ever convince them. The vision comes first. Figures are essential, but they come *afterward*, to support its feasibility.

I told Susan, however, that I had a suggestion. But I cannot reveal it at this point. As in any respected thriller, the solution to the puzzle will emerge in the final chapter.

Still, I will not mislead you here trying to demonstrate the financial value of design-driven innovation. We are talking about innovation—not throwing dice. The difference between profit and loss in innovation is not in the amount of the investment but in how you invest. Luckily, if you have had the patience to read this book to this point, it is because you do not want to be convinced; you want to know *how*. I will therefore show how design-driven innovation can bolster a company's economics: where the benefits come from and where the challenges are. In this way, when the right proposal is on your table you will see the threads that connect it to financial results, along with the challenges you might face.

Before I provide this analysis, two important notes. First, I am not talking about the value of design in general but of *design-driven innovation*, a very specific approach. Second, I focus especially on one benefit that is peculiar to the radical innovation of meanings: the ability to create products with a life cycle significantly longer than that of the competition. This ability is crucial in the current innovation race, where products tend to survive for a very short time, and firms are unwilling to waste resources in constant redesign.

The Value of Design-Driven Innovation

What happens when a company launches a product with a radical new meaning and people love it? Four threads connect an innovation to a company's economics: profits, assets, investments, and shareholder value. Design-driven innovation has significant implications for all of them (see figure 5-1).

Profits

First, design-driven innovation may act as a major source of profit. If successfully realized, it creates products with a strong and unique personality that stands apart from the crowd of undifferentiated competing products.

Such innovation often boosts a company's sales volume. For example, as you have seen, the Nintendo Wii has enjoyed the highest-ever

FIGURE 5-1

Model of the value of design-driven innovation

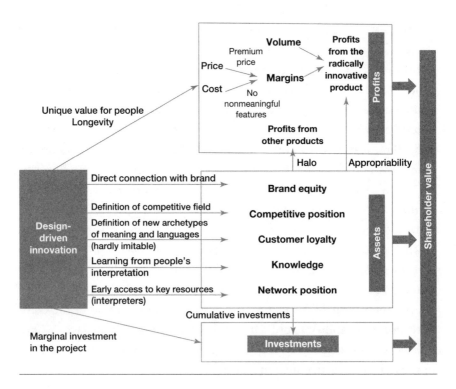

demand in the game console industry, with weekly unit sales twice those of the Xbox and four times those of the PlayStation 3. Similarly, the Swatch is the watch with the highest number of units sold in history. And the iPod has a 75 percent market share in portable music players.[2]

Uniqueness also yields higher profit margins per unit, even more often than it increases sales volume. People are always willing to pay a premium price for products that are more meaningful. However, this does not mean we are talking about high-end or luxury products. The Swatch costs $40! Nicolas Hayek estimates that the premium is about 10 percent, and this means that the price could have been even lower and that profit margins are remarkable. And, in fact, the Swatch Group ranked number 232 in revenues but number 22 in profit as a percentage of sales on the 1994 *Fortune* 500 list. And the Wii was the cheapest game console on the market (about half the price of its competitors) but the only one providing a profit on unit sales.

If a product is meaningful, there is no need to overburden it with powerful functionality. Profit margins are higher because when people love a product, they are willing to pay more than its pure utilitarian value, however low or high that is. However, the time distribution of profits from successful design-driven innovations is distinct: sales often start slowly, because people have to reset the way they think about a product and embrace a radical new meaning. But then sales grow and sustain themselves for a long time. The next section provides more detail on this dynamic.

Corporate Assets

Second, and often most important, design-driven innovation has an impact on corporate assets. Most significantly, it contributes to *brand equity*. Firms can create brand value in many ways—through advertisements, quality and customer satisfaction, technological innovation—but creating a radical innovation of meaning is the most powerful approach. That is because product meanings and languages intimately determine users' experience and therefore have a direct impact on a company's brand. Meanings are authentic and do not lie. And given a unique product, people are even willing to forgive some weaknesses in quality, because they usually consider them a personality trait (such us the noisy roar and uncomfortable sitting position of many Harley-Davidson motorcycles).

We have seen that after the release of the Wii, Nintendo's brand equity grew significantly. The brand value of the Swatch is so high that a watch that retailed for SFr100 was auctioned at SFr68,200. This direct and disintermediated connection between design-driven innovation and brand identity is crucial, because it allows the innovator to reap the benefits. In other words, competitors could imitate the product's function and even its form, but they will never be able to imitate its real meaning, because that remains inextricably knotted to the brand.

Chapter 8 explores the case of Kettle 9093, designed in 1985 by American architect Michael Graves for Alessi. In 1999 retailer Target invited Graves to design a new line of products, including a knockoff of Alessi's Kettle 9093. Well, Alessi continues to sell large numbers of model 9093 (its best seller, with 1.5 million units sold) for five times the price of Target's version. Because both original and knockoff are designed by the same person, the difference in price is undoubtedly attributable to the Alessi brand. It is the only thing that Target could not imitate. And when it comes to meaning, people are very sensitive to authenticity.

Even more important, thanks to its impact on brand equity, radical innovation of meanings creates a halo that enhances a company's other products, generating additional and sustained profits. The value of the Metamorfosi system is not only in its own sales but above all in the fact that it reinforces the value of the Artemide brand. In 2006 Artemide's best-selling product was the Tolomeo lamp, designed in 1986—priced four to five times as high as imitations. Why are people willing to pay that price for a Tolomeo lamp, whose meaning is still that of a beautiful contemporary lamp? Because it is an Artemide lamp. And how has Artemide created such a valuable brand? Not through advertisements (the company has a minimal advertising budget) but through a series of design-driven innovations such as Metamorfosi, which let the company push back the frontier of what lamps and light mean in modern culture.

The same holds true for Apple. The recent growth of its market share in notebook computers, and especially the frantic assault on shops after the release of the iPhone, reflects not only the merit of these products but also the halo that the iPod created around the Apple brand.

Design-driven innovation also enhances a company's assets in other ways, most of which stem from the typical advantages of the first mover. For example, being the first to create a new meaning allows a company to define the new rules of the game to better suit its own core competence. By overturning the meaning of a watch from an instrument to a fashion accessory, Swatch shifted competition closer to the historical strengths of the Swiss industry. These strengths include analog displays rather than digital, sophisticated modular product architecture (which requires mastery of micromechanics), and knowledge of trends in style. The Swatch's Japanese competitors had to comply with these new rules.

Design-driven innovation also enables a firm to create new archetypes of product meanings and languages. These archetypes act as cultural standards that dictate what people will look for when buying a product in the same or a similar category.

For example, with Family Follows Fiction, Alessi created a new archetype of meanings (household products as playful transitional objects) and a new standard of product language (anthropomorphic forms and colorful translucent plastic). These archetypes drove sales of other Alessi products because of compatibility: emotional compatibility ("I feel intimately affectionate toward Alessi's products. Why should I change?"); symbolic compatibility ("I buy an Alessi product because colorful anthropomorphic objects are now considered cool in my social world"); and aesthetic compatibility ("I will buy another Alessi product because it will look great when I place it next to the one I bought last week, and the products of other companies really do not match it").[3] In other words, just as with technological standards, customers will find it hard to move away from new standards in meanings and languages—especially if they have a strong signature—and will remain attracted by the innovator's other products.

However, when it comes to imitation there is a huge difference between technological standards and archetypes. Users typically expect all industry players to conform to a technological standard, and as long as imitators embrace it, that's fine. But when a company establishes new standards for meanings and languages, life for imitators becomes much harder. The more they use the same languages as the innovator, the more they are perceived as slavish copyists. If they want to avoid that perception, they need to find a different language, something that is unlikely right after people have found a new cultural archetype. Life is difficult for competitors after you have created a radical innovation of meanings.

Another contribution of design-driven innovation to corporate assets concerns knowledge. The first to invest is also the first to gain feedback on how people interpret the new concept. In other words, the company is the first to learn from its own investment, and this knowledge will drive better results in the later stream of incremental innovations.

Finally, a major benefit to corporate assets stems from the innovation process itself. In chapter 1 I introduced the concept of *key interpreters:* the external parties that conduct research on how people could give meaning to things. I have shown (and the ensuing chapters discuss thoroughly) how the process of design-driven innovation is rooted in a company's privileged interaction with key external interpreters. The company that moves first has the significant advantage of attracting these key interpreters when they are still untapped resources and therefore is likely to develop a more effective collaboration with them.

For example, Alessi was the first company to ask Michael Graves to design a product. Attracting the American architect was much easier and less expensive for Alessi in 1985 than for Target in 1999, after he was famous. And thanks to its repeated investments in design-driven innovation, Alessi occupies a central position in the network of designers and sociocultural interpreters. Hundreds of new ideas now flow to the company, sent by young (and less young) designers from all over the world. For free. Young design students even pay to participate in workshops organized by Laura Polinoro, head of the now-itinerant Centro Studi Alessi, and to provide fresh concepts. Alessi's network position is so strong that competitors find it very hard to undermine it.

Investments

The third variable and potential advantage to consider is investment. Does design-driven innovation cost a lot? No one answer applies to every situation, of course, but there are two considerations. On the one hand, many of my examples concern small and medium-sized firms with limited resources (including Alessi, Artemide, Kartell, Flos, and B&B Italia). Many do not even have a design department. Yet they are innovation leaders in their industry. As you will see, their unique innovation processes allow them to leverage the network of external key interpreters to whom they have low access costs. That is good news especially for large companies, which have a broader network of external collaborators (connections that remain untapped unless guided through a design-driven innovation process).

On the other hand, design-driven innovation requires a relentless, continuous effort to develop that network: a cumulative investment in relationships. Each event is small, but the cumulative impact over years is significant. That, by the way, is a major reason that when this process is in place, competitors are seldom capable of replicating it.

Higher profits, higher asset value, and limited investments in creating and sustaining an external network of key interpreters eventually produce significant growth in a company's share value and market capitalization. These results can be amazing: witness the 165 percent rise in Nintendo's stock price during the year after the Wii's release (and a market capitalization that topped that of giant Sony) and Apple's explosion in share price from $10 to almost $200 in less than four years.

Escaping the Innovation Race: Product Longevity

When my father came home with that new car, I could not believe it. What? A car with leaf spring suspensions?[4]

It was 1980 and I was a teenager. We were experts in cars. My father, an employee of Italian car manufacturer FIAT, used to replace his car every six months. He did not talk about his choice ahead of time, so each time it was a big event. But that March we were particularly anxious. FIAT, known for its tiny city cars (a famous example is the 500), had just released a brand new low-end, three-door hatchback called Panda. And I guessed that my father would buy one. But I could never have imagined that the boxy car would prove so unusual. It was surprising nonsense.

Almost ten years later, I was camping with friends in Corsica, using the warm flat hood of a Panda as a lunch table. I spent my college summers traveling around the Mediterranean in a classmate's Panda. Twenty years later, my mother—after decades in which she renounced driving for fear of damaging my father's gleaming new cars—finally decided to buy a car for herself. No one had any doubt about her choice: "I will buy a Panda." Twenty-three years later, in 2003, after two failed attempts at substituting new models for Panda, FIAT stopped making it, even though it was still second in monthly sales in Italy, because of problems complying with stricter safety regulations. It was basically the same car I saw that night in March 1980.

The FIAT Panda is an example of a long-lived product. Unfortunately, it is a rare example. We have been bombarded by experts who say that product life cycles are shortening and that companies must substitute for their products at an increasing pace. A study by Procter & Gamble found that the life cycle of consumer products halved between 1992 and 2002.[5]

But luckily, product life cycles are not exogenous, and their contraction is not an inescapable curse. They depend on a firm's innovation strategy. Design, in particular, may have a significant impact on product longevity—for better or worse. The popular incremental approach to design has dramatically accelerated product substitutions. Slight changes of style occur every other season; competitors rapidly imitate small creative ideas generated in quick brainstorming sessions in a crazy run toward a meaningless addition of unrelated features. Products intended to compete only on functionality quickly become obsolete every time someone invents a new function, coercing firms into continuous redesigns. Incremental design flows with the jagged and turbulent waves on the surface of the market, further stirring them by introducing flashy ideas that become indistinguishable after a few months. Many incremental innovations simply introduce what design theorist Ezio Manzini calls "semiotic pollution"—a noisy cascade of uncoordinated ideas that simply confuse people.

Are we really sure people want that? Of course, in the absence of great proposals, they can choose only what suppliers offer, and they choose the anonymous or stylish products that in a given moment have slightly better function or form. But when a company finally proposes a product with the right meaning, they have no doubts about what to choose and will keep choosing it even if it does not have the latest features, gadgets, or colors. Who cares, when you have the right product? A meaning is not a sum of functions; it is an integrated concept, and it is less sensitive to improvements in specific features.

One of the significant benefits of design-driven innovation is that it generates products with long lives. This innovation process works more deeply, on the profound movements underlying the flows, and is less sensitive to small movements on the surface. The average life cycle of Bang & Olufsen products, for example, is twenty years, compared with eight years for the products of its competitors. Alessi's two best sellers are the Kettle 9093, released in 1985, and the Juicy Salif citrus squeezer, designed by Philippe Starck in 1990. Swatch watches still lead the market twenty-five years after their first release.

This holds true even in fast-moving industries. Radical new products proposed by Apple, for example, tend to have a longer life cycle than their incremental siblings, and longer than the industry average.[6] Product longevity saves companies from breakeven fever, generates significant profits, eliminates the need for investments in continuous substitutions, and allows firms to focus their R&D budgets on more-substantial innovations.

Longevity in the Automotive Industry

The car industry has historically witnessed a number of larger-than-life products, such as the Citroën 2CV, the Volkswagen Beetle, the MINI, and the FIAT 500. The Panda, however, is an interesting case because it did not appear during the industry's pioneering times, when life cycles normally were longer. It battled in fast-paced times, when the average life cycle of competing cars was only 8.5 years (see figures 5-2 and 5-3).[7]

The Panda, launched in 1980, outlived its competitors in perfect shape for twenty-three years. The car was almost always first in the Italian city car market, and first or second across all segments of the car industry, even in 2003 when it was phased out. In twenty-three years FIAT sold 4.5 million Pandas worldwide, with minor changes and investments (the most significant were the introduction of a 4WD version in 1983 and a more efficient engine in 1986). Why was the Panda so long lived (lasting even longer than the classic FIAT 500)?

FIGURE 5-2

Sales of cars in Italy from 1980 to 2002

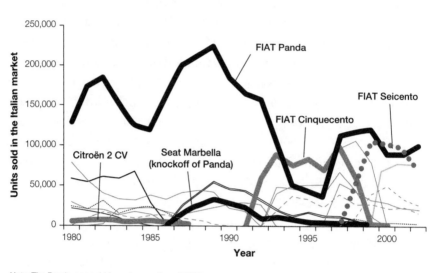

Note: The Panda was sold for only a portion of 2003.
Source: Data from Alessio Marchesi, "Business Classics: Managing Innovation through Product Longevity"
(PhD dissertation, Politecnico di Milano, 2005).

FIGURE 5-3

Comparison of market shares over product life cycle in the Italian city car segment (for cars launched after 1978 and phased out before 2005)

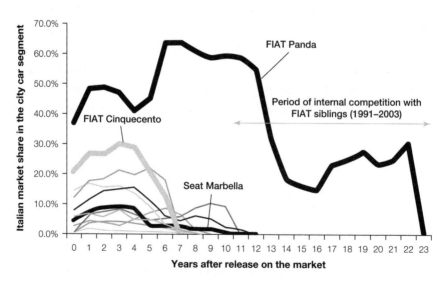

Source: Data from Alessio Marchesi, "Business Classics: Managing Innovation through Product Longevity"
(PhD dissertation, Politecnico di Milano, 2005).

Theories on management of innovation suggest that firms employ various strategies to support product longevity. The first explanation could be that FIAT used patents to protect a superior function from imitation. But the functionality of the Panda was definitely not superior throughout its entire life cycle, and it was not protected by patents.

To investigate this strategy, we compared the Panda's functionality— a score averaging passenger space, trunk space, fuel consumption, engine, acceleration, safety, and comfort, as rated by major industry magazines—with those of competing cars over the twenty-three-year life span (see figure 5-4). Although the Panda scored relatively well early on, its competitors rapidly caught up, and three years after the Panda's release its performance had already fallen to less than the industry average. The car's functional score rebounded in 1986, thanks to the new-generation engine, but then it slowly dropped again. From 1996 on, a rational buyer would never have bought a Panda. Like many FIAT models, it also suffered from quality defects. Yet it had an astonishing

FIGURE 5-4

Functional performance of the FIAT Panda relative to the average competition

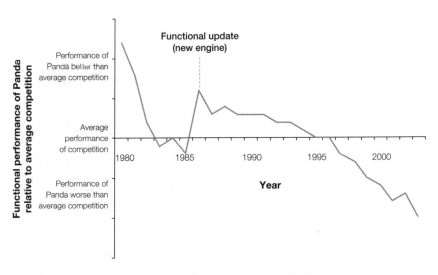

Source: Data from Alessio Marchesi, "Business Classics: Managing Innovation through Product Longevity" (PhD dissertation, Politecnico di Milano, 2005).

40 percent repurchase rate, compared with an average rate of less than 20 percent for other cars in its industry segment.

The second explanation could be that the Panda won because of price. That is true only in part. Its price basically tracked the inflation rate, starting at about 2,000 in 1983 and rising to 6,300 in 2003—slightly less than the industry average. According to FIAT's market analyses, only 38 percent of customers considered price a significant reason for buying a Panda in 2002. And the car's resale value topped that of competitors for its entire life, a clear sign that people valued the Panda more than competing products.

The third explanation provided by existing theories suggests that product longevity depends on market structure—that is, weaker competition (as with monopolies or market niches, or where a company controls complementary assets such as distribution channels) slows down product substitutions. But Panda was not competing in a monopoly or a niche but rather in the crowded city car segment, where it fought against twenty different models during its entire life. And its advantage did not simply reflect FIAT's market power in Italy. The proof is that FIAT itself tried to substitute for the Panda twice: first in 1991, with the Cinquecento (a dull car that shared only the name of the historical FIAT 500 of the 1960s), and then in 1998, with the Seicento (with the name again taken from a historical car of the 1960s, added to an improbable anonymous design). Although the Panda initially suffered from its internal competition in both cases, it eventually won out against its siblings.

The real reason for the Panda's outstanding longevity is that it was a breakthrough in *meaning* for city cars, especially compared with FIAT's historical approach. In the late 1970s, the dominant concept of a city car was to provide minimum performance for the minimal price by squeezing the occupants into minimal space. (The historical FIAT 500 was 117 inches long and 52 inches wide; its 1970s successor, the FIAT 126, was 120 × 54.) FIAT CEO Carlo De Benedetti asked Giorgietto Giugiaro, Panda's designer, to change the concept to the following: "What I want is a car with lots of room for passengers and their luggage, at the price of a small car."

It was 1976. Founded in 1899 (four years before Ford and nine years before GM), FIAT was enmeshed in one of the bleakest periods in its history, besieged by strikes and terrorism (a handful of its factory workers were enrolled in the Red Brigades, a terrorist organization that conducted sixteen attacks against executives). The world automobile market, meanwhile, was facing a crisis after the oil shocks of the 1970s, when global production dropped 20 percent (and FIAT's production dropped 30 percent). Thus wisdom and market trends suggested that the company should pursue a conservative, incremental innovation strategy, further squeezing people into a small, utilitarian, even less expensive car.

Carlo De Benedetti remained in charge of FIAT for only one hundred days. When he left, the company was drawn into other problems so dramatic that Giugiaro was given significant autonomy and total responsibility for vehicle concept and engineering design. Thus, to some extent, the innovation process that produced the Panda reflected unusual circumstances and would have been regarded as a mistake—not only at FIAT but also by many management experts. However, as you will see, the process exactly matched that of design-driven innovation.

Design for Longevity and Personality

Giorgietto Giugiaro, who founded the automotive design and engineering firm Italdesign in 1968, is one of the world's most prominent car designers. He has created several landmarks in the industry, at the high end of the market (the Maserati Ghibli in 1966 and more recently the Ferrari GG50) and especially the low end (the Daewoo-Chevrolet Matiz in 1998 and, most of all, the Volkswagen Golf in 1974). He is an expert at designing long-lived products. "Panda is the project I loved the most," says Giugiaro, "because I had maximum freedom with few requirements. And designing a low-end car is much more challenging, from a design standpoint, than designing a Bugatti."[8]

In creating the Panda, Giugiaro added another requirement to the equation: not only more space but also a deeper meaning amid average performance. He conceived the Panda as a "no frills, big thrills" car. It was in the realm of clever lightheartedness and freedom from concern— a fresh and practical car that people could use for any occasion, from traveling to serious appointments in town to carrying vegetables in the countryside. The car's myriad consistent details suggested hundreds of familiar uses and also proposed new ones.

The seats were based on a simple tubular structure, with a removable, washable cloth cover. The backseat was a cloth rectangle stretched between two tubes that suggested various uses in addition to sitting: it could be folded as a hammock to hold a baby or fragile parcels, unfolded flat to make a bed-sized mattress, or removed, rolled up, and stored in a slot carved out of the floor behind the front seats to create a van-class cargo bay with 1,060 cubic meters of capacity. The dashboard was also covered with cloth, and below it, instead of drawers and small compartments, was a generous open pouch running from left to right that invited people to simply throw objects into it and let them remain visible.

The exterior design was also clever. Giugiaro gave the car a strong personality that suggested rugged use: the rear suspensions were leaf springs, the door's hinges were visible, all windows were flat and thus easily replaceable, the body sides were almost flat, with wide plastic bands to protect them from small bumps and rust, and the "naked" wheels remained visible because they lacked conventional arches. These solutions not only allowed rapid assembly and low cost but also gave the car a clear identity, suggesting an all-terrain wagon ready to be used in the countryside. (The project's nickname was "rustic," and the 4WD version actually outperformed even the more exclusive and rugged SUVs on rough terrain with unexpected ease, thanks to its light weight.) The Panda's styling was so unconventional that it was still contemporary twenty-three years later.

A Car in Sneakers

Low-end products are often simply a poorer version of a more luxurious one: they pretend to keep the same meaning as their more affluent siblings, but their functions and quality are simply debased. When you buy a product like that, you feel as though you are saying, "I would have loved to buy a better car, but unfortunately I could not afford it." Panda, instead, had a different meaning from that of its siblings. It was not the small, poorer one. You bought it not simply because it was cheaper but because you *wanted* it, and being cheap was an essential part of its "no frills, big thrills" concept. The best metaphor that describes its meaning is that it was a car in sneakers. You buy sneakers not because they are cheaper but because you need them. And, as with sneakers, Panda's transformability, adaptability, and versatility helped it become a social icon that cut across age, gender, and social status.

"I got one thing incredibly wrong about the Panda," says Giorgietto Giugiaro. "I assumed that people on a limited income would purchase it as their only car. But, from the day it came out, I found that it appealed to professionals as well as elegant ladies from the Turin hills. The larger audience fell for it only later."[9]

Like many design-driven innovations, the Panda was not the result of market or user analyses. Initially even users were confused, but then they were enthusiastically converted. The car's peak market share came in 1987, and its peak volume in 1989—seven and nine years, respectively, after its release. (Competitors' cars reached their top market share in less than three years, on average.) Eventually the Panda was one of the most profitable cars ever produced, despite FIAT's limited investment. Unlike other cars, whose development took more than ten years, the Panda was conceived, designed, engineered, and launched in four years.[10] The project simply started from a different question: what is the real meaning people could love in a city car?

The Panda received the Compasso d'Oro, the most prestigious Italian design award, given to only three cars in history. Indeed, the Panda is a masterpiece that crushes common wisdom on design: it is not a simple product, nor limited to a niche, nor luxurious, nor stylish. It is a complex mass product that sees affordability and functionality as worthwhile values and meanings in themselves. And those meanings, once created, remained even as the car became much less functional than its competitors.

Creating a Business Classic

The Panda is a synecdoche for the way that design-driven innovation can generate one of the most desired benefits any executive is searching for: a long-lived product that yields high profit margins on a small investment. As this example shows, the life cycle of design-driven innovations often follows the model depicted in figure 5-5. It starts slowly, but then—at a time when typical, incremental products become obsolete (because their functionality is no longer best-in-class or because their stylish design is no longer fashionable)—the product keeps attracting users because it is more meaningful to them, regardless of functionality and style.

FIGURE 5-5

Radical innovation of meanings and the creation of business classics

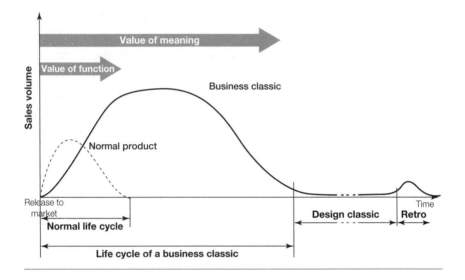

In other words, the unique meanings of design-driven innovations set them apart from their competitors and allow them to survive longer and in high volumes. They escape the law of imitation and obsolescence typical of functional products, simply because even though competitors may imitate and surpass the innovations' functions, they cannot replicate their meanings. Those remain attached to the authentic product and brand. Indeed, a competitor tried to imitate the Panda by launching a less expensive copycat, the SEAT Marbella. But the company sold one-tenth as many units as the Panda.

Of course, I am not suggesting here that firms should not provide their products with the best functions, patent them, and keep them updated. I am saying that radical innovation of meanings is what makes sense of those utilitarian moves and provides real long-term profit.

In the terminology of Susan Sanderson, the Panda was a business classic.[11] It not only was long-lived but also enjoyed significant sales and market share throughout its entire life. This distinguishes it from a design classic (such as the 1948 Citroën 2CV, a car that still sold in the 1980s to a few nostalgic hippies) and from a retro product (such as the new Volkswagen Beetle, released in 1998, which exploits only the brand name and style of its elder sibling, with a different meaning: not the "people's car" but a niche vehicle for the fashion addicted).

One of the greatest benefits of design-driven innovation is that it is likely to produce business classics, yielding great profits from both the product itself and the halo it bestows. Apple, for example, has been a serial creator of business classics (the Apple II, the Macintosh, the iMac, the iPod, the iPhone) that have built and sustained its brand.

The Challenges of Design-Driven Innovation

Although the benefits of design-driven innovation can be significant, many companies neglect this untapped wellspring of competitive advantage and simply wait for a competitor to introduce the next dominant meaning in their markets. Just as with technological breakthroughs, the innovator often comes from outside the industry, disrupting the leadership of established firms.

In the past decade, figures on household spending on furniture and fittings show that people spent the largest share of their budget on kitchens, followed by bathrooms. Living rooms come in third. Formerly the hidden and forgotten "functional" areas of a house, bathrooms have become surprisingly important. People buy the latest modern faucets, minimalist cabinets, supershowers, and pool-like bathtubs, in precious materials and sporting the latest spa gadgets. Bathrooms have moved from being simply functional to becoming wellness rooms.

Leading this radical shift in meaning were not industry incumbents such as American Standard, which kept selling traditional products with style adjustments, but small new entrants such as Boffi, an Italian manufacturer formerly focused on kitchen furniture, which released a new range of high-end wellness products for furnishing bathrooms. American Standard eventually left the industry in 2007, selling its bathroom and kitchen businesses.

That's not a new story. Incumbents have observed Apple redefining the meaning of listening to and selling music, as well as personal communication. Levi Strauss has seen its market share eroded by a start-up named Diesel, which understood that the meaning of jeans could change radically from that of a uniform (the icon of identification with the working masses in the 1970s) to an individualistic symbol of freedom and nonconformity. Even the Swiss watch industry had to wait for an outsider (Nicolas Hayek, formerly an engineering consultant) to discover that a watch could have a radically new meaning.

Why do incumbents often fail to seize the opportunities offered by design-driven innovation? There are many reasons, most of which can be traced to the typical barriers to innovation (lack of vision, fear of change, lack of competencies, the not-invented-here syndrome). However, I focus on two particular challenges of design-driven innovation: strategy and process.

Believing That Meanings Do Not Change

First, many companies simply do not ask themselves the right questions: "What is the profound, ultimate reason people buy our product? Will this meaning remain unchanged in the next few years? How can we make people more gratified and content by providing products with a different meaning?" In other words, firms do not view design-driven innovation as part of their innovation strategy, for several reasons.

The most common reason is that they believe that meanings do not drive competition in their industry. They believe that design is interesting only in mature consumer markets for simple luxury products. I hope, after these few chapters, that you have no remaining doubts about the crucial role of design-driven innovation in any industry and market segment, especially when linked to breakthrough technologies.

Some companies do realize the importance of meanings, but with a limited perspective: they think meanings are simply a given in the market and that they cannot be innovated but only understood. These firms therefore consider meanings only as part of a market-pull strategy, and not as the object of radical innovation.

Fearing Risk and the Innovation Borderline

More often, however, companies are scared to even ask the key questions. Design-driven innovation is radical, and, like any radical innovation, it is as complex and risky as it is rewarding—sometimes even riskier than breakthrough technologies (although less expensive). Transforming a corkscrew from a tool into an object of affection, as Alessi did before anyone else, is as challenging as moving from analog to digital transmission in telecommunications. It requires basic research on sociocultural models, and the outcomes are uncertain. What's more, the process does not start from data on what people want now, but from research on what people could want and are not yet aware of.

Marketing figures (which one can blame in case of failure: "Users asked for this!")—the typical safety net for innovation—are not available, nor is feedback from focus groups, nor are early sales (which often start more slowly than those of incremental products, only to soar later). Managers are uncomfortable in these situations, which require that they rely on their own insights and vision, built through a precise process (described in part 2). And they are afraid of risk. But if you do not accept the challenge, there will always be others who, for reasons such as the need to recover from a weak competitive position (Nintendo) or the opportunity to enter a new market (Apple), will try and will succeed.

I find Alberto Alessi's explanation of his company's attitude toward risk, and especially his theory of the innovation *borderline*, inspiring:

> We tend always to work, almost spontaneously I would say, in a land inhabited by desires, the desires of people, still largely undiscovered . . . and this, as we know, is a zone with high, extremely high, turbulence . . . We walk on streets that have not yet been opened, on unknown paths to reach the heart of people . . . We move on the enigmatic borderline between what could become real (objects really loved and owned by people) and what will never become real (objects too far from what people are ready and willing to want). This practice of the borderline is difficult and risky, and asks for awareness and commitment from each one of us, in each of our roles. Our mission is to stay as close as possible to the borderline, although we know it is not clearly drawn and that there is a risk of going beyond it . . . but what an emotion when with a new project we get close to it. Mass manufacturers instead keep as far as possible from the borderline because they want to avoid any risk . . . but in this way, slowly, they all produce the same cars and the same TVs.[12]

Alessi knows that if all his new products are successful, the company has been too conservative and has stayed away from the borderline. This is not good, because it opens the field to competitors. So the company periodically pursues more-radical projects. And even when these efforts apparently fail (proposing products that are too extreme—beyond the borderline), that failure is the revealing moment in which the firm finally sees where the borderline was and is in the best position to make a breakthrough with the next project, before and better than its competitors.

Lacking the Needed Capabilities

The second reason incumbents often avoid design-driven innovation is simply because they do not know how to implement it. Their processes and abilities are framed around incremental innovation. Most companies know how to understand user needs, do ethnographic analysis, and organize brainstorming sessions; and if they don't, they involve a design consultant. But they have no idea where to start, and they have no capabilities when it comes to radical innovation of meanings, which requires them to step back from close observation of people's current needs.

A significant challenge is that design-driven innovation is based on interaction with a network of interpreters (as you will see in the next chapter). Thanks to their research and knowledge, these interpreters provide insights on how people could give new meanings to things. Many companies, however, have no relationship with interpreters; these firms exist outside the dynamics through which society investigates and creates new meanings. Or companies do have such relationships but do not value them. For example, they interact with manufacturers of components simply as technology suppliers and not as interpreters of possible new meanings.

Locking a Firm In to Obsolete Capabilities

Alternatively, a company may have strong relationships with a network of interpreters, but this network is obsolete and focuses on translating past sociocultural models rather than anticipating changes. In other words—as Clayton Christensen shows about the failure of incumbents to deal with disruptive technological innovations—many companies have close links with a "value network" of actors who lock them in to old interpretations rather than help them understand and shape future breakthrough meanings.[13]

Consider, for example, Bang & Olufsen. The Danish company has been a radical innovator of meanings in audio and video products, as well as a great interpreter of apartment lifestyles, for several decades. But the advent of digital media technologies has dulled its cutting edge. The way people listen to music and watch shows is changing and will change even more radically in the future.[14] However, the challenge is not technological. Bang & Olufsen has acquired electronic technology in the past without jeopardizing its innovativeness, and it could acquire digital technology in the future.

Instead, the challenge stems from a transition in lifestyles. Stereos and TV are no longer the modern household fireplace (basically the metaphor for Bang & Olufsen products). People do not sit down in their living rooms to listen to music or watch TV. Instead, they pursue those activities in the kitchen, in bathrooms, in cars, in offices, in the street. To make new proposals, Bang & Olufsen must reconfigure its value network, finding the key new interpreters who can help it understand how new media could make people happier.

The challenges of design-driven innovation therefore concern risk, process, and capabilities. These are hard challenges. Radical innovation is never easy. But it always happens, and it will happen again very soon, as this analysis has shown. And the companies that realize this will reap the greatest value.

The next two parts of this book face these challenges. After learning from persistently successful design-driven innovators, I provide guidelines on how to implement the process, build the necessary capabilities, and boost your chances of success.

Part Two

THE PROCESS OF DESIGN-DRIVEN INNOVATION

THE INTERPRETERS

[Doing Research with the Design Discourse]

Mondrian and the scientists at the corporation were pursuing the same type of activity: exploring new possibilities, recombining others' findings, experimenting, identifying promising results, sharing them with others, exploiting their discoveries. In other words: research.

OW DO YOU CREATE design-driven innovations? Every company would love to be the one that changes the paradigm, that radically redefines the meaning of things. We know why. Previous chapters show the value of design-driven innovation—its contribution to profit, brand value, product longevity, and asset generation. We also know that, like any type of radical innovation, it is a risky and complex challenge.

In part 1 you learned what design-driven innovation is not: it is not user-centered. You have seen that the closer companies get to users, the more they get stuck in the way people currently give meaning to things. In contrast, design-driven innovations are proposals about radical new meanings. They are visions of a possible future. Yet these proposals, these visions, are not dreams without a foundation. These proposals eventually emerge as the products users were actually looking for—and thus are great market successes.

Companies that master design-driven innovation are repeatedly successful. They are global leaders in their industries because they have pursued this strategy for decades. Their innovations are not simply flukes nor the results of a sudden spark of creativity. They have a process and capabilities, built and led by entrepreneurs and managers.

This chapter illustrates the basic principle underpinning the process of design-driven innovation: the need to leverage the work of interpreters to envision how people could give meaning to things. You will see that as a company steps back from users and takes a broader perspective, it discovers that it is not alone in its effort to understand changes in society, culture, and technology. Many other parties share its interest. In other words, firms can tap in to an external research process that focuses on the meanings of things. I call this informal, diffused research process—which is like a collective discussion—the *design discourse.*

This chapter illustrates this basic principle by analyzing the nature of the design discourse and outlining the overall process of design-driven innovation. The next chapters then show in detail how companies can create design-driven innovations by listening to, interpreting, and influencing the design discourse.

You Are Not Alone

Let's consider Artemide, the manufacturer of lighting fixtures that created the Metamorfosi system. As you have seen, if Artemide had aimed at incremental product improvements, it would have asked, "How can we create a better way to replace a lightbulb?" However, when Artemide pursues radical innovation of meanings, its question is different. It asks, "How can we make a person feel better when she comes home after work at seven at night?"

Although apparently simple, this question has three implications. First, the context is broader: it is not use, such as changing a lightbulb, but is instead *life*, such as living in a home, alone or in relationship with other households and friends. Second, the subject is broader: not a user of a specific product but a *person*, with her entire psychological, cultural, and social background. Third, the purpose is broader: not the pragmatic need to change a bulb but the *reason* (utilitarian as well as emotional) people do things in that context.

From this broader perspective, a richer innovation environment emerges. Artemide is not alone. Many other actors share the same question: "How can we make a person feel better when she comes home after work at seven at night?" These actors include companies in other industries, such as producers of TV sets and audio systems, that look at the same person in the same context of the domestic lifestyle. Although these manufacturers design electronic appliances, whereas Artemide designs lighting fixtures, all have the same interest in understanding the aspirations of households and discovering how people could give meaning to things when they come home from work.

Manufacturers of furniture, personal computers, and game consoles, even broadcasting firms, all look at the same person and contribute, with their products and services, to creating household experiences. Product designers also share the same question (they develop their own vision of a domestic lifestyle by working with firms in these industries), as do architects (who design houses and living spaces), editors of magazines and other media (which publish articles on domestic scenarios), suppliers of raw materials (which, like Bayer Material Science, are interested in possible new uses in household products), universities and design schools (where professors and students often conduct workshops on designing domestic products), hotel and exhibition designers (who explore new organizations of spaces), and consultants in the sociology and anthropology of consumption.

All these actors may act, for Artemide, as *interpreters*. Although they do not make lamps, all of them pursue, through their own processes and approaches, research on domestic scenarios, developing knowledge about how people could give meaning to things in their homes. And they may be willing to share that knowledge. It is the interaction with these interpreters that makes Artemide better able to envision new meanings and translate them into radically new products that are likely to be successful.

By stepping back from a user performing a specific action and taking a broader perspective on the context in which that person lives, every company may discover that it is not alone. Every company is surrounded by several interpreters. These interpreters have two

FIGURE 6-1

User-centered design versus design-driven innovation

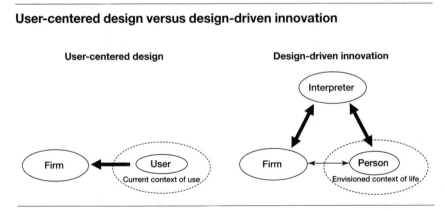

characteristics. First, as noted, they share the same question. In other words, they conduct research on how people (the same people who are also our users) could give meaning to things. Second, they are also *seducers*, in that the technologies they develop, the products and services they design, the artwork they create will help shape sociocultural models and influence people's meanings, aspirations, and desires.[1] Because of these two characteristics, interpreters are the keystone in the process of design-driven innovation (see figure 6-1). A company willing to propose breakthroughs can leverage the efforts of these noncompeting interpreters who are also investigating and influencing future meanings.

The Design Discourse: A Circle of Researchers

Companies that produce design-driven innovations value highly their interactions with this network of interpreters. These companies understand that they are immersed in a collective research laboratory through which firms, designers, artists, and schools are conducting their own investigations. These researchers are engaged, explicitly and implicitly, in a continuous dialogue: they exchange insights, interpretations, and proposals in the form of artwork, studies, speeches, prototypes, and products. They test the robustness of their assumptions and share their visions. This diffuse and networked research process on the possible meanings of things is the design discourse.[2]

Most companies are not aware that they are immersed in a design discourse, because this process unfolds in forms that differ from those of the research we usually think of: technological R&D. Interpreters are seldom insulated within the walls of a few company labs, but rather are diffused throughout many industries and contexts. Their protocols for interacting are informal and unpredictable. They tend to coalesce into circles and provide their most insightful interpretations only to other members. And most of all, they are not only scientists or engineers, and they are unlikely to call themselves researchers: they encompass many professions (see figure 6-2). Let's examine them a little more closely.

FIGURE 6-2

The design discourse

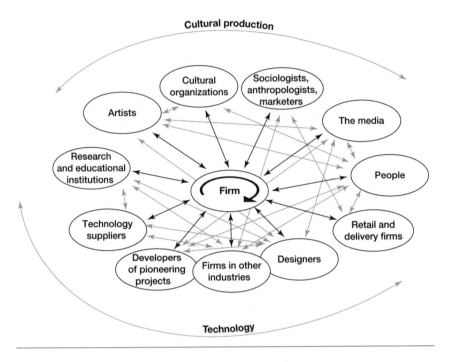

Interpreters in the World of Cultural Production

In the upper part of figure 6-2 are clustered interpreters who belong to the world of *cultural production*—that is, people who are directly involved in the production and investigation of social meaning.[3] These may be artists, cultural organizations, sociologists, anthropologists, marketers, and the media, who make the exploration of culture and meaning an explicit component of their core mission.

Artists

Poets are the unacknowledged legislators of the world.

—Percy Bysshe Shelley

Anthony, CEO of a well-known company in the computer industry, had not yet spent an entire day with his son. Michael was turning eight, and Anthony felt he was grown enough to enjoy extended time with his father, without mom and sisters. It should be a boys' Saturday.

In the morning they visited the R&D labs at Anthony's firm. Michael was thrilled by the idea of wearing a white suit to enter the clean rooms. It was hard to understand what was happening there, with all the machines, wafers, and workers busy with graphs and numbers on their calculator screens. But his dad, who had begun his career in the labs as an engineer, explained how the firm would transform everything occurring there into new computers. It would be only a matter of years, sometimes only months, until what the labs discovered would become the next personal computer on the boy's desk.

Leaving the labs and heading toward the baseball stadium to watch the Saturday afternoon game, they came across a poster for a new exhibition at the museum of modern art. The exhibit would feature Piet Mondrian, a Dutch abstract painter of the early twentieth century. The poster included two images. On the left was a painting, with a caption that read "'Composition with Yellow'—1930." The artwork appeared to be typical Mondrian: the canvas was white, crossed by a grid of black lines, perfectly horizontal and vertical, which formed a few rectangles, one of which, very small, was filled with primary yellow. Next to the image of the painting was a photo of a small-scale reproduction of Mondrian's studio. The exhibition explored the life, inspirations, and masterpieces of the artist.

Michael could not refrain from spontaneously asking his father what was special about that geometric painting and why that painter was so famous, given that his artwork was not so different from drawings the boy could easily make (and actually often did make, in his exercise book, fooling around during boring classes). Anthony had hoped that his son would not ask that question, which he had been asking himself for years without finding an explanation. How could it be that such simple artwork—which looked more like children's drawings than beautiful compositions—could be considered masterpieces? What had the modern painters contributed to humankind? What were they trying to achieve? He did not know what to answer.

Yet the exegesis would have been simple: the painters were doing *research*, just like the researchers the father and son had met that morning. There was not much difference between the clean rooms they had just visited and the studio of Mondrian. They were both labs. And both helped shape our world of objects and products. Just as a subtle thread connects the research that scientists conducted in the early twentieth century on the physical properties of semiconductors with today's integrated circuits, a thread also connects the research of Mondrian on the essentiality of pure abstract form with the current form of computers. Without this research on reduction and simplification by abstract artists, who dared to challenge dominant assumptions about aesthetic language accepted for centuries, computers would have Victorian decoration (as did many machines in the late nineteenth century). If every morning we wake up and turn on a computer with a sleek minimal design, or we drive a car that does not look like a Louis XVI wagon, we can thank Mondrian.

The scientists and engineers at Anthony's corporation were pursuing the same type of activity as Mondrian: exploring new possibilities, recombining others' findings (artists leverage the work of their predecessors just as scientists leverage existing theories), experimenting, collecting feedback from various avenues, identifying promising results, sharing them with other researchers, exploiting their discoveries.[4] In other words, research.

The only difference between those engineers and Mondrian is that they were doing research in different dimensions: the former on science and technology, the latter on meanings and languages. From the perspective of design-driven innovation, painters, writers, filmmakers, musicians, and choreographers are among the most powerful symbol creators in our society.[5] As Percy Bysshe Shelley reminds us, poets do research, and they do have an impact on everyday life. But we seldom acknowledge it.

Italian manufacturers turn a watchful eye to artists, even if their work does not appear to relate directly to their industry and market. For example, Artemide has recently developed a close collaboration with Luca Ronconi, a well-known theater and opera director who has worked for La Scala in Milan and the Salzburg Festival and who is now artistic director of the Piccolo Teatro di Milano. Ernesto Gismondi, president of Artemide, has asked Luca Ronconi to help the company conceive a new lighting fixture.

What does a theater director share with Artemide? They both do research on how light can become meaningful and how it creates emotions, and both make proposals to the same people (users of lighting fixtures and spectators of theatrical pieces). Some theater directors conduct novel experiments on light design. Ronconi, especially, is well known for his avant-garde attitude and explorations. And conversely, he involves interpreters from industry in his productions, such as architect Gae Aulenti and fashion designer Karl Lagerfeld, thus pursuing a continuous exchange of knowledge about meanings and languages with other interpreter-researchers.

Of course, Gismondi did not expect Luca Ronconi to design a lamp. Rather, this was Gismondi's assignment to Ronconi: "Imagine a room in a house, and tell me what light you would like to experience there. A light that would make you feel better. Do not think about the lighting fixture, because we will take care of that. Just think about the light."

Ronconi started to think about his own bedroom and had Artemide build a small-scale model of it (matching precise details of the carpets, blankets, books, and even the dog's bedding). His initial suggestions and requirements were limited to utilitarian features (such as a lamp that, when a person wakes up thirsty during the night, can detect a certain arm movement and gently illuminate a bottle of water or glass on the nightstand). In other words, he initially acted as a lead user trying to provide pragmatic pointers to improve existing products. But then, progressively, the director's sensibility crept in, allowing more emotional and intimate aspirations to arise.

"You know," said Ronconi to Gismondi, "I always come back home very late at night, after my shows, and I hardly see my room in daylight or at sunset. Well, what I would really love is that when I enter the room, artificial light coming from the window would re-create the natural light of different seasons and phases of the day. For example, dawn, sunset, twilight in winter, a summer afternoon, a springtime morning . . . " This theatrical vision clearly benefits from his years of research on using artificial light to replicate natural light to create deep feelings among opera goers (the same people who use lamps in their homes). The resulting product is actually a lighting system, in the form of a window, that generates eleven different atmospheres, such as a night with moonlight.

Cultural Organizations

Cultural organizations, such as associations, foundations, and museums, are also involved in the interpretation and production of social meaning. Some of these institutions represent a given culture and may actually help preserve the status quo. Others, however, promote novel visions and interpretations of meanings, which often contrast with dominant and institutionalized culture. And toward this end they perform research and experiments.

An example is Slow Food, an international movement and organization founded in Paris in 1989 by a group of food lovers. Slow Food promotes a vision designed to counter the drift toward poor-quality fast food and poor eating habits. The group aims to make people more conscious and responsible about what they eat, in terms of both the taste of food and the way it is produced.

Slow Food sustains the entire agricultural culture and society behind good food. The group supports biodiversity in grains, vegetables, and animal breeds; creates educational programs and learning experiences in food tasting and food culture (it even founded the Graduate School of Gastronomic Science in Italy's Piedmont region); and organizes fairs and events in various countries to showcase local produce and allow consumers to meet small producers. It is one of the most advanced and innovative cultural forces in the world of food, and innovative firms in the industry, such as Barilla, follow its activities and interact with it in investigating new visions and meanings.

Sociologists, Anthropologists, Marketers

A third category of interpreters in the world of cultural production includes, naturally, all those who perform research on meanings and languages as a professional service. Such people include consultants and researchers in the sociology and anthropology of consumption, in marketing, in branding, and in communication.

With their expertise in observing and analyzing society, culture, and markets, such interpreters can rapidly provide a picture of how people give meaning to things, and of emerging trends. Although these efforts are useful predominantly in incremental innovation, understanding the state of the art can also serve as a foundation for radical innovation, allowing companies to identify the challenges and the avenues others have already explored. Interacting with such interpreters becomes especially interesting when they can help detect cultural phenomena that are emerging in industries other than the companies' own but that could transfer to their markets. This is especially true of consultants who do not focus on specific market segments and can therefore detect phenomena that transcend a given product category and apply to a broader life context.

The Media

Finally, the world of cultural production is populated by the media: editors and writers for journals and magazines, broadcasting organizations, and Web sites. These people observe society, culture, policy, and the economy: they interpret events, and thus influence how people will internalize them.[6] Although most of these interpretations result from observation more than research and vision, some are occasionally forward-looking, and companies can use them to build consistent scenarios about possible new meanings.

Interpreters in the World of Technology

The second group of interpreters in the design discourse are those who, with their discoveries, technical innovations, and new products and services, actually change the world of things and, implicitly or explicitly, propose new meanings. Technology is indeed one of the most influential factors that, in the long term, shapes the way we live. And actors who explore radical changes in technologies often also explore the implications of those changes for culture and life.[7]

Research and Educational Institutions

Research and educational institutions, such as schools, universities, and public research organizations, often investigate the evolution of technologies and their impact on culture and society. People conduct such investigations not only in technical schools but also, and above all, in schools of design, which explicitly address the interactions between technology, languages, and meanings. Firms are eager to cooperate with design schools by challenging professors and students with innovative projects, promoting workshops, inviting young scholars for internships, and sharing labs and resources.

Alessi, for example, has institutionalized these interactions. Its former Centro Studi, directed by Laura Polinoro, has become an itinerant research center, organizing workshops at prominent international design schools such as the University of Art and Design Helsinki, the Royal College of Art in London, and the Politecnico di Milano.

Nokia also cooperates extensively with schools and research centers. For example, the Finnish company has recently cosponsored (with the government) an ambitious research project, based at Finland's University of Tampere and UIAH, that uses eye-tracking technology to assess people's perception of product languages.

Nokia also sponsors a global student project called Only Planet, which investigates how product design can express cultural influences in Estonia, Israel, Brazil, and several other countries. The project consists of two phases. The first asks students to explore key influences (including commercial, familial, and aesthetic values) on their country's visual culture and discover how these factors might affect the design of global products. The second phase asks students to create concepts, scenarios, and products that integrate findings from the first phase with the technological opportunities developed by the firm, such as multimedia and entertainment technologies and new production systems.

Nokia acknowledges that this project aims not so much to discover specific new ideas but rather to improve its knowledge of local cultures, spur creative reflection on significant social phenomena, and, not least, spot new talent. Unlike other firms, which often approach design schools with the illusory hope of finding ready-to-use solutions, Nokia sees this effort as contributing to its larger research process.

Technology Suppliers

Technology suppliers are a second category of cultural interpreters in the technical world. Chapter 4 shows how new technologies—especially the real meanings quiescent in those technologies—often trigger design-driven innovations. That chapter also shows how these technology epiphanies may emerge thanks to cooperation between manufacturers and suppliers of components and materials.

The most innovative Italian furniture manufacturers seek intense cooperation with upstream technology suppliers that both invent new materials and foresee the sociocultural and aesthetic implications of their inventions. Thanks to this cooperation, furniture manufacturers can explore the emotional possibilities of new materials as soon as they emerge and can promote the product languages that best fit their capabilities and identity.

Consider Kartell, the innovative manufacturer of plastic furniture and creator of the Bookworm bookshelf. The collaboration between Kartell and advanced suppliers of polymeric materials such as Bayer is so intense that they often challenge each other to explore new solutions. Results of these explorations can be seen, for example, in La Marie, a transparent chair designed by Philippe Starck that is manufactured in a single polycarbonate mold.

Piero Ambrogio Busnelli, founder and chairman of B&B Italia, a leading furniture manufacturer, has devoted much of his own time to interacting with technology suppliers in the quest for new materials. Indeed, he founded B&B Italia in the 1960s when he was exploring applications of polyurethane in the manufacture of sofas. The company was the first furniture firm to use this technology, which Busnelli scouted at the Interplast fair in London and then developed by cooperating with Bayer. It allowed B&B Italia to create a new language and touch in the industry.

One of the most famous products resulting from this interaction is the armchair UP5, designed by Gaetano Pesce in 1969. This icon of design—a bold metaphor for an enormous female figure—receives the sitting person in a warm and snug womb, tied through an umbilical cord to a ball-shaped ottoman symbolizing a shackle. One of this armchair's most outstanding features is that it was delivered compressed into a small vacuum-packed box; once unpacked, the chair took its intended shape, making the opening of the box an emotional experience in itself. Today B&B and Kartell are among Bayer's closest partners in exploring new product languages and meanings.

An interesting example of interpreter in the world of innovative materials is Material ConneXion. Headquartered in New York, with offices in Bangkok, Cologne, and Milan, Material ConneXion acts as a mediator: it scouts suppliers around the world, including small companies and major global manufacturers, to identify new materials that manufacturers and designers could use. The firm has a library with physical samples of more than thirty-five hundred materials and processes, and gallery space where quarterly exhibits investigate scenarios associated with new materials. The firm also publishes a magazine and hosts conferences.

In its explorations, Material ConneXion investigates not only the functional properties of materials but also their implications in languages and meaningful applications. The firm's approach is design-driven: in its own words, it helps form "creative circles" connecting suppliers and industrial users of innovative materials that "determine the shape of things to come."[8]

Participants in Pioneering Projects

Other interpreters are those involved in pioneering projects. In many industries, innovators use products in special settings outside the normal market stream, where they have greater freedom to explore new solutions.

For example, architects who design hotels, institutional headquarters, and public buildings need to consider lighting in their work. Some of the most advanced architects, such as Norman Foster and Philippe Starck, approach these projects with an experimental attitude, doing research on novel ways of organizing human spaces and expressing symbolic languages. In so doing they consider not only a building's architecture but also its interior, including illumination and lamps, and usually design lighting fixtures to suit occupants' particular needs.

Artemide often cooperates with architects on such special projects. For example, in 2002 it collaborated with Swiss architects Jacques Herzog and Pierre de Meuron on headquarters for the insurance company Helvetia in St. Gallen, Switzerland. During the project (which received England's prestigious Royal Gold Medal), the two architects worked with Artemide to design lamps for the internal offices. Artemide added the special lamp that resulted from this effort (which received the prestigious Compasso d'Oro design award in 2004) to its consumer catalog under the commercial name Pipe.[9]

Artemide is not the only company that sees participation in special projects as an opportunity to pursue research and develop innovations. One of the best-selling products of Flos, an Artemide competitor, is Miss Sissi, a small table lamp originally designed by Philippe Starck for the Paramount Hotel in New York. Similarly, Molteni created one of its most popular products—the table Less, designed by Jean Nouvel—for the Fondation Cartier in Paris. B&B Italia performs advanced experiments when designing interiors for large cruise ships.

Any industry has opportunities to experiment with design-driven innovation through special projects, which can range from special cars designed for specific races to new food products created for specific events. Such projects are particularly well suited to innovation for several reasons.

First, clients of such projects are more prone to delve into new avenues and create new landmarks, and therefore they provide more freedom to explore radical solutions. Note, however, that these are not simply "concept" projects, like the experiments firms often conduct: rather, they are real implementations used by real clients who provide real feedback. Simply, given their special nature, they offer interesting ground for experimentation. An example is the $100 PC developed under the One Laptop Per Child initiative led by Nicholas Negroponte. This project has spurred several firms and designers to jointly explore both new technological solutions (such as the clever idea of making each laptop both a router and its own communication device, thus creating a mini-network that enables even the most remote child to connect to the Internet) and new meanings (PCs as educational and social tools rather than machines).[10]

Second, these special projects are usually led by *advanced interpreters* (such as architects, designers, scientists, and top chefs), who convene and challenge researchers from several settings to pioneer new meanings and languages in a given context. Such projects therefore provide firms a unique opportunity to share and develop new knowledge with noncompeting interpreters who are at the forefront of research and exploration.

Third, these projects act as beacons of cultural production. They receive significant attention from other interpreters, including the media, cultural institutions, and the public, and thus often eventually influence how people give meaning to products.

Companies in Other Industries

Among the most interesting interpreters in the design discourse are companies in other industries that address the same life context that a firm is targeting. In citing Artemide, I mentioned other companies that also look at how people live in their homes, including manufacturers of furniture, TV sets, audio systems, personal computers, and game consoles, as well as broadcasting firms.

In the bicycle industry, interpreters from other industries might include manufacturers of sport apparel, portable music players, and street food; music producers; and firms providing wireless services and tourist services. These companies are not competing with bicycle manufacturers. However, all are conducting research on how people live, move around, and work out in the streets, and all help create people's outdoor experiences.

Every company, in any context, is surrounded by these kinds of interpreters. When we want to develop design-driven innovations, therefore, an interesting question is, What other companies in other industries are targeting the same people in the same life context? Which kinds of other products or services are these people using, or could they use? All these interpreters have some knowledge of the meanings and languages we are investigating. And they would probably be eager to share it and to understand our interpretations, as they confront the same problems and have the same interests.

Philips, for example, has developed several collaborations with firms in other industries, such as Artemide, Alessi, Cappellini (furniture), Levi Strauss, Nike, Douwe Egberts (coffee), and Beiersdorf (personal care). These collaborations, which can take the form of workshops, concept products, or even products launched in the market, allow Philips to explore breakthrough opportunities, exchange insights, and test its vision with companies that it esteems as forward-looking interpreters.[11]

Developing a scenario with noncompeting firms also makes it more likely that a coherent way of living will occur in the market, because the actors will create products and services that fit together both functionally and symbolically.

Designers

Design firms, of course, are also important interpreters of how people could give meaning to things, especially design firms that conduct research by focusing on a given life context. This does not necessarily mean that design consultants have research projects like those undertaken by universities or corporations, although some design firms deliberately invest in exploring new scenarios and developing advanced knowledge to anticipate clients' future requests.

Design firms research and learn through repeated projects in various industries that target the same life context. Designers who design lamps, sofas, kitchens, and consumer electronics have iterative chances to collect information about domestic lifestyles, test new proposals, gain feedback, and interact with multiple interpreters in this context. Chapter 7 illustrates several design-driven innovation projects in which designers have played a central role.

Retail and Delivery Firms

Finally, firms involved in the delivery of products and services are interesting interpreters. These companies might include, for example, retail shops and restaurants for consumer goods or maintenance and repair services for durable goods and machines. Some of these actors perform research on how people buy and use the products they complement with their services. For example, some furniture showrooms present sophisticated explorations of new scenarios in domestic living. Avant-garde architects design these interiors, which sometimes even assume the connotations of pioneering projects.

When Samsung designed its Bordeaux TV—an LCD set that people like not only because of the performance of its screen but also because of its unique look and feel (the apparently one-piece glossy shape resembles a glass of wine)—it analyzed furniture shops. The company wanted to let the product speak the emotional language of the ambience in which the TV was meant to live and to stimulate the emotional purchasing pattern people follow when they buy furniture.[12] The Korean company has even created a retail space at the Time Warner Center in Manhattan, where it showcases its own interpretations of the digital lifestyle.

Similarly, restaurants are an interesting category of interpreters in the food industry. Some restaurants explore not only new recipes and ingredients but also entirely new experiences, experimenting with how to enjoy food in a social context.

Users

Of course, the design discourse includes users. Although design-driven innovation is not user centered, that does not mean users are pure recipients. The bidirectional arrows that connect users with the other actors in our model underline their active role in the network of interpreters. Eventually they are the people who give the actual meaning to new products. Even more important, some users perform research. This is true especially of so-called lead users, who anticipate new cultural patterns and explore new ways of giving meaning to things.

The introduction of sport wheelchairs provides an interesting example. Most innovations in this industry have not come from incumbent manufacturers of hospital devices. Instead, they have come from users, especially people who loved playing sports before experiencing a disabling accident.

Rory Cooper, for example, is a successful wheelchair runner (he was a bronze medalist at the Paralympic Games in Seoul in 1988) as well as a successful wheelchair innovator, being a professor at the University of Pittsburgh's Human Engineering Research Laboratories. Bob Hall, the first person to compete in the Boston Marathon in a wheelchair and the winner of the first wheelchair marathon in 1974, designed sport wheelchairs in his mother's basement, eventually founding his own firm New Halls Wheels in 1984.

What prevented incumbents in this field from realizing innovations was not technology. It was mainly a matter of meanings. Manufacturers of hospital devices designed wheelchairs in a way that segregated people instead of integrating them. Designing wheelchairs for competition did not simply require functional innovation. Above all, it required a change in cultural interpretation. This new proposal came mainly from lead users.[13]

The Process: Participating in the Design Discourse

Creating design-driven innovations requires two assets: knowledge of how people could give meaning to things, and the seductive power to influence the emergence of a radical new meaning. In exploring the design discourse, I have shown that companies are not alone in their research endeavor: they are immersed in a collective research laboratory where these two assets are diffuse and shared.[14] Whereas the core capability in user-centered design is getting as close as possible to users, the core capability in design-driven innovation is participating in the design discourse.

More precisely, the process of design-driven innovation is rooted in three actions (see figure 6-3):

- *Listening to the design discourse:* This action entails accessing knowledge about possible meanings and languages of new products. It implies understanding where this knowledge is and how to internalize it. And it requires continuously identifying and attracting key interpreters in the design discourse.

- *Interpreting:* This action entails generating your own vision and proposal for a radical new meaning and language. It implies integrating and recombining knowledge gleaned from the design discourse, as well producing novel interpretations. It requires that you conduct internal research and experiments.

- *Addressing the design discourse:* This action entails diffusing your own vision to interpreters. You may benefit from their seductive power and thus eventually influence how people give meaning to things. It implies defining the most appropriate means through which interpreters can discuss and internalize your new proposal.

FIGURE 6-3

The process of design-driven innovation

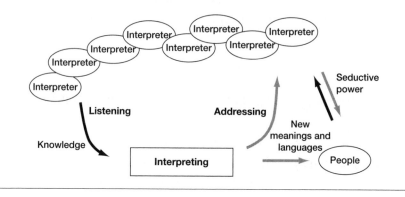

These three actions—which the next few chapters analyze in detail—are the foundation that enables companies to leverage the design discourse. On the one hand, the actions are aimed at securing privileged and distinctive access to external assets: knowledge and seductive power. "Privileged and distinctive" means that your dialogue with the design discourse is better than that of your competitors. It is, in other words, a source of competitive advantage. It may therefore require you to create relationships with key interpreters before your competitors do, or in a more intense form, or in a unique overall configuration.

On the other hand, these actions also are aimed at developing internal assets. Generating design-driven innovation does not simply imply sharing knowledge with the design discourse. It is a proactive process that entails generating a new and proprietary proposal. It requires the internal ability to absorb external knowledge more effectively than competitors, to find unidentified combinations, to generate unique visions through internal experiments. That is why I talk about *participating* in the design discourse: it requires active interpretation, through which a firm develops its own vision. Without this central action, there is no innovation but mere replication.

This process is significantly different from the user-centered processes you are used to. First, the process speaks of deep research rather than fast brainstorming, of developing and sharing knowledge rather than pursuing extemporaneous creativity. This process resembles engineering research (although targeting meanings rather than technologies) more than the work of a creative agency.

Second, the process of design-driven innovation is based on participation more than observation. It entails modifying dominant cultural paradigms and producing possible new meanings, rather than simply observing what is happening in society.

Third, the process is based on the ability to build and sustain an external and internal network of relationships rather than on a specific method or sequence of steps. For that reason, in the next chapters you will not find a handbook on how to analyze sociocultural trends. Rather, you will find guidelines on how, for example, to value the work of sociologists and anthropologists, how to spot them, and how to integrate their interpretations of trends with those of other interpreters.[15]

The model of the design discourse in figure 6-2 does not show how meanings and languages evolve in society. Rather, it shows how interpreters who do research on meaning and languages interact. It points out where the two assets of design-driven innovation—knowledge and seductive power—are and how they are shared. It is a model aimed at highlighting the role of executives in generating design-driven innovations. If you think that the secret of success of companies such as Alessi or Artemide or Apple is a specific tool or method, I am sorry to disappoint you. There is entrepreneurial and managerial acumen. The next chapters try to distill it.

7
LISTENING

[Finding and Attracting Key Interpreters]

The collective of Memphis was engaged in challenging, radical research. They provide one of the most interesting examples of how basic research on product meanings moves to applications. [IN THE ILLUSTRATION First room: the studio of Memphis's Ettore Sottsass. On the wall: a sketch of the Carlton sideboard. Second room: A laboratory at Alessi. On the table: a prototype of the Mandarin citrus squeezer. Third room: the office of Jonathan Ive at Apple. On the table: a prototype of the iMac G3.]

S O, YOU ARE TELLING ME that I should hire a superstar designer and trust him?" interrupted a man from the back row of the audience.

I was caught unaware by this sharp comment midway through my presentation. "No, I'm sorry. We are talking about design-driven innovation, not design*er*-driven innovation."

People who approach design for the first time are often biased by a preconceived stereotype. They imagine a scenario in which firms execute what a superstar designer has decided to do because "she knows what people dream." Some go even further, envisioning nightmarish situations in which executives are at the mercy of design gurus and surrender to their whims. Observers in the media, some designers, manufacturers themselves (especially newcomers who overstate the contribution of a celebrity master to gain press attention), and even crafty competitors boost this mythology.[1]

Curiously, this designer-centric perspective is also gaining a foothold in accounts of user-centered innovation, which often point to the central role of an external design firm to which companies outsource a significant part of the process. In this case the terminology is different (the trendy tag has changed from *guru* to *evangelist,* making the scenario more familiar to Western cultures), and the narration is closer to management jargon (brainstorming, creativity, teamwork); but the mythology that all you need is a designer (or a design firm) out there to solve your innovation problems remains intact.

This is not the kind of approach I am talking about. Would that it were so simple! You could then merely hire a famous designer and a successful innovation would miraculously materialize, at arm's length.

Some companies have indeed tried to implement such a designer-driven strategy, with unlucky outcomes. In 1995 Aprilia, an Italian motorcycle manufacturer, asked French architect Philippe Starck to conceive a new bike. Well positioned in the scooter market, Aprilia needed to strengthen its position in powerful high-end bikes. The company withdrew Motò 6.5, the motorcycle designed by Starck, from the market in 1997, only to release it again in 1999, and finally canceled it in 2002. Although the bike received significant press acclaim, thanks to the designer's name, and won a small niche among design-addicted bikers who became passionate for it, Motò did not allow Aprilia to make its way into the large-bike segment (where the firm did not overcome the 3 percent European share, compared with the 20 percent share of Japanese competitors). In 2003 Piaggio acquired Aprilia.

Another example of fatal reliance on a designer-centric approach is the Halley lamp, designed in 2005 by Richard Sapper for Lucesco. Sapper is considered a master of design, his effectiveness in designing lamps proven by Artemide's Tizio, a business classic released in 1972 that is still young-looking in the market after having sold 20 million units. Halley, however, was a failure. "Going for an iconic designer and for Richard was not a mistake," says Curtis Abbott, cofounder of Lucesco. "Our mistake was starting from too weak a base of knowledge about the lighting business. We didn't have the market research to help us understand the sales potential for this product."[2]

I am not saying that designers and design firms do not provide a substantial contribution. Far from it: they are an essential voice in the design discourse and may be among the primary contributors to an innovation project. However, they are never the sole interpreters. The process we have observed among successful companies—including those in Italy that appear to depend on individual designers—is actually based on a web of interactions with a multitude of interpreters in various categories (including, for example, technology suppliers, artists, and firms in other industries). Italian entrepreneurs do not trust anyone when it comes to investing money from their own pockets. They listen to several voices, even when they name a product after one designer, and eventually make up their mind. Thus the process of design-driven innovation pivots on the integrative capabilities of executives rather than on individual interpreters. It can hardly be outsourced, because it combines insights from a company's unique network of relationships.

In this chapter I analyze how firms implementing design-driven innovation build a privileged dialogue with the design discourse to

TABLE 7-1

Dynamics of the design discourse and guidelines for gaining privileged access to interpreters

Dynamics of the design discourse	Guidelines for identifying and attracting interpreters
Debates	Listen to multiple voices.
Skewed distribution of interpreters	Find key interpreters.
Transfers	Harness forward-looking researchers.
Bridges	Leverage brokers and mediators.
Whispers	Immerse the company in the discourse.
Two-tiered geography	Hybridize the local and the global.
Elite circles	Attract interpreters by acting as an interpreter.
Obsolescence	Keep searching for new interpreters and circles.

effectively tap knowledge of product meanings and languages. I show how they spot unidentified key interpreters, attract them before their competitors do, and develop a preferential, fruitful relationship with them. Table 7-1 summarizes these practices, which reflect the dynamics of the design discourse. I briefly examine each dynamic and then illustrate its implications. My aim is to provide guidelines that enable managers to assemble a unique circle of interlocutors that may become an inimitable wellspring of innovation.

Multiple Voices

The design discourse is not a plain, straightforward dialogue wherein participants present novel interpretations, discuss them one by one, and then accept a single interpretation as dominant and reject the rest. Rather, it is a noisy and confused debate wherein several interpretations coexist.

Proposals and feedback become increasingly unintelligible and ambiguous as participants move from utilitarian features to emotional and symbolic meanings. Everyone would agree that designing a car engine that halves fuel consumption is useful (the problem is then to find a practical way to produce such an engine). But when we investigate the meanings that people associate with spending time in a car and the importance they give to interior space and ways to use it, then interpretations are multiple and often in striking contrast to each other. No company will ever find a single definitive view: the insights in the design discourse are scattered among several interpreters. A company develops its unique vision by distinctively combining all these insights and perspectives.

Indeed, successful Italian manufacturers interact with multiple interpreters. A study of the Italian furniture industry that I conducted with Claudio Dell'Era investigated differences in the portfolio of designers between the most innovative companies and their imitators (see table 7-2).[3] We found, first, that innovators tend to rely on external designers more than their competitors do. Well-known companies outside Italy confirm the benefits of this strategy. According to Brian Walker, CEO of Herman Miller, for example, "This external network ensures that we are always taking a fresh look at problems faced by our customers without subjecting it to our own filters. If you only have an

TABLE 7-2

Italian furniture manufacturers' portfolio of designers

	Innovators	Imitators
Percentage of products designed by external designers	90%	77%
Average number of external design firms in the portfolio	11.9	4.4
Percentage of designers with a degree in architecture	45%	33%
Percentage of designers with an engineering degree	6%	0%
Percentage of designers with a degree in industrial design	31%	52%
Percentage of non-Italian designers	46%	16%

internal design staff, even an enormously talented one, you are inherently limited by their existing world view and experiences."[4]

The difference between the percentage of products designed by external designers, however, was not remarkably higher in innovators (90 percent) than in imitators (77 percent). Collaboration with outside interpreters is a somewhat common practice in the industry and therefore is not enough.

The picture became more interesting when we examined the number of design firms with whom Italian manufacturers cooperate. Successful manufacturers have an average portfolio of 11.9 external design firms, compared with 4.4 for imitators, with companies such as B&B and Kartell having about 30 each. That average does not include Artemide and Alessi, which cooperate with more than 50 and 200 external design firms, respectively, each with a different voice in and opinion on the design discourse. Not all these designers participate in projects that focus on radical innovation of meanings; most are involved in incremental development. But these findings do suggest the variety of insights that leaders gain by participating in the design discourse, along with the breadth of talent that they can tap when eventually investing in more-radical innovation.

The first task in developing a dialogue with the design discourse, therefore, is to identify multiple interpreters—not only designers but an array of unrelated sources. What matters is the variety of their perspectives: heterogeneity is essential.

Consider Barilla, the leading manufacturer of pasta and other flour-based products. To extend its reach beyond its traditional businesses, the company recently pursued an innovation project aimed at understanding people's unmet aspirations in preparing and eating food in their homes, and thus at creating radically new meal experiences. Toward that end, Barilla integrated its own research and market insights with those of interpreters it invited to its headquarters in Parma to share visions of how people live in their kitchens.

These interpreters included the innovation unit of the white goods manufacturer Whirlpool, the R&D manager of the kitchen manufacturer Snaidero, and the design manager of kitchenware producer Alessi. Barilla also invited two designers from the design firm IDEO to discuss their insights on food preparation and consumption. A chef who had explored the merging of two culinary cultures (Italian and Japanese) commented on people's openness to experimenting with new eating habits. And, finally, a food columnist from the German magazine *Stern* revealed his insights on why people are more interested in watching others cook on TV than in cooking themselves. His interpretive ability reflected his unusual background: a degree in theology allowed him to bring a scrutinizing eye and profound perspective to cultural developments.[5]

Where to Look

A company should therefore base its dialogue with the design discourse on multiple interactions. But where to look for possible interpreters? Chapter 6 provides a map and directions. First, a company should define the *life context* that its innovation project is addressing. For Barilla, that life context is a home kitchen.

Second, a company should ask, Who are the interpreters who conduct research on how people could give meaning to things in that same life context, and who are likely to influence the emergence of new meanings? The framework in figure 7-1, introduced in chapter 6, can serve as a checklist for typical categories of interpreters. Of course, different innovation projects—even within the same company—will require their own circle of interpreters. For example, in pursuing another project more focused on pasta, Barilla interacted with an array of interpreters who were different from those involved in the project mentioned above: a winemaker, a professor with expertise in designing restaurants and "happy hour" experiences, an entrepreneur in modern catering services, a semiologist, a sociologist with expertise in food and the history of food culture, a vice-president of the cultural organization Slow Food, a chef who had been doing research on molecular gastronomy, and a food critic.

Key Interpreters in a Skewed World

Only a few interpreters have the ability to contribute effectively to design-driven innovation. For example, thousands of chefs may populate the design discourse, but only a few do advanced research on the

FIGURE 7-1

Categories of interpreters

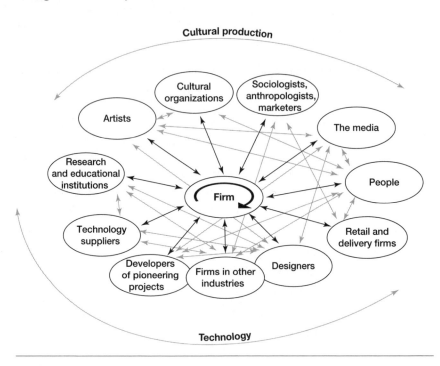

meaning of food, and even fewer can envision new possibilities and constructively participate in the teamwork that innovation requires. Thus, when you ask yourself, "Which actors can help me envision how people could give meaning to things?" the problem is not that you will find no one. The problem is finding the right person among a multitude.

For example, Barcelona is home to more than three hundred design firms, Milan to more than seven hundred, and London to more than a thousand.[6] These firms may be very creative in supporting a company's incremental innovation projects. But only a handful have generated or have the potential to generate *radical* innovations of meanings. Indeed, my data on the Italian furniture industry (table 7-2) shows that a significant number of imitators also collaborate with external designers. Mere collaboration with a design firm therefore does not guarantee success. The difference between innovators and imitators seems to stem from *which* interpreters firms choose.

Indeed, the number of interpreters in the design discourse who can provide radical insights is small. The distribution of the quality of their interpretations is therefore positively skewed (see figure 7-2). In this context collaboration with a generic interpreter is counterproductive: with a random choice you are more likely to end up on the left side of the diagram. You need instead to identify the *key* interpreters who stand at the extreme of the long tail: those who can provide the two assets (knowledge and seductive power) you need. According to Bruno Murari, scientific adviser for MEMS at STMicroelectronics, "Breakthrough innovation in a given field is envisioned by few people around the world. Perhaps three or four. I really mean people, not organizations. You better know them."

Unfortunately, companies and policy makers sometimes fail to understand the highly skewed nature of the design discourse. Many times have I heard a company exploring its first use of design say, "Why don't we launch a design competition? We could get tons of great ideas for free!" This shortcut is a trap. Companies end up spending their energy screening thousands of poor ideas that lie on the left side of the curve, lacking the ability to make sense of them and often

FIGURE 7-2

The skewed distribution of key interpreters in the design discourse

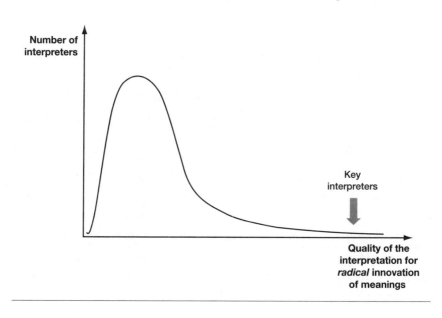

missing the good ones—if they are ever submitted. If you were a talented interpreter, would you invest significant time and risk losing your interpretation among thousands of others by submitting it to a company that lacks interpretative abilities?

Large numbers of responses create *adverse selection:* the best interpreters avoid such competitions and try to develop direct personal relationships with the most advanced companies. Firms may still find competitions useful for more incremental innovation or to gather insights as a part of a larger, more integrated project. Design competitions may also help diffuse an innovation throughout the design discourse. For example, suppliers that want to make designers aware of new materials adopt this approach (see chapter 9). Yet many companies still think that design competitions are the best and only way to find great, packaged ideas, and this technique is becoming so popular that it is spurring competition among design competitions (all fighting for space on the left side of the diagram in figure 7-2).

Policy makers sometimes fall into similar traps. I have been exposed to several innovation and design programs promoted by governments in various countries. Most of these programs share a common trait: they start from the assumption that manufacturers should cooperate with (local) designers and pursue activities that favor these encounters. Again, this approach can be highly detrimental—not only to manufacturers, which are more likely to encounter designers on the left side of the diagram, but also to designers themselves. Promoting a vision in which every designer is alike (see the dashed line in figure 7-3) implies transforming design into a commodity: the same qualities appear wherever you look.[7]

These strategies often ensue from a shallow and misleading analysis of the behavior of successful firms. Companies such as Alessi and Artemide do not resort to the innovation techniques for which IBM, Procter & Gamble, and Eli Lilly, for example, have become known: they do not rely on an anonymous horde of code writers or the equivalent to perfect an existing product. These open and crowded techniques work when several contributors can provide fair-enough quality (see figure 7-3).[8] But when the world of interpreters is skewed, competition is based on close, privileged relationships with key interpreters rather than on numerous ideas: Claudio Luti, chairman and CEO of Kartell, says, "I choose the designers with whom to cooperate before I choose the solutions, and not the other

FIGURE 7-3

Two possible distributions of the quality of interpretation and related strategies of collaboration

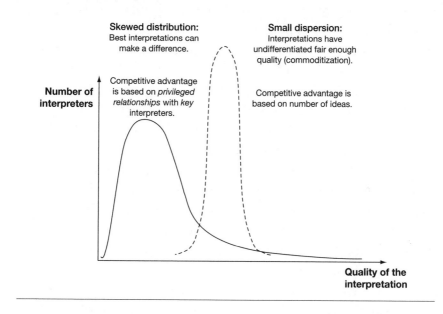

way around. For this reason projects that are submitted spontaneously to our firm are not even considered. Innovation comes from collaboration."[9]

These companies carefully select dozens of key designers after years of cumulative investment in building relational assets. And to pursue radical innovation of meaning, these firms tap this familiar resource or further invest in searching for new talents and attracting them before and better than their competitors do. These firms pursue experiments, succeeding with some and failing with others, until they find the key people.

The following sections provide guidelines on how to identify and attract—among the multitude of potential interpreters—the few key individuals who can support design-driven innovation.

Forward-Looking Researchers

Many people overlook the fact that Italy had no graduate schools of industrial design until the late 1990s.[10] Those Italian "designers" with whom local manufacturers collaborated were mainly architects.

I once asked a friend at the school of design of Politecnico di Milano to explain the conundrum: how was it possible that a country often cited as preeminent in design lacked industrial designers? His explanation was enlightening. "Italian design is so unique, so radical," he said, "because of the approach to innovation brought by architects instead of designers. Think about it. Have you ever heard of an architect taking a marketing course?"

Indeed, I had been recalling how fellow engineering students and I had joked about stereotypical architects: they never listen to their clients. Tom Wolfe parodied this attitude in *From Bauhaus to Our House*, in which architects, in their intellectual monasteries, are more engaged in inaccessible discussions than in understanding people's needs.[11]

My friend continued, "Architects design buildings, and most buildings will outlive the tenancy of their present owners. So why should architects listen to them if they will not be the only users of the buildings? A building also has an urban presence in a larger community, serving more people than merely those who live inside."

Actually, architects are trained not to listen to clients but rather to take a step back and design from a broader perspective: broader in time (connecting a building with the history of the urban context and envisioning the way of life of future generations who will take up residence there) and broader in space (considering the social environment in which the building will stand). When architects were asked by Italian furniture manufacturers to design furniture, they brought this forward-looking attitude from designing buildings to designing products. Their process did not start from market analysis; instead, it began from an investigation of sociocultural phenomena triggered by the new materials and technologies made available by the manufacturers.

"Designers shouldn't accept false suggestions from the market. The market never suggests anything good." So says Michele De Lucchi, an architect who is a major interpreter for Artemide. Architect Michael Graves mirrored this perspective when he designed the well-known Kettle 9093 for Alessi (see chapter 8): "I stayed true to what I thought was good design no matter who it was for."[12]

The most innovative Italian furniture manufacturers still tend to rely on architects more than industrial designers for their most advanced projects, despite the growing supply of graduates in industrial design.

In my study of the industry (see table 7-2), I found that innovative companies collaborate with more architects (45 percent of their collaboration portfolio) than with industrial designers (31 percent).[13] These companies sometimes even outsource concept design to engineers, who do not have a typical user-centered education. Imitators, in contrast, tend to cooperate with more industrial designers (52 percent of their portfolio) than architects (33 percent) or engineers (0 percent).

Of course, architects are not the only radical interpreters in the design discourse (nor do all architects have this capability). There are also designers who are capable of moving beyond market trends. For example, Giorgietto Giugiaro, who designed the FIAT Panda, says, "The public doesn't ask for anything. You are the one offering them something. When car manufacturers say that the public demands this or that evolution in style, it is not true. If that were the case, then marketing people, as organized and expert as they are, would be able to propose a strategy that guarantees success. Something that we all know doesn't happen very often."[14]

Language Transfers: Moving Upstream in the Design Discourse Toward Basic Research

When pursuing design-driven innovation, companies should therefore seek interpreters having the forward-looking attitude needed to move beyond dominant interpretations in the market. Unfortunately these interpreters are as rare as they are precious. Where can companies find them?

An effective strategy is to look in the communities of basic researchers who do advanced exploration. The flow of knowledge on meanings and languages in the design discourse resembles that of science-based R&D: it moves from basic research to applications.[15] Just as scientists conduct basic exploration and then technicians develop products based on their findings, some interpreters are engaged in radical, untargeted experiments exploring new languages, and others later suggest more-focused targets, transferring the results of those experiments into market applications.

In other words, knowledge transfers move from the left side of the model of design discourse in figure 7-1 (educational institutions, artists, technology suppliers) to the right side (the media, professional consultants, retailers). I highlighted this dynamic when noting the role of artists as basic researchers in creating cultural symbols. The density of basic researchers is therefore higher among parties that are positioned upstream within the design discourse. That is the first place to look. I have shown, for example, how Artemide has cooperated with theater director Luca Ronconi, who is known for his experiments in stage design. However, forward-looking researchers can also be found—albeit more rarely—among interpreters who are typically oriented to the short term, on the right side of the design discourse. The example of Barilla shows that you can also find researchers among chefs and journalists if you search carefully.

Memphis: A Research Lab on Languages

Memphis—a 1980s collective of architects and designers—provides one of the most interesting examples of how basic research on product languages and meanings moves to applications.

Memphis was founded by Ettore Sottsass, an architect by training, who was born in Austria, studied in Turin, and then moved to Milan to establish his studio. He was a consultant for Olivetti in the 1960s, designing products such as the iconic Valentine typewriter. In 1981, during the upending of norms that occurred in the wake of the youth movements of the 1960s and 1970s, Sottsass, then in his sixties, joined with emerging talents less than half his age (such as Michele De Lucchi, Matteo Thun, Javier Mariscal, and Aldo Cibic). The new collective's vision was to challenge the institutional culture and dominant connotations of "good design."

For example, Memphis cultivated an irreverent liking for intense primary colors (in contrast to the dominant use of "appropriate" black and white, or brown) and the uneasy juxtaposition of materials. Said Sottsass: "The challenge was to put together materials that are significantly different from the perspective of meaning. For example, plastic laminate beside precious wood or marble. Sensorial stories. Vulgar plastic and noble marble combined and, as such, questioned."[16]

Memphis represented the conflation of high and low art, luxury and simplicity, in a democratization of taste. Its proposals were lighthearted and ironic and were meant to make an emotional rather than a rational,

utilitarian appeal. In short, the circle engaged in a pioneering exploration of postmodern philosophies and languages applied to experimental artifacts.[17]

In seven years (Sottsass dismantled Memphis in 1988 because it had
lost its innovative drive) the group produced a collection of about forty
pieces—ranging from furniture to ceramics, lighting fixtures to textiles—
meant not for the mass market but for interpreters in the design discourse. Of course, critics in mainstream institutional culture dismissed
these proposals, claiming that only affluent Dallas psychiatrists would
ever buy such designs.[18] However, these pieces were not the sterile results of a bizarre and extemporaneous spark of creativity. The collective
was engaged in challenging, radical research. According to Sottsass, "I'm
always offended when they say that I play when I do Memphis work; actually I'm very serious, I'm never more serious than when I do Memphis
work. It's when I design machines for Olivetti that I play."[19]

We know the final outcome: postmodernism, with its emotional drive
and language of symbolic objects, made its way into mainstream markets via breakthrough consumer applications by firms such Artemide
and Alessi.[20] Other firms hired the architects who left Memphis, and the
works of the collective influenced some of the most popular designers
of the 1980s, such as Philippe Starck and Marc Newson.[21] Emotional
objects became commonplace in many industries.

Entrepreneurs immersed in the local design discourse had a privileged opportunity to recognize the potential of those experiments.
Ernesto Gismondi, president of Artemide, saw Memphis as an opportunity to explore breakthroughs in meanings and languages: "Ettore
Sottsass needed some funding for Memphis. I gave them the money and
left them free to do what they wanted. For me, this was a laboratory."

I want to underline here that Gismondi did not provide funding
because of a sense of patronage or his love of the artistic avant-garde.
Rather, Gismondi invested in Memphis with the same intent of CEOs
investing in new technological ventures and spin-offs: to create breakthrough innovations. He supported interpreters in their research
process.[22]

I also want to emphasize that Gismondi talks about Memphis as a
lab and not a creative think tank. Key interpreters are researchers who
are exploring and experimenting in depth with one specific vision,

TABLE 7-3

The contrasts between radical researchers and typical creative teams

	Forward-looking researchers (radicals)	Creative teams
Output	Proposals, vision	Answers
	Framework	Ideas
Process	Depth	Speed
	Research and experimentation	Brainstorming
Dynamics within the circle or team	Convergence	Divergence
Assets	Knowledge	Methodology
	Scholar (unique expertise)	Neophyte (ignorance of constraints)
	Relationships	Processes
Quality metrics	Robustness of the vision	Number and variety of ideas
	Impact of the vision on society	Solution to a problem
Vision of society	A strong personal vision	Culturally neutral
Attitude toward existing sociocultural paradigms	Challenging the dominant paradigm	Playing with the existing paradigm

rather than tossing out hundreds of brainstormed, unrelated ideas. We have recently been smothered by treatises on the importance of creativity, and the word is losing any meaning. Fast brainstorming might be useful for incremental, user-centered innovation, but people involved in radical innovation of meaning work differently (see table 7-3).

Brokering and Mediating

Those who do not want to imitate anything, produce nothing.

— Salvador Dali

Like transfers of product languages and meanings from research to applications, there is another dynamic in the design discourse that recalls the movement of technologies: the process of transferring languages and meanings across industries.

Studies of technology management have shown that innovation often occurs as a novel recombination of existing pieces of knowledge.[23] Actors who identify new combinations (called *brokers*, *bridges*, or *gatekeepers)* link previously unconnected technical communities.[24] Designers, for example, may act as technology brokers. A study on IDEO has shown how this Palo Alto–based design firm—which develops projects for manufacturers in as many as forty industries—harnesses its network position to move solutions across industries.[25]

A similar dynamic holds for design-driven innovation. Interpreters who operate at the intersection of unconnected worlds may help move languages and meanings around.

Language Brokering in the Apple iMac

The iMac G3, released in 1998 by Apple, is an illuminating example. The iMac—which signaled the return of Steve Jobs to Cupertino, and Apple to the forefront of innovation—was acclaimed as one of the most revolutionary personal computers ever released. It had resurrected earlier connotations of Apple products, such as the compact all-in-one architecture, which wrapped the monitor and circuit board into a single body, and the focus on simplicity. But it also adopted a design language that was novel for the industry: a friendly shell in translucent colored plastic and an ovoid form that challenged the dominant paradigm of unsympathetic beige boxes. However, that language was not novel in other industries. The same translucent plastic and the same colors had spread into household products in the early 1990s.[26]

I am not implying that the iMac was not innovative. Rather, I am saying that Apple relied on inspirations from existing products to stimulate its breakthrough. The history of progress—both technical and artistic—shows us that no innovation stands alone. Advances always take off from the achievements of others. Raffaello Sanzio spent his early years as an apprentice in the workshop of Pietro Perugino, who significantly influenced his work. Thomas Edison spent his entire life recombining inventions from disparate industries. Breakthroughs are often based on elements that were previously nonexistent in a given environment.

The emerging language of objects in homes inspired the iMac because it was meant to live in houses. It was the first computer in the Internet era, when people started to use desktops at home even for their jobs, thanks to remote connectivity. Apple understood that personal computers should speak the friendly language of modern household products rather than the cold, remote language of business and offices.

Jonathan Ive, Apple's senior VP for design, acted as a *broker of languages:* before joining Apple, he had been an independent design consultant in London. His firm, Tangerine, was involved in designing household products (for example, Tangerine was a consultant for Ideal Standard, then a player in the bathroom and plumbing industry). Ive held the perfect network position to give Apple access to a world of household meanings and languages unknown to any other computer company.

Firms often tend to involve only interpreters who already have a central position in their own industry. This strategy may appear to be safe. But it is inspired by the past rather than the future. The result is that everyone looks in the same directions and involves the same type of interpreters; consultant budgets rise, and industry products all look alike. What seemed to be an irrational choice by Apple (having a former bathroom designer design a computer) was instead the proper identification of a key interpreter in the design discourse.

The brokering of languages is a central dynamic in the discourse. The difference between that process and the one used to develop technological knowledge is that languages are more culturally dependent and less industry dependent. They are culturally dependent because meanings evolve within a given life context and may face barriers in moving across different sociocultural worlds (such as different countries: the language of luxury furniture in Russia differs from that in Western countries). However, product languages move more fluently than technologies across industries. The emergence of new signs in a sector easily fertilizes products that live side by side (moving from furniture, to lamps, to computers, to telephones, and vice versa).

An important criterion in identifying key interpreters, then, is to look for people who can act as bridges—that is, those who do not belong to your industry but who target your same life context. The more you create bridges to worlds that are relevant for your users but that are unusual for your competitors, the more you have a chance to end up with breakthrough proposals.

Brokers

Two types of bridges, in particular, are important. The first is language brokers. These individuals provide knowledge about meanings emerging in a subnetwork of the design discourse that is inaccessible to a firm. This is Jonathan Ive's role in the iMac example, and the typical role of designers and consultants. For example, an automotive company that wants to explore new in-car experiences may look for an expert in the entertainment and digital media industries, asking for his interpretation of the evolution of language in entertainment on the go.

Mediators

The second type of bridge is mediators. These individuals do not provide knowledge but rather access to other interpreters. For example, a car company might ask an expert to provide access to other interpreters in the field of entertainment with whom the company might interact and share insights. Mediators create connections to other people.

An example is Material ConneXion, a firm described in chapter 6, which acts as a bridge between suppliers of novel materials, product manufacturers, and designers. Alessi's Tea and Coffee Piazza project provides another example. Alessandro Mendini, a well-known architect, was a central interpreter for Alessi in that project. Mendini's role was not to provide new designs but rather to introduce the firm to ten foreign architects doing experiments in postmodern architecture. He was a mediating bridge to other interpreters.

This mediating role is unusual in the design industry (design firms are not likely to provide access to other interpreters, and clients seldom pay designers to provide contacts instead of projects), but it may be the cornerstone that opens up access to worlds that are unknown to a firm. Indeed, a company that wants to start to create design-driven innovations, but has not yet built an extensive dialogue with the design discourse, may find this second type of interpreter, who helps build the firm's network, much more useful than brokers who provide solutions directly.[27]

Immersing a Company in the Whispers

Most of the interactions in the design discourse—new products, artworks, prototypes shown in exhibitions, articles, public reports— occur in forms that are visible to a large audience. In other words, to use the terminology of technological innovation, knowledge about how people could give meaning to things may be embedded in a *codified* form.[28] This allows interpretations to spread more readily. However, it also makes them easily accessible to everyone, including competitors. Thus the value of this embedded knowledge is lower than interpretations that are not yet codified but that are instead whispered—exchanged timidly when they are still in the form of insights.

A recent book by Giulio Castelli (the founder of Kartell), Paola Antonelli (the curator of the Department of Architecture and Design of the Museum of Modern Art in New York), and Francesca Picchi (a journalist at the architectural journal *Domus*) narrates in great detail how dialogue between entrepreneurs and designers has unfolded during fifty years of Italian design. Entrepreneurs interviewed by the authors often mention that discussions occurred while people were sailing on boats or skiing in the Alps.[29]

I am not implying that you need to improve your skills in sailing and skiing to raise your chances of creating radical innovations. Rather, I am saying that gaining access to the most valuable knowledge in the design discourse does not entail reading reports on sociocultural trends or scanning the Web. Instead, it requires *immersion* in the discourse. You need to be there, to listen to the whispers and promote experiments. The most effective forms of knowledge creation and exchange typically take the form of verbal dialogue, workshops, and joint projects. That is why top executives of design-driven companies often interact directly with external interpreters (designers, students, researchers, and suppliers), without intermediating figures.

Interpretations that take the form of codified knowledge may still be valuable. Monitoring exhibitions and fairs for artwork and conceptual products, scanning magazines and Web sites, and analyzing reports are essential to building a foundation. (And a growing number of interpreters such as trend-analysis agencies, scenario-building institutes, and sociologists are available to support firms in this monitoring activity.) However, it is highly probable that this information is also available to your competitors and thus is seldom a source of differentiation. Your ability to interpret codified knowledge differently and more effectively depends on what others do not have: privileged access to key inter- preters' whispers before they become broadly diffused. Whispers allow you to discern in the crowded and noisy sea of products, reports, articles, and experiments signs that others do not see even when they are in front of their eyes.

Genius Loci: The Geography of the Design Discourse

The design discourse is both local and global. On the one hand, the local density of the network is essential, because interactions based on tacit knowledge benefit from geographic proximity. On the other hand, interactions among interpreters worldwide allow them to en- large the quantity and variety of their insights and provide a global per- spective on the evolution of meanings.

The Design Discourse Is Everywhere

Proximity to a region where the design discourse is flourishing is a significant advantage for a company. For example, the literacy of the design discourse on domestic lifestyles in northern Italy is a major contributor to the success of local furniture manufacturers. Some may therefore think that design-driven innovation can thrive only in sur- roundings as visually sophisticated and culturally rich as Milan and its hinterlands, or Helsinki, or Copenhagen, or San Francisco. You should not, however, underestimate the (often untapped) resources in your own region. In fact, the potential for a design discourse exists everywhere.[30]

Let's take one unpromising candidate: the Finger Lakes region of upstate New York, more than two hundred miles northwest of New York and culturally no more connected to that metropolis than is west- ern Pennsylvania. Upstate New York has high rates of unemployment and one of the slowest-growing economies in the United States. But it has the raw material for a design discourse.

Rochester, the largest city in the Finger Lakes region, with a population of 212,000, was once the headquarters of Xerox and the Gannett newspaper chain, and it remains the headquarters of Bausch & Lomb (the lens manufacturer) and Kodak. Fiber-optics maker Corning is based in a nearby town of the same name. Smaller local companies manufacture high-speed digital equipment and do custom printing.

The city is also home to the Center for Electronic Imaging Systems, a New York State–funded advanced technology lab that involves collaboration among Xerox; Kodak; the University of Rochester, a medium-sized research institution with excellent professional schools (including its engineering school, which houses the Institute of Optics); and the Rochester Institute of Technology, one of the world's premier schools of print media. Less than an hour away is Alfred University, which has world-class programs in ceramics and glass sculpture, and its Division of Expanded Media, which promotes collaboration among printmakers, designers, video artists, and computer programmers. Cornell, an outstanding research university, is in nearby Ithaca.

The arts are far from neglected in the Finger Lakes region, which can claim 270 members of the American Institute of Architects, famous craftsmen such as Wendell Castle and Albert Paley, and a cluster of design studios in Skaneateles, which sits on a lake as serene as Lake Orta, north of Milan, where Alessi is based. Rochester also boasts Eastman House, perhaps the world's preeminent photography museum, and other fine arts museums are nearby. So we shouldn't be surprised that Richard Florida, in *The Rise of the Creative Class*, rated Rochester the twenty-first most creative among large cities in the United States, and second among large cities in its percentage of "super-creative" people.[31]

Yet despite the region's concentration of optics, imaging, and the related technology of offset printing, and its abundance of resources, Rochester has not emerged as a prominent center for design. Why? The shortcomings lie not in the quality and number of local interpreters but in the lack of a close dialogue among them and local firms. As in many other regions, the resources are there but local companies have failed to leverage them.

"Information sharing has been partial, creating cross-town rivalries rather than a center of the global economy," according to one local manager. Says another, "Creative resources do abound in this area, and I believe our corporation could do a much better job of utilizing them. I think a major reason is our mind-set of product design, which historically has been an internal activity. We as a company tend to resist the sort of outward collaboration that defines the design discourse concept."

Yet the possibilities in the Finger Lakes region are evident even to the people working there. According to one scientist and manager at Xerox, "In the past, it was rare for local communities such as Kodak, Bausch & Lomb, Corning, Xerox, and a cluster of small firms to collaborate. But collaboration in design-driven innovation could allow each firm to create competitive advantages in its respective industry. Xerox could get inspired by Kodak's camera design and Corning's glass fiber. Who says Xerox could not use transparent glass as a copier's frame? It is artistic, modern, and trendy. It also could serve the functional purpose of providing a clear view of paper-jam locations."

In a study I conducted for Finlombarda, the financial body of the government of Lombardy, Italy, twenty-six international design experts agreed that the components of the design system—schools, studios, and manufacturers—were not significantly better or worse in that region than elsewhere. What distinguished Lombardy was the number, strength, and quality of the links between these components.[32]

In short, a lack of resources need never keep a cluster from forming. Just as in Milan, where dialogue on household scenarios and goods for personal style is intense, or the Finger Lakes region, with its untapped potential for cultural experiences related to imaging, every region in the world has a wealth of local discourse on design and meanings. And every region where this discussion occurs values the unique aspects of local culture. The growing software industry in Dublin could tap the local storytelling cluster (which stretches from the heyday of Joyce, Beckett, Wilde, Shaw, Synge, and J. B. Keane to contemporary writers Binchy and Banville); think of how we would all enjoy enterprise resource planning software plotted like a play rather than a boring and incomprehensible set of instructions conceived by technical developers! Firms in Norway or New Zealand could take advantage of local expertise in extreme outdoor culture, sport, and entertainment.

The design discourse is everywhere. Companies need only immerse themselves in it and leverage the local resources that are not as accessible to competitors in other regions.

Hybridizing the Local and the Global

Companies cannot rely, however, only on local dialogue. The combination and hybridization of local peculiarities with interpretations from other cultures are the practices that create original visions.

My study of the design portfolio of Italian furniture manufacturers shows that successful companies tend to cooperate with foreign designers much more often than their less innovative competitors (see table 7-2). The former have a balanced portfolio that is split equally among Italian (54 percent) and foreign designers (46 percent), whereas imitators have a much narrower share of international collaboration (16 percent).

Again, this should sound a warning for all policies and programs that aim purely at stimulating cooperation between local manufacturers and local designers. The share of foreign designers among successful Italian manufacturers attests to the importance of looking beyond the connections that firms may easily find right outside their doors.

Identifying key interpreters in the global arena before competitors do requires investment and support. Alessi invested significant resources to find, attract, and test talented American architect Michael Graves before any other manufacturer. Only later, after the Italian firm had demonstrated his value, did he become a major interpreter for U.S. companies such as Target.

The need to reach for interpreters in the global setting underlines the importance of supporting mediators (such as Alessandro Mendini for Alessi) who can expand a company's network beyond national borders. Global corporations, especially, have access to interpreters worldwide if they leverage local branches. Samsung, for example, has design centers in Tokyo, Shanghai, San Francisco, Los Angeles, London, and Milan. However, most companies use regional centers only as antennas to detect local trends rather than to mediate local talent. The result is that large corporations often have no knowledge of the rich web of local relationships developed by their units, and they seldom leverage the full potential of global design.

Attracting the Interpreters

Once a firm has identified key interpreters, it needs to attract them, before and better than competitors. As the skewed nature of the design discourse reminds us, key interpreters are a scarce asset. How can a company develop a privileged relationship with them? How can it convince them to participate in radically innovative projects, which often imply a significant amount of risk and whose financial outcome is not clearly defined up front?

Not a Matter of Money

Architect Alessandro Mendini has been one of the prominent figures in the history of radical design. He has been the director of major architectural and design journals such as *Casabella, Modo,* and *Domus,* a key consultant and art director for companies such as Swatch, Philips, and Swarovski, and a recipient of the Compasso d'Oro design award. He is one of the major interpreters of postmodern design, now one of the most popular product languages.

How would you attract such a key interpreter to collaborate with your firm? The laws of economics imply that you would have to pay significant fees to secure access to a critical but scarce asset. Yet if you ask Mendini why he cooperated with Alessi, his answer has a completely different tone: "It is hard for me to distinguish if I'm working for Alessi or if Alessi is working for me."

The interaction between Alessi and Mendini is clearly not that of a client and a supplier. It is hard to understand who is providing a service and who is paying for it. Actually, designers who cooperate with Italian manufacturers are often not even paid on a project basis, but rather on royalties from sales. Designers, in other words, share the innovation risk with manufacturers, in a relationship that resembles that of a publisher with an author: it's hard to distinguish whether the supplier is the writer or the publisher. Both contribute to proposing a creative product to people. Designers are often eager to collaborate with Alessi regardless of financial implications, and interpreters sometimes even pay to work for the company.[33] Says Alberto Alessi, "When you ask an unspotted talent—for example, someone who has never designed products before—to cooperate with you in an experiment, she is so curious and involved in this new challenge that she is not even concerned about how much you will pay her. That is, of course, not true when you work with famous designers, and you ask them to do the normal job of designers."

Acting as an Interpreter

Another type of currency clearly attracts key interpreters. Remember that we are talking here of radical innovation—we are in the realm of *exploration* rather than exploitation. What is an interpreter looking for in this context? She is looking for the same things we ourselves are looking for: knowledge about how people could give meaning to things, and seductive power. In other words, she is looking for key interpreters.

Accounts of designers working for Italian manufacturers underscore that the capabilities they find at these companies are a major reason for the cooperation. They find technologies, flexibility, vision, and a brand—assets they seldom find among competing manufacturers.[34] Through cooperation they experiment with new technologies, stretch their talents, develop a reputation as avant-garde interpreters, and develop their own assets, which they can later harness more profitably.

According to artist-designer Ron Arad, "Northern Italy is the center of the design world above all because of its manufacturing culture. There is no other place in the world where you can find such a vast array of manufacturers who know the value of design." And Karim Rashid, an Egyptian designer raised in Canada: "In Italy, you can find entrepreneurs who stimulate designers from all over the world to work for them." Designers also value the climate of mutual esteem and exchange of experience, which foster experimentation, and an open door even to top management. Michael Graves says, "As a designer, you and your people are brought in and treated as a member of a family—it's a very personal relationship between designer and manufacturer. It is what ties everything together."

Philippe Starck attests, "When a project is presented to Claudio Luti of Kartell, to Enrico Astori of Driade, to Piero Gandini of Flos, to Umberto Cassina of Cassina . . . they love the project, they love it with a passion. When a prototype is taken to Alberto Alessi, he thinks it is

Christmas. It is a splendid gift. I have never heard an Italian manufacturer say, 'This will make a lot of money.' I have always heard, 'People will really like this.' And that is how it should be." The attitude of paying back designers with a currency composed of capability and flexibility is typical of design-intensive companies worldwide. Says David Lewis, a major designer for Bang & Olufsen, "All the people here are enormously interested in technology and mechanics. They will go a very long way to resolve any issue that looks promising or interesting. Which is great for us designers. It's really in their culture, just give them a challenge and they go way out for it."[35]

The manufacturers themselves underscore the importance of empowering the creativity and expression of their key external interpreters. Giulio Castelli, chairman of Kartell, recalls how his firm's technological capabilities and explorative attitude sustained cooperation with talented interpreters. "I knew that he was in Milan," said Castelli about his first cooperative effort with Philippe Starck, "and I invited him to Kartell because I had an idea of getting him to do a desk set." Castelli continues, "He did not seem to go for the idea, and, of course, he immediately sold me a product he had designed several years before, which no French businessman had had the courage to manufacture. It was the Dr. Glob chair: instead of being made of a single material, it combined a plastic seat with a steel backrest; instead of having rounded-off corners, they were sharp. Then it was also made in colors that were absolutely new, and the plastic was no longer glossy but had a matte finish. In brief, it went completely against any other chair on the market. He managed to do it in Italy and he was not able to do it anywhere else in the world."

Castelli talked about the La Marie chair, also designed by the French architect: "The research carried out by our engineering department was enormous and very difficult. Finding the material with the right technical characteristics and the right mould was a real undertaking. Just imagine, not even Bayer would have guaranteed the result." And here is how he describes his collaboration with Ron Arad, who designed the Bookworm bookshelf: "That was the first time the company worked with Ron Arad, the first of a long succession of such cooperative efforts. Today Arad sends us one project a week, and sometimes it is necessary to keep him happy. He is a nagger but soooo good."[36]

All major players in design-driven innovation share this open attitude toward exploration and experimentation as a stimulus to innovation and a technique for attracting talent. "When a designer makes his debut with Flos, we give him carte blanche so that he can express himself to the best of his ability," says Piero Gandini, chairman of the lighting company. And Claudio Molteni, chairman of the homonym furniture company, notes, "Sometimes I think, 'This is crazy.' But before cutting any further development, we think about it twice. We do not take anything for granted. Otherwise we would keep on doing only things that have already been done. These masters force you to study things that still do not exist, to solve problems."

His approach mirrors that of Herman Miller, according to CEO Brian Walker: "The central thing we've learned is a willingness to follow and give ourselves over to these designers—not to lose ourselves, but to be open to following them to places we may question in the beginning. We give our creative network an outline of a perceived problem, and let them share their insights as to whether we're on the right path, and then enable them to bring their own gifts to the search for a solution. We follow them in their journey without judging too quickly . . . The genius of our R&D folks . . . is their ability to know how to put the right constraints in place to push the creative network to a different place."[37]

We need not be dazzled, as shallow observers might be, and confuse this attitude with the stereotypical designer-driven process epitomized at the beginning of this chapter. These senior executives are not handing over leadership of their firm to design gurus. Rather, once they have identified a key interpreter (an essential premise), they want to leverage his interpretative capabilities as best they can. To attract him before their competitors do, to develop a privileged relationship, to allow him to express his abilities, they know they must be open and free of unnecessary limitations, and they must provide the interpreter with ground for experimentation. These managers are not mere executors of a designer's caprices, nor are truly talented designers attracted by executors who do not provide them with challenges and knowledge.

Design-driven companies pursue radical innovations in meanings because they master technologies. Their innovation processes are flexible. They are not afraid of small production lots, so they encourage interpreters to take chances as the companies fashion their prototypes. And the designers can be confident that top management will carefully assess whatever results. When Antonio Citterio designed his first lamp (named Lastra) for Flos, the manufacturer created thirty-two prototypes to identify the right nuance for the white light diffusers. This relationship is significantly different from the typical one between a design firm and a manufacturer in a user-centered project, where the manufacturer outsources a significant portion of the innovative task to the design firm, including finding technical solutions and manufacturing technologies. Here, instead, companies ask external interpreters to bring in the results of their explorations on the meaning of things, and technology remains an asset in the hands of the manufacturers.

According to Federico Busnelli, codirector of the Center for Research and Development for furniture manufacturer B&B Italia, "The designer who wants to propose a project doesn't have to bring drawings, because what can be drawn has already been done. He has to present new ideas, new proposals, even if he doesn't know how to implement them. It is our Center for Research and Development that gives life to the project." Flemming Møller Pedersen, director for design and concepts at Bang & Olufsen, similarly emphasizes, "We don't want [designers] to be [unduly] influenced by other parts of the organization, [which have] to worry about optimizing the daily business. [Designers] don't need to understand our industrial limitations, manufacturability, or what sound can come out of which form. Designers have to be free to look in an unconditioned way at what's happening in our society, how people live and furnish their homes, and then come up with proposals that could be good for B&O. It's up to our engineers to make it work."[38] According to Flemming, "At B&O, we do not do design for manufacturing, but rather we manufacture for design."

The best way to attract key interpreters and empower their expressions and visions is to pay them back not merely in cash but with assets: technological capabilities, experimentation ground, seductive power (the capability to deliver a new message to the market because of your brand and distribution channels), and your own knowledge of meanings. In other words, if you want to be more attractive to interpreters, you need to be an interpreter yourself. That is why I talk about participating in the design discourse, and not simply exploiting it. You need to have a vision—something to say to the design discourse—and bring assets to the table.

Design Circles

The importance of being an active contributor to the design discourse becomes even more manifest if we consider how breakthrough interpretations emerge. One of the most interesting dynamics of the design discourse is that radical innovations are often developed by collaborative circles: interpreters who share a common vision and revolve around a common center (perhaps a school, a cultural institution, a major scholar). Most breakthroughs in the history of design are associated with more or less institutionalized circles: the Wiener Werkstätte in Vienna and the Bauhaus in Germany in the early twentieth century; the School of Ulm, again in Germany, in the 1960s; and Alchimia and Memphis in Milan in the early 1980s, to name a few.

Circles of radical interpreters can emerge in any industry and life context. Slow Food—the cultural association that promotes change in food and nutrition paradigms and now one of the most innovative cultural players in the world of food and beyond—was born as a circle of a few pioneers led by founder Carlo Petrini.

A study by Michael Farrell explains why radical innovations often occur within collaborative circles.[39] By analyzing major shifts in literature, painting, and science, he shows how breakthrough thinking benefits from the interaction, mutual trust, and sense of mission typical of circles. They provide an encouraging, familiar, segregated environment where pioneering minds can explore new avenues. Within this environment, members are more likely to survive skepticism and criticism by the dominant culture. They realize they are not alone, and they sustain each other in early experiments through the frustration of failure. Circles provide trusted colleagues with whom to share progress in explorations and the effort of communicating a new vision. However, unlike the creative circles that Farrell investigated, composed mainly of peers (such as the impressionist painters), circles in the design discourse embrace interpreters in different categories, including managers.

For example, the design discourse in Milan developed in the 1950s around small circles of entrepreneurs (such as Cesare Cassina, Giulio

Castelli of Kartell, and Ezio Longhi of Elam), architects (such as Gio Ponti, Marco Zanuso, and Gaetano Pesce), innovative retailers (such as Osvaldo Borsani of Tecno, Maddalena De Padova, Dino Gavina), and technology suppliers (such as Carlo Barassi, an engineer at Pirelli). Some participants met regularly.

Alberto Alessi recalls participating as a rookie during his early years in Milan in debates of the "group of nine"—a small circle of entrepreneurs from several industries whose product lines revolved around the home. These entrepreneurs shared visions of the world of domestic lifestyles, promoted exhibitions, and founded avant-garde design journals such as *Modo* and *Ottagono*.

This collaborative attitude is alive today. In 2005 I conducted with Claudio Dell'Era an analysis of two thousand products (lamps, tables, chairs, and sofas) from the catalogs of Italian manufacturers.[40] We compared the product lines of the most innovative companies (those that had received at least one design award) with firms that were less innovative in terms of design. In particular, by using the Gini index, a common measure of heterogeneity, we analyzed to what extent products released by innovative companies use a variety of signs (materials, colors, shapes, surfaces, styles).

The heterogeneity of the cluster of innovative companies turned out to be significantly *lower* than that of the cluster of non-innovators. In other words, innovative companies use similar signs and a more homogeneous product language among themselves, whereas followers tend to move in various directions until they grasp the new dominant product meaning in the market and eventually imitate it. This indicates that innovators share insights through a small circle, bolstering their ability to both understand and influence the world of signs.

The emergence of a new circle may be a symptom of turmoil in the design discourse, and an early sign of possible change in dominant meanings. A company may gain significant advantage by identifying promising circles in their early stages and developing privileged relationships with their members. However, that exercise may present challenges.

New circles, in their initial stage, are by definition outside the dominant stream of discussion. They tend, initially, to perform tacit, intimate experiments until they reach internal consensus and develop confidence. And to protect the proprietary value of their experiments and information and to prevent untrustworthy outsiders from offering destructive criticism, they also develop a sense of membership. In a way, members consider themselves part of an elite.

Identifying emerging circles therefore implies immersing yourself in the design discourse to detect the most muted whispers, and investing to ensure that the circle will invite you in. That implies becoming a *member* of circles—an active participant in the design discourse. This further underscores the importance of being perceived as a key interpreter, as someone who brings value to the table: a vision and ground for experimentation.

Obsolescence

It is easy to make a list of the top 10 designers of the past 10 years. But I'm virtually certain that fewer than half of them will be among the top 10 designers of the next 10 years. By then their language won't be novel anymore, or will be widely imitated. Also, their interest and vitality may fade. Sometimes, too, they are spoiled by success. We need therefore to continuously search for new talents if we want to create radically new languages and stay ahead of competition.

—Alberto Alessi

Building a distinctive dialogue with the design discourse requires significant effort. It asks for immersion and direct involvement by a firm's senior executives. Most important, it is the result of *cumulative* investments. In the beginning, before you have developed a reputation as a key contributor, it is hard to gain membership in a circle and attract interpreters. But then, after you have started a dialogue—perhaps with the help of mediators—you progressively acquire a central position in the discourse. Insights and interpretations then flow smoothly and easily.

Alessi now receives hundreds of unsolicited designs every month. Should the firm rest on its laurels and reduce its investment in new network relationships? Alberto Alessi's answer leaves no doubt. The design discourse unfortunately suffers from obsolescence: the key interpreters of today are not those of tomorrow. At a given point, relying on the same interpreters—those who were the key drivers of past successes—may even become a barrier to further innovation.[41] You should therefore keep refreshing your network.

Interpreters become obsolete for several reasons. First, an endogenous dynamic occurs. As Farrell has shown, collaborative circles follow a parabolic life cycle, moving from an initial stage of formation and development, through a central stage of creative work and collective action, to a final stage of loss of creative drive and group disintegration.[42] Memphis, for example, lasted seven years.

From a strategic perspective, the value of interpreters may decline even before the final phase. Once an interpreter becomes well known as a talent, her attitude often moves from exploration to exploitation. She starts focusing on incremental reinterpretations of her breakthrough vision (a practice that is fine for incremental innovation but not for design-driven projects), others imitate her, or sometimes she ends up working for your competitors (as happened with Michael Graves when he became a major collaborator of Target).[43]

The second reason for the obsolescence of interpreters is exogenous: a change in the context (in culture or, more often, technology) may displace the network and spoil its ability to investigate future changes in meanings and languages. A major challenge for Bang & Olufsen, for example, is the emergence of digital audio and video technologies, as well as new media for entertainment. Artemide must face the diffusion of LED technology, which is transforming the value of lighting fixtures and providing novel options for creating ambient light.

The challenge for both firms is not only changes in technology but also the need to refresh their network of interpreters. Because technologies are changing how people live in their homes, they require new visions and interpretations. The past success of these firms even inflates the threat. The more central their position in the design discourse, the more they are tempted to avoid moves that destroy this asset and to make marginal investments to sustain their position. Bang & Olufsen launched a competition, with blind judging, to find new designers for flat TV screens. When the identity of the winner was disclosed, the company discovered he was David Lewis, the firm's own acclaimed designer.[44]

Italian furniture manufacturers, such as Alessi, B&B Italia, and Kartell, that have succeeded for several decades by surfing different waves of parabolic change in culture and technologies tend to maintain a large network of interpreters in a dual configuration. This structure includes a core of well-established designers who are prolific generators of the current product portfolio, along with a larger periphery of looser collaborations that explore connections with new worlds. Interpreters periodically move from the periphery to the core, only to be later displaced.[45]

Alessi launches a radical research project every five to ten years not only to develop design-driven innovations but also to identify new interpreters. In one such project, Tea and Coffee Piazza, launched in 1979 (which chapter 8 describes in detail), the company started with ten architects who had never designed products, eventually selecting two as promising new designers: Aldo Rossi and Michael Graves. Then, in the early 1990s, came projects such as Family Follows Fiction (see chapter 3) and Memory Containers. The firm launched Tea and Coffee Towers more recently (2001–2003), enlisting about twenty new architects, including three Japanese and one Chinese.

Alberto Alessi expects the advent of computer-assisted design to inspire new forms: "These architects know how to use the computer like a pencil. They are so good with the PC that the design comes directly from the heart, just as a traditional designer's pencil is directly linked to the heart. This permits the creation of a wealth of shapes never seen before in products." Seven of these architects are now developing products, which many consumers await with the anticipation they might feel about the next movie from their favorite director.

8

INTERPRETING

[Developing Your Own Vision]

Many people think that Kettle 9093 was the result of a sparkle of creativity. Perhaps, one morning, the image of a kettle with a whistling bird popped into Michael Graves's mind. No speculation could be further from reality. Kettle 9093 is instead the result of years of research led by Alessi. [IN THE ILLUSTRATION Alessi's Kettle 9093.]

D EVELOPING A PRIVILEGED RELATIONSHIP with interpreters in the design discourse is only the first action in
the process of design-driven innovation. This action is essential, because it allows companies to gain access to
knowledge and interpretations. But it is not sufficient.

This knowledge then must feed a process through which a company
creates its own vision and proposal: internal research and experiments
that allow the firm to eventually develop a radical new meaning and
language.

This chapter uses examples to show how this process of interpretation and creation may unfold: Alessi's Tea and Coffee Piazza, Artemide's
Light Fields, Barilla's Beyond Primo Piatto, and Arthur Bonnet's Design
Direction Workshops. You will see that there is no one best way to approach this process: it can take different forms. All the examples, however, share a common feature: the process of design-driven innovation is
a research project—that is, it is exploratory, it aims at creating an entire
breakthrough product family or new business, and it occurs before product development (see figure 8-1). It is not the fast creative and brainstorming sessions that are typical of concept generation but rather a
deep investigation that, like technological research, escapes attempts to
imprison innovation in simple, sequential ten-step rules.

Alessi's Tea and Coffee Piazza

By now everyone has seen architect Michael Graves's whimsical cone-
shaped kettle with the little plastic bird affixed to its spout. Since introducing the kettle in 1985, Alessi has sold more than 1.5 million units
of what is, as kettles go, an expensive item. Kettle 9093 is one of the
first examples of postmodern design. Earlier kettles came in various
shapes and sizes, but their purpose was, almost without exception,

FIGURE 8-1

The process of design-driven innovation as research and its position relative to other phases of innovation

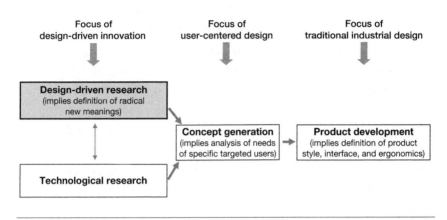

utilitarian. Thus their form followed their function (to boil water), the first precept of modern design.

Although undeniably clever in its synthesis of pop art and art deco references, model 9093 showed its greatest originality in broadening people's expectations of what a kettle was and did—and, indeed, the nature of the breakfast experience. Far from being an annoyance or merely a signal, the birdlike whistle emitted by the kettle draws its owners to the breakfast table as powerfully as the aroma of coffee. The little plastic bird visually confirms that beckoning sound, and the delightfulness of its shape is its own reward. In an interview on Business-Week.com, Graves said he once received a postcard from a French poet who wrote, "I'm always very grumpy when I get up in the morning. But when I get up now, I put the tea kettle on, and when it starts to sing it makes me smile—goddamn you!"[1]

As a scholar of management of innovation, I love this project because it defies common wisdom and trivial stereotypes of design. Many people think that Kettle 9093 was the result of a spark of creativity. Perhaps, one morning, Michael Graves was taking a shower and suddenly the image of a kettle with a whistling bird popped into his mind. No speculation could be further from reality. Kettle 9093 is instead the result of years of research, which formally began in 1979 with a project called Tea and Coffee Piazza, whose roots date back to the early 1970s.[2] The main driver behind this project was not even the designer but Alberto Alessi, CEO of his company, who had conceived of the research as a process of design-driven innovation: "We needed to do something completely new, to be radically innovative . . . and to do so, we needed to find new talents, who had never practiced in this field before, who could create new languages."

At that point Graves had never worked on a consumer product but had designed a few notoriously postmodern buildings in the United States (their surfaces were both decorative and referred to earlier architectural idioms—modernist taboos). It was Alessi who first contacted him and spotted his talent in industrial design. "We were very timely," says Alessi. "When we visited him in the U.S., he told us that we came at the right moment, as he was willing to work in the future on product design for 50 percent of his time."

Now Graves is a well-known designer. But U.S. manufacturers dismissed his talent until Alessi discovered him. The success of model 9093 attracted the attention of Target, a retailer known for offering sophisticated designs at popular prices, which in 1999 invited Graves to design a new line of products, including a knockoff of the bird kettle. It is a testament to the mystique of the original that Alessi continues to sell large numbers of model 9093—for five times the price of Target's version. As a researcher, I find this situation intriguing and unusual. Because the same person designed both original and knockoff, the critical variable in the success of model 9093 would appear to be the company itself. How did Alessi structure its research process?

At roughly the time Michael Graves was only a twinkle in Alberto Alessi's eye, Ettore Sottsass started the Memphis collective (described in chapter 7). Alessi was immersed in the design discourse in Milan. He met with other entrepreneurs at the Triennale (the local cultural center for architecture and design) a few times a year, had helped found the avant-garde design journal *Modo*, had already pursued a project with local architects. And he already had close contacts with Sottsass, who had designed popular products for the company in the late 1970s.

Drawing on those discussions, Alessi recognized that his firm's kitchenware needed a sharply new design language, and he believed that mostly foreign architects who had never designed consumer goods were the ones to invent its vocabulary and grammar. He called the project Tea and Coffee Piazza and asked a Milanese architect and close friend, Alessandro Mendini, to select ten other architects and coordinate their activities. Mendini's choices included Austrian Hans Hollein and American Robert Venturi—now also famous postmodernists—as well as Graves.

Alessi asked the eleven architects to design a tea and coffee service by bringing the language of postmodern architecture to the dimension of industrial products (hence the name Tea and Coffee Piazza). Alessi typically led product development projects on the basis of four requirements: cost, functionality, communication, and sensation (discussed in more detail later in this chapter). But this was not a development project aimed at designing a new product. The architects were to consider it a *research* project aimed at exploring new possible meanings. Alessi told them to concentrate exclusively on the communication and sensation requirements (which in our framework relate to the product symbolic and emotional meaning). Issues of cost and functionality would be pondered only later, during development.

Once they had received general direction from Alessi, the eleven worked independently for three years. There was no brainstorming; there were no multidisciplinary teams. It was individual research and exploration.[3] Among the architects, Graves was one of only two whom Alessi invited to move into concept generation and product development. The CEO asked him to design a commercial kettle that would maintain the prototype's meaning and language but that also would comply with requirements of cost and functionality.

Model 9093 had a broad base, which facilitated rapid heating; visible rivets, which recalled a kind of vintage artisanship; a superimposed plastic handle in cool blue, which was decorative as well as heat resistant; and a little bird, which flew in the face of modernism's insistence on abstract form. Indeed, because of the company's success with a previous kettle (model 9091, designed by Richard Sapper), which emits two low, harmonizing whistles evoking ships passing in the night, a whistle was one specification that Alessi imposed on Graves.

Alessi knew that before the company could present groundbreaking products to the public, the ground itself had to be prepared, or else the public, which had not been consulted about what kinds of products it wanted, would not know how to make sense of them. Therefore, while Graves was working on the commercial kettle, Alessi addressed the design discourse by showing its participants the results of his Tea and Coffee Piazza research project. The idea was to leverage the seductive power of the interpreters to start diffusing the new language and emotion of postmodern design applied to kitchenware.

In so doing, Alessi took the following steps. First, he convinced cultural centers, such as the San Francisco Museum of Modern Art and the Smithsonian, to exhibit the eleven coffee and tea service prototypes the architects had created. He also produced these prototypes in limited editions of ninety-nine, selling them to museums and influential collectors for $25,000 each. Alessi then created a book about the prototypes and distributed it to the extended design community. High-end department stores around the world showed a traveling exhibit of the prototypes, and Alessi invited the press in Italy and abroad to write about the exhibits and the project. He closely followed the reactions of design aficionados. By continuing to talk and write about the product's role and meaning, the members of the design discourse disseminated knowledge of it to a wider audience. In the end they acted as amplifiers of a message they had helped to construct (see figure 8-2).

FIGURE 8-2

Alessi's Tea and Coffee Piazza research project and the development of Kettle 9093

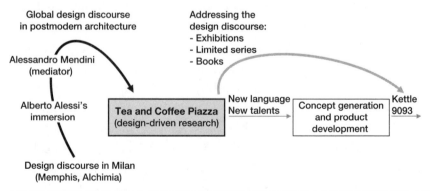

Artemide's Light Fields

Light Fields is the research process that Artemide conducted to develop the Metamorfosi product family—lighting systems (introduced in chapter 2) that create personalized colorful atmospheres. Artemide launched the project with the specific purpose of identifying a radical change in meanings that encroaching global competitors would never think of first: that people would buy a lamp not because of its beauty or its technical features but because of the light it emits and the emotions it generates.

Metamorfosi is the result of an articulated research effort in both meanings and technologies (see figure 8-3). In 1995 Ernesto Gismondi, company chairman, and Carlotta De Bevilaqua, managing director for brand strategy and development, assembled a group of close friends to launch a project to investigate the biological, psychological, and cultural dimensions of light. The team, coordinated by a professor of social psychology with a background in medicine (Paolo Inghilleri), included two design theorists and professors (Andrea Branzi and Ezio Manzini, the former with a background in architecture and the latter both an engineer and architect), three designer-architects (Michele De Lucchi, Pierluigi Nicolin, and Denis Santachiara), and a marketing expert. Participants used team meetings to share insights and visions.

FIGURE 8-3

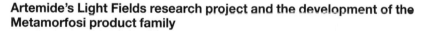

Artemide's Light Fields research project and the development of the Metamorfosi product family

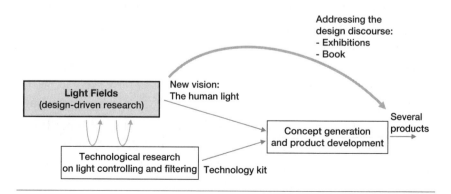

The firm was simultaneously interacting with other external inter-preters, such as a joint workshop with Philips Design at the Politecnico di Milano. When after six months the team identified the concept of a human light—that is, a light that makes people feel better—the inno-vation process shifted to technological research. Artemide's in-house R&D department perfected the technology for allowing the cus-tomized creation of colored ambient light.

The resulting patented system took the form of a technology kit (eventually also sold as a stand-alone product). The technology kit and the new vision of a human light then became the input for a more tradi-tional product development phase, during which individual designers focused on giving form to the product. These designers included some from the Light Fields research project (such as Ernesto Gismondi and Carlotta de Bevilacqua) and others newly involved (such as Aldo Rossi, Richard Sapper, and Hannes Wettstein). As Alessi had done with model 9093, Artemide arranged exhibitions and publications to accompany Metamorfosi's introduction. In particular, *Light Fields*—a small book that the company distributed to the design community, with chapters written by team members—summarized the findings of the initial ex-ploratory project.

Barilla's Beyond Primo Piatto

The processes used by Alessi and Artemide differ in their organiza-tion and dynamics. Whereas the latter focused mainly on developing a design-driven innovation, the former also aimed to identify new talent for the next decade. Both, however, shared a common trait. The initial driver for these explorations was mainly *sociocultural:* the advent of post-modernism for Alessi, the growing attention to well-being for Artemide. In other instances, new technologies can conversely give impetus to the search for new meanings—that is, for a technology epiphany.

That is what happened with Barilla, the leading pasta manufacturer. In this case, the design-driven process was activated by the firm's R&D director of the Pasta Meal Solution business, who had a background in chemical engineering. His team had developed new processing and con-servation technologies that allowed the company to produce genuine food while also addressing a major trend in the industry: convenience. Observations showed that people had less time to buy and cook food. However, rather than merely apply these technologies within this evolutionary industrywide road map, the director of R&D wanted to discern whether Barilla could also open up new, more-powerful meanings.

To search for a technology epiphany, the firm activated a design-driven research project aimed at investigating people's unmet aspirations for preparing and eating food in their homes. The project—which explored new meal experiences beyond Barilla's traditional core business, and hence the name Beyond Primo Piatto—consisted of three phases over five months designed to progressively focus the concept for a new product family (see figure 8-4).

The first phase was a workshop where some fifteen Barilla managers (from R&D to marketing, from food services to packaging) shared their insights on new scenarios for preparing and eating food. Barilla's employees are constantly immersed in the design discourse.[4] The company assumed that it needed a process to collect, share, and focus these insights. This workshop aimed to capitalize on internal knowledge that would otherwise have been lost. It helped participants envision various scenarios, some of which confirmed the more incremental vision of food convenience while others shed light on radically new contexts in which people would linger in a more exciting social experience of food preparation and consumption.

FIGURE 8-4

Barilla's Beyond Primo Piatto, a design-driven research project

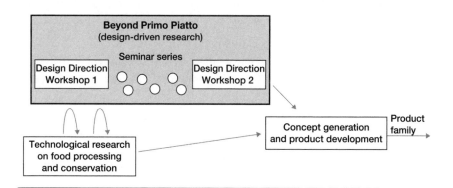

After conducting this workshop, the company moved into checking the results with external interpreters (as noted in chapter 7): a cook, a journalist from *Stern*, managers from firms in other industries that look at how people experience life in kitchens, a design firm. The company met with these interpreters individually to share visions and experiments; at the end of each meeting, Barilla's internal chefs prepared prototypical meals that gave form to the project's emerging insights. Finally, a second workshop—like the first, limited only to internal interpreters—focused on conceiving the product strategy.

The Design Direction Workshops

Barilla's process was much more structured than the one used by Alessi and Artemide. Those firms rely on less-formal approaches, given that they concentrate their interactions with the design discourse in a few hands—namely, those of their top entrepreneurs. Larger firms like Barilla have even greater potential for interacting with interpreters, because their external interfaces are richer and more articulated. However, to fully leverage this potential, companies need a proper process through which they can channel and share knowledge from the design discourse and turn it into novel visions. Barilla's experience shows how a firm can create a structured process: a sequence of workshops, interactions with interpreters, and experiments that progressively lead toward a design-driven innovation.

The workshops have a specific format (which we call Design Direction Workshop) and play a central role in this process. My colleagues and I have observed and participated in several Design Direction Workshops that were aimed at sharing knowledge from the design discourse and identifying new meaning and languages. Our observations and experimentations revealed that these workshops typically share several characteristics, which the next few sections briefly illustrate (see figure 8-5).[5]

Envision

The first activity in a Design Direction Workshop involves producing insights. If a company has identified key interpreters who are immersed

FIGURE 8-5

The Design Direction Workshop

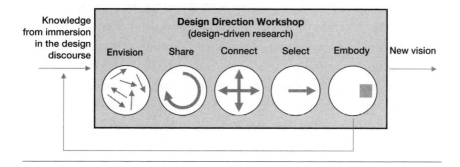

in the design discourse (see chapter 7), then these interpreters have been conducting their own research, explicitly or implicitly, for months or years, and have developed their own interpretations. The convener of the workshop asks the participants to envision the implications of their own research and explorations triggered by the specific project. Participants use this generative and experimental activity to apply knowledge from the design discourse to the problem at hand, giving form to their insights through various media: metaphors, analogies, stories, prototypes. For example, by developing their prototypes, the eleven architects of Alessi's Tea and Coffee Piazza envisioned the implications for kitchenware products of their previous architectural research.

This activity can last for a few weeks or even months: it does not involve fast generation of several creative ideas. It is, rather, real research. The possibility that each participant will envision new scenarios is based not on his creativity but on the extent to which he has previously tapped in to the design discourse and developed his own path of exploration. If there is no knowledge base, there is no envisioning.

Share

The second activity is to share the insights—typically in team sessions. The aim is to bring together, compare, and discuss the results of the previous activity and enrich them through modification or further identification of new interpretations.

Connect

The third activity entails building possible design scenarios by finding connections between the proposals envisioned by the participants. An effective approach is to identify several dimensions, with aspects of each clustered into opposing polarities. Figure 8-6 shows an example of two dimensions from a workshop conducted by Arthur Bonnet, a French manufacturer of kitchen furniture. One dimension concerns the centrality of the kitchen in the home, organized into two extreme polarities: a "front office," where kitchen functions are visible and accessible; and a "back office," where the kitchen is separate and kept as a specialized hidden function. The other dimension concerns whether households are willing to reinterpret traditional living habits and experiment with new lifestyles.

FIGURE 8-6

Scenarios identified during a Design Direction Workshop convened by kitchen manufacturer Arthur Bonnet

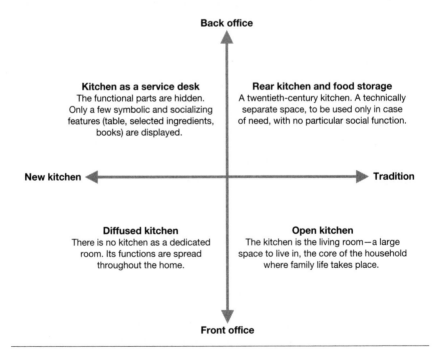

A firm may identify several dimensions through which to organize participants' insights—the two most promising of which, once polarized, offer four scenarios of meanings and languages. Some of these scenarios may be closer to the current dominant meaning, and others, such as the diffused kitchen in the Arthur Bonnet example, may envision radical change.

Select

"My colleagues kept on asking me how I select the projects in which to invest," Alberto Alessi once told me. "So I wrote down on paper the criteria I used. It is a kind of scoring system. We call it our 'formula for success.'" He looked at me with an amicable smile, as if to say, "Would you believe I use a scoring system?"

This model describes the product dimensions Alessi is considering and clarifies which factors he uses to gauge them when investing in radical innovation of meanings (see figure 8-7). The first two dimensions are those any innovation project weighs: on the one hand, functionality—the product's utilitarian value—and, on the other hand, its cost and therefore its price. The other two dimensions—communication/language and sensation/memory/imagery—are the most interesting and the most peculiar to design-driven innovation. (They also reflect the framework for product and user needs introduced in figure 2-1.)

Communication/language refers to the product's symbolic meaning and to the social motivation that can lead people to buy it. Does the product help the user interact with others? Which need of self-representation does it satisfy? What status and style does it suggest? How does it communicate a person's culture and beliefs?

Sensation/memory/imagery refers to the product's emotional and poetic meaning and to the intimate motivations that can lead people to buy it. Does it grip the user's memory or imagination? Does it stimulate affection? Does it please the senses?

Alessi usually screens out products that rank in the middle of the scale in figure 8-7 (those deemed standard, neutral, and acceptable). However, the company may decide to market products that are weak on one dimension (whose function is questionable, for example, or

FIGURE 8-7

Alessi's "formula for success"

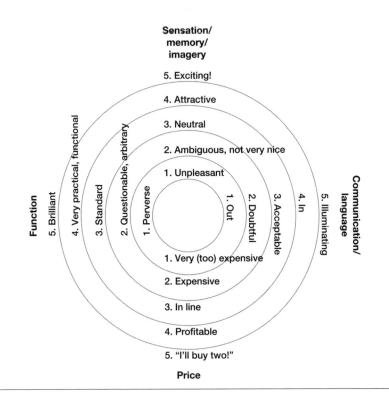

whose price is high) if they are strong on other features (they are particularly illuminating or exciting). Interestingly, Kettle 9093 earned the highest rating in Alessi's history.

Another important criterion that firms can use to select ideas to pursue—used intensively, for example, by Bang & Olufsen—is a product's potential for a long life cycle. Does it fall outside current short-term trends? Does it have a distinctive language and a personality that can survive aging? Does it satisfy deeper needs and earn people's loyalty? Is it clearly linked with the company's brand identity so that imitators can appropriate only little value through imitation? Does it help start a learning process for the firm and an interaction with the design discourse that could last for a while? In other words, to what extent does the product help build a firm's long-term assets (those noted in chapter 5)?

Embody

The last activity of a Design Direction Workshop typically entails giving form to a new meaning and language. The purpose is to facilitate its communication: on the one hand, to the company's board or to the team that will pursue concept generation and development, and, on the other hand, to the design discourse, to leverage its seductive power. The books and exhibitions that Alessi and Artemide promoted are examples of such efforts. (Chapter 9 illustrates in more detail strategies for embodying a firm's interpretation and addressing the design discourse.)

Holding to the Path During Product Development

Once design-driven research has led to a new vision and meaning, the innovation process moves into the more-traditional phases of concept generation and product development. With this transition, the focus expands to include a product's specific utilitarian features. In Alessi's Tea and Coffee Piazza, for example, entering product development meant considering price and functionality in addition to the concept's emotional and symbolic dimensions. In Artemide's Metamorfosi, this phase entailed giving form to the vision and technologies of a human light, which meant applying traditional industrial design skills to express the right product style.

In other words, the approach to innovation shifts from design driven (and technology push) to user centered as the firm translates its radical vision into products bereft of functional shortcomings. Bang & Olufsen describes this as a shift in the product requirements targeted during each phase of the process (see figure 8-8). First, design-driven research is aimed at defining a product's identity: its differentiating requirements and customer delighters that are the profound reasons people will buy it. Next, concept generation focuses on features that customers expect, that can be observed and understood through user analysis, and that, if properly designed, can provide incremental value (such as an effective user interface on a TV's menu). Finally, product development focuses on the product's mandatory elements: those that people take for granted and that the product cannot lack (such as a TV remote control).[6]

FIGURE 8-8

How Bang & Olufsen shifts its focus during the innovation process

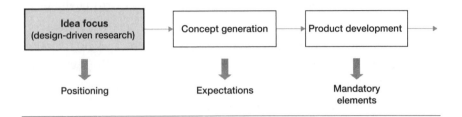

Scholars have deeply investigated the practices that are most effective in managing concept generation and product development.[7] Their findings—for example, that multidisciplinary teams, heavyweight project management, and top management support are critical—also apply to design-driven innovation. However, firms engaged in radical innovation of meanings must carefully consider another central concern: they need to avoid being diverted by constraints emerging downstream in development that can jeopardize the identity of the vision. Once they have identified the proper new radical meaning and language, they should not compromise its integral nature and personality. Unfortunately, acknowledged best practices in product development sometimes push in the opposite direction.

Design-intensive companies are masters of remaining faithful to the vision devised during research. This practice reflects their capability and flexibility in product and process technologies—and their organization. In particular, they introduce interfaces between the interpreters who participate in the initial research and the engineers and marketers involved during implementation. At Bang & Olufsen, for example, Flemming Møller Pedersen, director of design and concepts, plays this role; at Ferrari, Stefano Carmassi; at Snaidero, Paolo Benedetti; at Alessi, Danilo Alliata. These interfacing managers have been carefully bred and are trusted by both communities: designers trust them because these managers go to great lengths to implement a new vision and do not yield to constraints unless there is no reasonable way to escape infeasibility. Engineers trust them because these managers have the skills to carefully consider technological problems and provide pointers and support.

Firms should also be thoughtful when analyzing feedback from market testing and focus groups. As noted, users seldom seize on the implications of radical innovations of meanings, even though they could fall in love with them later. Firms therefore should not rely on market tests to decide whether to launch a product: they can better gauge that by interacting with the design discourse. Market tests should be aimed instead at identifying possible improvements in the product's features or at understanding how to make the new product language more comprehensible, such as by adding a few familiar signs to give users "conceptual handrails."[8]

Product development should also preserve the uniqueness of the product in every detail. For example, engineering features can provide a psycho-cognitive performance that is not easily imitated, such as a superior texture and touch or sound. The surface of the Bookworm bookshelf (explored in chapter 2) is not perfectly smooth but has little bubbles. This solution, which requires a complex extruding process that is not easily imitated, provides softness in both sight and touch.

Companies can also introduce features that provide an aura of emotional magic, wit, and charm. Examples include the whistling bird on Alessi's Kettle 9093, the "dream" function in Artemide's Metamorfosi (which allows the light to automatically fade and slowly switch off at a scheduled time at night, gently driving a person into her dreams), the whir of the tiny electric motor that gracefully unfolds the Bang & Olufsen's Serene mobile phone, the image on the screen of the Apple iPhone that automatically shifts from landscape to portrait as a person rotates the device.

For a company to hold to the path initially envisioned, the key is leadership. "This process is not democratic," says Lowie Vermeersch, a chief designer at Pininfarina, well-known automotive design and engineering firm. "To design distinctive products with a clear personality, you need a leader to protect that personality."

9
ADDRESSING

[Leveraging the Seductive Power of the Interpreters]

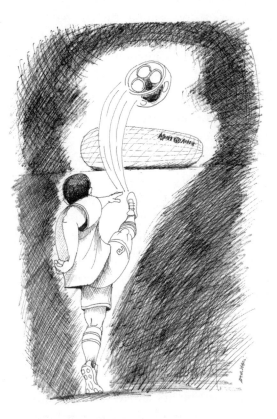

Interpreters have a double nature: they not only conduct research on how people give meaning to things; they also have seductive power, as they influence the context of people's lives. [IN THE ILLUSTRATION An Artemide Metamorfosi lamp kicked into the glowing Allianz Arena stadium in Munich, Germany.]

F REUD AND WITTGENSTEIN" READ the title of chapter 8. I was browsing through the table of contents of the book *Light Fields*, which Carlotta De Bevilacqua of Artemide had just handed to me. It had been written by the Metamorfosi team.

We are all accustomed to buying a product and also receiving a small slick booklet with brief stories about the company brand and riveting images evoking the emotional value of the product. But this book was different. It was not sleek like a marketing brochure, not short (it was fifty-eight dense pages), and not an easy read that you would flip through while awaiting your turn at the hairdresser. It was definitely not meant for typical customers of a lamp. And indeed, it was not delivered to customers. Rather, it had the language, the structure, the content (and the appeal) of a research book. It was meant for researchers.

This chapter discusses the third action in the design-driven innovation process. After you have defined a new vision for a product family, you must effectively propose that vision and product to the market. We know what the challenges are. People may be confused by a radical new proposal, even though they may eventually convert and became passionate about it. Design-driven innovation implies a change in sociocultural paradigms: if it is successful, the market—and consumption culture—will not be the same.

Thus, rather than simply launch the product and wait for customers to embrace the proposal, a firm needs to support this paradigm change through proactive investments aimed at facilitating the understanding, assimilation, and adoption of the new meaning. Design-driven manufacturers—large corporations as well as small firms such as Artemide and Alessi—pursue this process. The latter cases are particularly puzzling. How do small firms, with limited communication budgets, manage to diffuse their radical innovations? How do they end up with so much influence on how people around the world give meaning to products—in their own industries and often beyond?

These are not marginal questions for large corporations either, especially when they want to maximize the effectiveness of their communication strategy when budgets are slim.

Talking to the Interpreters

When it comes to radical innovation of meanings, advertising is not the ideal medium. Traditional communication tools provide little room for explanation, because they are meant to be consumed rapidly: they may include a photo in a magazine or on a Web site, a slogan on a billboard, or fifteen seconds in a commercial. These tools are effective in conveying straightforward messages that are close to what people expect to hear. Apart from rhetorical devices that sometimes may provoke surprise and curiosity, they are based on a few utilitarian or emotional messages that fit current patterns of consumption. They may be effective in diffusing incremental, market-pull innovations.

To support radical innovation of meanings, design-driven companies need to adopt a different strategy, again by leveraging the interpreters in the design discourse (see figure 9-1). Indeed, as chapter 6 notes,

FIGURE 9-1

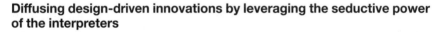

Diffusing design-driven innovations by leveraging the seductive power of the interpreters

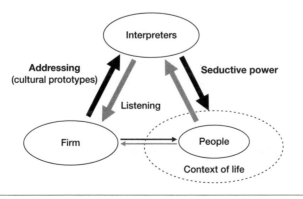

interpreters have a double nature: not only do they conduct research on how people give meaning to things, but also they *influence* the context of people's lives. Thus they eventually shape the sociocultural and technological scenario: artists with their artworks, cultural organizations with their dissemination activities, companies with their new products and services, suppliers with their technologies, pioneering projects with their landmark experiments, schools with their programs, designers with the designs they propose to several clients, early adopters who play with innovative proposals, and, of course, the media that look at all this. In other words, these interpreters have *seductive power*, because they influence how people will give meanings to things.[1]

If we want our new vision to become part of that scenario, then it must enter the collective process that shapes it. We need to diffuse our new vision into the design discourse and become part of the interpretations that its participants will eventually propose to people. The books and exhibitions promoted by Alessi, through its Tea and Coffee Piazza project, and Artemide, through its Light Fields project—both described in chapter 8—served this purpose. Artemide distributed the book *Light Fields*—with its chapters on the biological, philosophical, anthropological, and psychological basis of light—to designers, researchers, architects, schools, other firms, and the media. As noted, it was a research book addressed to researchers: no customer has ever seen it. However, customers have seen articles talking about the importance of the color of light in our lives, have appreciated proposals by firms such as Philips—which, leveraging the intuition of Artemide, has designed the Ambilight LCD TV screen to generate ambient colored light from the back of the panel—and have admired landmark projects by architects who increasingly use colored light to create emotions.

From Light Fields to Soccer Fields

On June 9, 2006, millions of people around the world were seated in front of their TVs, craning to watch the opening ceremony of soccer's World Cup in Germany. The broadcast began with an aerial panorama of the Allianz Arena in Munich, where the ceremony was being held. People were stunned: in the German night, the stadium appeared surreal. Its façade was lit from within by colored lights that made the entire arena glow. The stadium's operators achieved this atmosphere by illuminating the 2,874 polymeric air cushions of the arena's outer skin with 4,200 sources of blue, red, and white light.

This memorable image contributed significantly to people's changing approach to illuminating public spaces and their homes. The image was also one of the best testimonials to the emotional value of colored light that Artemide could have thought of. The company had no specific role in the event, but it did have noteworthy indirect connections to it through the design discourse. Jacques Hertzog and Pierre de Meuron had designed the Allianz Arena in 2002, right after the two Swiss architects had cooperated with Artemide on designing a new lamp (see chapter 6). They had shared insights with Artemide and had known about its new vision for Metamorfosi, described in *Light Fields*. It is hard to discern to what extent this collaboration eventually influenced the stadium design, because interpreters develop their innovations from multiple insights. But the cooperation with Artemide had left a mark. And through the opening ceremony of the World Cup, the architects diffused that mark into people's lives.

Note that interpreters are not paid to exert their seductive power. Artemide did not reward Hertzog and de Meuron for covering the Allianz Arena with colored light. We are not talking about testimonials here. We are talking about the natural inner dynamics of the design discourse, wherein interpreters themselves need access to insights that they can embed in their projects. Interpreters, especially the most advanced, create novel proposals for their own sake. We need to ensure that they are exposed to our vision and assimilate it during their research.

The process of collective interpretation through which our vision will eventually reach the market is seldom predictable and controllable. It may be reinterpreted, and its meaning—embedded in the work of others—adapted and modified. We cannot plan up front the quantity and intensity of people's contacts with the vision. Artemide could not predict whether and how Hertzog and de Meuron, as well as Philips, would embrace the company's vision and amplify it in the market. However, a firm can enhance its ability to leverage the seductive power of the interpreters, despite a limited investment, by following a few guidelines, discussed next.

Talking Through Cultural Prototypes

To address the design discourse, design-driven companies rely on *cultural prototypes*. These can include books, exhibitions, cultural events, concept products shown at fairs, journal articles, presentations at conferences, the firm's showrooms, a Web site, special products for landmark pioneering projects, and design competitions.

A cultural prototype is a medium that embeds the results of a manufacturer's research. It codifies and diffuses the company's new interpretation and vision. It is *cultural*, because rather than being a specific product (which the company may not yet have conceived), it is an articulation of a new meaning or language.

Artemide's *Light Fields* book did not show any lamp (the firm had not yet designed any Metamorfosi lamp). Instead, the book illustrated the findings of the design-driven research process and the firm's new vision: that light and colors have a significant relationship to people's biological, cultural, and psychological balance. The book is a prototype because it is not the final output of the innovation process but rather an interim interpretation to be shared and discussed by the design discourse. Alessi's Tea and Coffee Piazza exhibitions did not show Kettle 9093 (that was still to come) but rather the experimental prototypes created by the eleven architects, who focused only on emotional and symbolic dimensions.

Philips has a composite strategy for addressing the design discourse that entails multiple cultural prototypes. In 1995 the Dutch company conducted a research project called Vision of the Future to explore new scenarios suggested by sociocultural changes as well as technological developments. The company reported the results of the project in a well-known homonymous video that featured fragments of a day in the life of people interacting with the firm's prototypes. Philips also set up a Web site illustrating the project's outcomes, a permanent exhibition in Eindhoven, a traveling exhibition (shown in New York, Milan, Paris, Hamburg, Vienna, Tel Aviv, and Hong Kong), and a book.

Philips perpetuated and enriched this strategy during ensuing research projects. Between 1995 and 2005 Philips Design—the corporate unit that coordinates design-driven research—published eight books. The company's Web site is becoming ever more sophisticated, allowing it to receive feedback on the firm's interpretations (the most recent of which is Design Probes, which envisions a scenario in which products are "sensitive" rather than "intelligent," including garments and fabrics that express the wearer's emotional status). The company also produces *New Value by Design*, a quarterly magazine posted on its Web site that reports on the firm's interpretative research.

Yet "this testing process goes beyond providing useful feedback on the suitability of our scenarios," says Stefano Marzano, CEO and chief creative director of Philips Design.

> It also plants in people's minds what Swedish neuroscientist David Ingvar has called "memories of the future." The work of Ingvar and American scientist William Calvin has shown that thinking about potential future developments opens your mind so that you are ready to see the signs relevant to those developments if and when they occur. The brain uses plans and ideas just like real memories and experiences to filter information and guide decisions. These memories of the future potentially lead to new aspirations and desires. Exhibitions also encourage other potential partners, both within the company and outside, to join us.[2]

The Features of Cultural Prototypes

When developing cultural prototypes to address the design discourse, a company should keep in mind a few tenets. First and most important, cultural prototypes are not brochures promoting a product. They are not meant for final users but for interpreters. Therefore, as noted, firms need to conceive them as research outputs. The design discourse views cultural prototypes as interesting and assimilates them if they offer novel visions, if they are conceptually deep and challenging, and if they leave room for further interpretation.

Because cultural prototypes should speak the language of research, and not of marketing and communication, the company brand should not be immoderately visible. It should appear instead through the symbolic language of authorship and copyright. The prototype should be seen as a book, a Web site, or an exhibition *authored* by the firm or its affiliates.

Analogously, a firm is not necessarily supposed to make a profit from cultural prototypes, unless doing so helps the diffusion and assimilation of the vision. For example, Alessi sold the prototypes conceived by the eleven architects in its Tea and Coffee Piazza in limited editions of ninety-nine pieces to collectors and museums for $25,000 each. This helped signal the innovative value of Alessi's interpretation to the design discourse.

Finally, one type of cultural prototype is usually not enough. The examples cited here show how firms target different types of cultural prototypes to different types of interpreters, and at different moments in the diffusion process. For example, early in that process key researchers and seducers should perceive cultural prototypes as elite pieces of information so that they appreciate the advantage of embracing them. Remember that research and interpretations occur through circles (see chapter 7). If you want to effectively address those circles, you should think of a specific type of prototype tailored to them and not available to everyone (such as the books of Artemide and Alessi).

You can use various types of cultural prototypes later to address larger numbers of interpreters. Design competitions, for example, may support broader diffusion during this stage. Rather than uncover new ideas, such events are a way to let more players know about the new vision, experiment with it, and embrace it. In the late 1960s, for example, DuPont, a U.S. chemical company, invented Corian, a polymeric solid-surface material used by prominent designers such as Ron Arad, Ross Lovergrove, Ettore Sottsass, and James Irvine. DuPont is still launching design competitions to promote the product's broader assimilation in the design discourse. For example, more than three thousand designers participated in The Skin of Corian competition in 2006.

Protecting Your Vision

Cultural prototypes have other important roles beyond enabling innovators to address the design discourse and therefore diffuse a new vision into the sociocultural context. For example, prototypes facilitate communication of the new vision to the product development team. Companies usually provide such teams with long lists of requirements. In contrast, cultural prototypes allow a team to assimilate an interpretation's intimate emotional and symbolic value, rather than spoil its integrity and identity in the face of implementation details and constraints.

Cultural prototypes are also central in allowing a firm to profit from a design-driven innovation. Indeed, a major concern in design is how to capture the value of innovation.[3] Innovators typically try to appropriate value and prevent imitation by erecting protective barriers around an innovation. However, visions that have emotional and symbolic value—once disclosed—are relatively easy to imitate. Legal instruments for protecting intellectual property, such as patents and copyrights, are only somewhat effective when it comes to product languages and signs.

A better option is to capture a significant portion of the profit despite (and even thanks to) imitations. How? By profiting from your reputation as an innovator. When people buy purely functional features, they pay less attention to distinguishing the original innovator from imitators: they look instead for the best utility-price ratio. But when people also seek emotional and symbolic value, possessing the authentic original product makes a formidable difference. In design-driven innovation, people do look for the innovator. Competitors can easily imitate a product's function and even its form, but they will never be able to imitate its real meaning, because that meaning is inextricably attached to the innovator's brand.

Cultural prototypes anticipate the moment when a firm declares ownership of an innovation. It can develop such prototypes even before releasing an end product to the market. Prototypes make authorship manifest so that the interpreters in the design discourse can help the innovator build and defend its reputation. From that moment on, other companies in the industry will seldom use a similar vision, unless they acquire a reputation as imitators—not only among customers but also among interpreters. And imitators are not considered attractive by elite circles.

Some companies may be less concerned about being perceived as imitators and therefore may try to copy a novel vision. However, research my colleagues and I have conducted shows that imitation requires a very complex strategy when it comes to radical innovation of meanings. In our analysis of the Italian furniture industry, we compared the product languages of innovators and imitators.[4] We found that innovators invest in a few languages they have carefully identified through design-driven research, whereas imitators include a greater variety of signs in their product portfolio. One might have expected the opposite, given that innovators perform experiments and investigate uncertain avenues, whereas imitators wait, observe what innovators do, see how the market reacts, and invest only in successful languages.

What makes this imitative strategy ineffective is that market feedback is—at an initial stage—very ambiguous, with several languages coexisting. As we have seen, the design discourse consists not of linear discussions but of open debates, as participants consider different visions simultaneously. Imitators—less skilled at design-driven research—can hardly interpret the meaning of these debates. In the beginning, it is unclear which product will be the winner, as new meanings introduced by an innovator often convert users slowly and take off gradually. Imitators perceive semiotic chaos and eventually chase everyone and imitate everything, launching products with different meanings and languages, further jeopardizing their brand.

Our study shows that in this context imitators need to wait several years (even as long as four or five years) to clearly discern whether a radical new meaning is actually successful and then respond with their imitation. Meanwhile, your company has had considerable time to establish authorship and reputation, thus profiting from design-driven innovation.

Part Three

BUILDING DESIGN-DRIVEN CAPABILITIES

10

THE DESIGN-DRIVEN LAB

[How to Start]

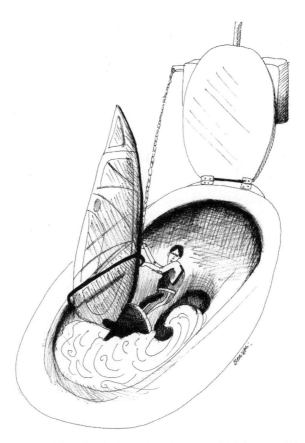

The assets that back design-driven innovation are embedded not in tools but in relation-ships among people. Their tacit nature makes them hardly imitable. Once you have developed a distinctive relational asset, competitors can hardly scratch your competitive position. [IN THE ILLUSTRATION Henkel's Fresh Surfer.]

I F A COMPANY WISHES to become a leader in the radical innovation of product meanings, where should it start? What assets and organizational arrangements should it develop? And how should it sustain and improve them over time?

Part 1 of this book frames the value of design-driven innovation and its role in a firm's innovation strategy. Part 2 analyzes the process that leads to design-driven innovation. This final part explores the underlying capabilities that enable a company to deploy such a strategy and implement such a process. In particular, this chapter focuses on the critical capabilities a firm should develop within its organization, and the next chapter focuses specifically on the vital role of top executives.

After reading part 2 of this book, you may wonder whether design-driven innovation requires any internal capabilities. After all, the process is based on leveraging external interpreters. You have seen examples of firms that succeed despite the lack of an internal design unit, such as Ferrari, Alessi, Artemide, and Kartell.[1] However, this surprising fact should not confound you: all these firms have clear internal capabilities that allow them to beat the competition.

Design-driven innovation requires firms to develop distinctive, proprietary capabilities, regardless of the size of the firm or whether it employs designers. This chapter shows how to invest to create such capabilities. You will see how a company often already has some of them but does not recognize or value them, or target them toward design-driven innovation. This is especially true of large companies, which often enjoy a much greater stock of knowledge and relationships with external interpreters, proprietary technologies, and complementary assets than smaller firms—yet nonetheless fail to harness the powerful potential of these assets.

The Capabilities

Three capabilities underpin design-driven innovation: relational assets with key interpreters, internal assets (your own knowledge and seductive power), and the interpretation process.

As part 2 shows, pursuing design-driven innovation requires building your own network of privileged relationships with key interpreters in the design discourse. "Privileged" implies that a key interpreter is more likely to cooperate with your firm or offer you her better insights, or that your firm can better leverage her knowledge and seductive power. In either case, this privileged network of relationships becomes a core asset—an engine of innovation that competitors can seldom replicate. Relational assets are not external to your firm and not freely accessible to others. They reside along the edge of your boundaries, in the unique interaction between external interpreters and your own people.

The second capability concerns your own proprietary assets: unique ingredients that cannot be found elsewhere. On the one hand, this capability includes your knowledge of the evolution of sociocultural models and technologies stemming from your research projects, investigations, and investments. On the other hand, it includes your own seductive power—your ability to suggest and influence the emergence of new meanings—which comes mainly from your brand.

The third capability is embedded in the interpretation process: the ability to integrate external insights with your internal assets and identify your own vision. As chapter 8 shows, the capability to select the right vision and translate it into physical products and services must eventually become substantially internal.

These assets are essential to attracting key interpreters, who look for firms that can provide the same currency the interpreters offer: knowledge and seductive power. If you do not produce your own vision, if you do not master unique technologies, if your manufacturing systems are not flexible and advanced enough and they limit rather than enable innovation, then you likely will not develop a privileged relationship with key interpreters. "No interesting designer in the world will collaborate with a company that does not know where to go," says Eugenio Perazza, founder of Magis, one of the fastest-growing furniture manufacturers in Italy.[2]

Among these three capabilities, the most challenging for a company that wants to start investing in design-driven innovation is the first: creating relational assets. Building internal assets, in contrast, is not a novel problem for firms. A significant literature shows how to create technological capabilities and brands, and companies similarly know how to build their capacity for process integration, teamwork, and project management. However, companies are less used to creating relational assets with key interpreters. This intriguing process therefore merits a closer look.

Building Relational Assets

Managers tend to be attracted by codified approaches to innovation. They love tools, step-by-step processes, applications, instruments. They implicitly assume that innovation systems can be bought and replicated at once. Indeed, one reason for the acclaim for user-centered innovation, with its ethnographic methods and brainstorming tools, is that it has been codified and packaged in a form that is digestible to executives. Highly codified approaches, however, have a downside: competitors can easily replicate them.

The relational assets that back design-driven innovation are of a completely different nature. They are embedded not in tools but in relationships among people. Relational assets rest on how one or more people in your organization know the interpreter, his skills, his attitude, and his behavior; know how to attract him; have built trust over time; and also know where to look for new talent. This relational knowledge cannot be codified in address books but rather is *tacitly* preserved and nurtured by people. Like any form of social capital, it cannot be bought immediately but must be built over time. Such knowledge requires *cumulative* investments, punctuated by attempts, failures, and successes.

The Strength and the Challenge

The tacit and cumulative nature of relational assets is both the strength and the challenge of design-driven innovation.

It is the *strength*, because the tacit nature of these assets makes them hardly appropriable by competitors. Others could hire a key interpreter once you have found her, but they are not likely to replicate your capability to interact with her and to value her contribution. And the cumulative nature of these assets creates a positive reinforcing loop: the more privileged relationships you have with the design discourse, the more you are capable of developing breakthrough and seductive visions, making you even more attractive to key interpreters. In other words, once you have developed a distinctive relational asset, competitors can seldom overtake your competitive position. Indeed, many Italian manufacturers have been worldwide leaders in their own sectors for decades.

The nature of relational assets is also the *challenge*, because the process of building them is sluggish at first and entails much suffering. You start moving into a complex, multifaceted, and noisy design discourse—an unfamiliar territory. You need to gain membership into elite circles while you are not yet perceived as a central contributor.[3]

How can you accelerate the process of creating relational assets and rapidly activate a positive loop? Three complementary strategies are essential: valuing, searching, and acquiring (see figure 10-1).

Valuing Your Existing Relational Assets

Often companies already have significant relationships with interpreters in the design discourse. A scientist at a major U.S. office automation firm wrote me, "I am aware that my corporation has numerous close contacts with various interpreters in the print industry, universities, graphics arts, supplier base, and both internal and external design communities. However, we have such a strong technical strength that it tends to overshadow efforts to improve design via these interactions."

You can only imagine how many relationships with external experts, scholars, suppliers, artists, journalists, designers, sociologists, and marketers a firm with more than ten thousand employees might already have. You may simply have never valued or empowered this treasure. Most firms have no idea of the richness and extent of their existing web of relationships with the design discourse, because they remain disconnected assets of individual employees rather than a coordinated asset of the organization.

FIGURE 10-1

Strategies for building relational assets with interpreters in the design discourse

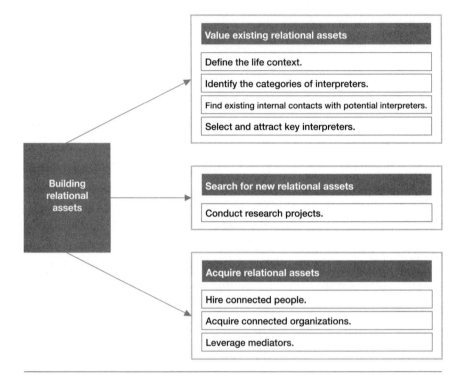

External experts may already cooperate with your firm, but not in design-driven research. For example, you have seen how a German journalist with a degree in theology made a major contribution to Barilla's Beyond Primo Piatto project, thanks to his ability to read long-term changes in society and meanings. This journalist was introduced to the innovation team by someone in the communication department, who had contact with him for different purposes and never envisioned he could act as an interpreter for a radical change in meanings.

The first strategy in building relationships with the design discourse, therefore, is to transform the individual links that people already have with interpreters into company assets. Toward that end, as chapter 7 shows, you should first identify the life context that is the focus of your innovation strategy. Next you should identify the categories of interpreters who are concerned with that life context. Then you should ask your firm's organizational units that already have significant contacts with people in those categories to help identify potential interpreters.

Note that your design department (if you have one) might be a significant source of such contacts, but it is definitely not the only one: relationships with the design discourse are spread throughout your organization. (Figure 10-2 shows internal units that typically already have relationships with external interpreters.) Finally, you select from among the roster of potential interpreters those who can really act as key interpreters (using the guidelines in table 7-1).

Searching for and Acquiring New Relational Assets

Unveiling and empowering your existing treasure of relationships form an important initial strategy, but often they are not enough. Your current links with the design discourse will not provide access to all the key interpreters you will need. This is especially true when you make your

FIGURE 10-2

Existing relational assets spread throughout various units of an organization

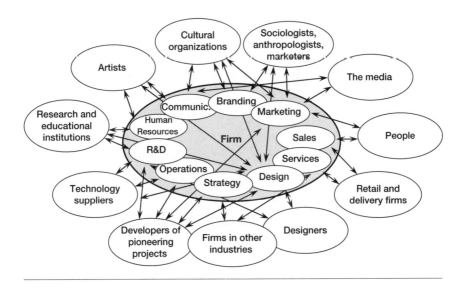

first move into design-driven innovation and can tap only an existing web of relationships that has unfolded spontaneously for different purposes—a web that you have not strategically planned, oriented, or nurtured. To fill the empty spots in your relational assets, you need two additional strategies.

The first strategy is to invest in the search for interpreters. Chapters 7 and 8 provide examples of such searches. For instance, you have seen how Alessi periodically conducts research projects in unexplored sections of the design discourse specifically to find unidentified interpreters.

The second strategy is to acquire relationships. You can do this by hiring people who already have those missing relationships with the life context you are targeting. Apple adopted this strategy when it hired Jonathan Ive, a designer with experience in domestic products (see chapter 7).

Or you might acquire entire organizations that are already significantly immersed in a section of the design discourse you are interested in. Philips, for example, recently acquired Color Kinetics, a Boston-based firm specializing in applications of LED technology. Through this acquisition Philips, a supplier of LEDs, has begun a more intense interaction with creators of downstream applications in both public and private life. Color Kinetics had developed significant experience and relational assets through several pioneering projects, such as illuminating the London Eye (one of the world's largest Ferris wheels) and Philadelphia's historic Boathouse Row.

Finally, you can acquire missing relationships by involving mediators—external people who can guide you through the unfamiliar land of the design discourse and direct you to unidentified key interpreters. Alessandro Mendini played such a crucial role by introducing Alessi to international architects who were pioneering postmodern design languages. You can find mediators in every category of interpreter. For example, companies often approach our team at Politecnico di Milano because they value the mediating role that an academic institution can play with a broad range of interpreters, given that it sits at the crossroads of various disciplines (from engineering to design to management) and that it is research focused and therefore inherently attractive to external interpreters.[4]

The Design-Driven Lab

This analysis of the capabilities critical to design-driven innovation has so far examined the *what* (what are the capabilities?) and the *how* (how can you build them?). Our next question is, *Who?* Who should drive, support, and monitor the process of building and renewing these capabilities?

This question is not marginal. As noted, firms often have the seeds of design-driven capabilities. But they do not recognize them or transform them into organizational assets by nurturing them, modifying them, crossbreeding them, and using them. These latter processes do not happen spontaneously. They need to be led.

Leadership by Functional Units

In some companies this role is played by a functional unit: R&D (for example, at Barilla), business development (at Bayer Material Science), strategy (at STMicroelectronics and Intuit), design (at Philips, Nokia, and Samsung), innovation (at Coca-Cola), product development (at Lego), marketing and branding (at Ducati motorcycle company). At all these companies, these functional departments have expanded their roles to embrace the deployment of design-driven capabilities.

This expansion may reflect the firm's explicit choice (such as at Philips), its historical evolution (such as at Intuit, where the founder, Scott Cook, is the design leader), its particular mission and industry (technology suppliers such as Bayer and STMicroelectronics tend to concentrate this role in strategic functions rather than R&D, which is highly technical), or the attitude and skill of the functional executive (such as at Barilla, where the VP of R&D had an eclectic attitude that drove him to search not only for radical technologies but also for radical meanings).

This does not imply that these firms realize design-driven innovation within the walls of those functional units. These companies spread their assets (relationships, knowledge and seductive power, integrative processes) throughout various departments. However, they have a key unit to activate, coordinate, and monitor the development of such assets.

At other companies, multiple departments explicitly share responsibility for promoting design-driven innovation. Indesit, a large manufacturer of white goods, recently launched a major initiative to propose new radical meanings for domestic lifestyles. Both its innovation and technology unit and its marketing and branding unit are managing this initiative. They are jointly leading it, promoting it within the organization, defining its scope, and gaining relational assets for it—to ensure that the firm leverages both technological and sociocultural drivers and cultivates a broad perspective.

Leadership by a Dedicated Lab

Other companies, finally, have created a dedicated design-driven lab: a small unit whose mission is specifically to support the development and monitoring of design-driven capabilities. An example is Zucchi Group, a leading European manufacturer of home textiles.

The textile industry is entering one of its most fascinating (and turbulent) periods, as Western firms significantly redefine their strategies and business models given encroaching competition from Eastern countries. For most Western companies, innovation will be the sole craft for riding the rapids. Although the industry has long been known for fast but incremental changes in product lines dictated by fashion, opportunities for radical innovation are now emerging, thanks especially to breakthrough technologies.

New synthetic fabrics have already revolutionized competition in the most technical segments of the industry (for example, sports textiles). Now waves of technological opportunities are also swamping the most traditional sectors: those that use cotton and other natural fabrics for clothing or home decor. These technologies include new chemical treatments, the use of cyclodextrins to release drugs, and the embedding of microelectronics and nanotechnologies to make the fabric intelligent, to name only a few examples.

Despite this wealth of exotic technologies, however, firms are still struggling to find applications that can fulfill people's real needs and aspirations. Textiles worn by people or used in homes have a remarkable emotional and symbolic content. Thus functional innovation is useless if not supported by a reinterpretation of meaning. The industry is entering an exciting period wherein design-driven innovation—especially the search for technology epiphanies—may make a significant difference. In this context Zucchi has created a dedicated lab, led by the former VP of product development, to promote radical innovation in both technologies and meanings.

The firm chose to create a dedicated lab that cuts across functional units for two reasons. First, the textile industry, like many others, is characterized by turbulence and speed. Marketing and product development are under pressure to deliver a new collection every other season. This forces these units to focus on fast, incremental innovations that reinforce existing meanings rather than overturn them. Daily activities drive the agenda and make it difficult for the company to focus on radical, long-term endeavors. Because Zucchi's lab is dedicated to design-driven innovation, it is protected from this short-term pressure.

The firm also chose to create a dedicated lab that cuts across functional units because it can combine multiple perspectives—from material technologies to process technologies, from marketing to branding, from distribution to services—that seldom exist within a single unit.

Snaidero, the kitchen manufacturer discussed in chapter 2, has stretched this approach even further by creating an external lab, the Rino Snaidero Scientific Foundation. The foundation promotes research on the quality of domestic lifestyles, merging investigations into sociocultural changes with technological explorations. Although an autonomous external research unit would seem to make transferring findings to the firm more challenging, it helps facilitate access to interpreters. They perceive the foundation as less focused on the needs of a specific firm and product category and more oriented toward exploring the future—and therefore as an interesting interpreter with which to interact and collaborate. Indeed, the Snaidero Scientific Foundation has more than twenty partners, including universities (such as Technische University in Dresden), design schools (such as Domus Academy in Milan), and firms that are interested in design-driven innovation in the same life context (such as the Zucchi Group).

The Role of the Design-Driven Lab

Whether you create a design-driven lab within an existing department or as an autonomous unit, it will take the lead in developing your firm's design-driven capabilities. In particular, the design-driven lab embraces four activities.

The first concerns strategy. The lab is the most attentive observer and champion of opportunities for design-driven innovation. It ensures that your company is first in the search for new meanings and does not leave this strategy in the hands of competitors. In other words, the design-driven lab is responsible for positioning design-driven innovation within your innovation framework (recall figure 3-1). It finds empty spots in the map, avoids unbalanced plans (such as those too focused on incremental innovation), anticipates the need to launch new projects (before the dominant meaning promoted by your company loses momentum or before a radical change in sociocultural paradigms affects the market), promotes synergies among various efforts (for example, by joining technology-push projects with long-term analysis of sociocultural scenarios in the search for technology epiphanies), and monitors the evolution of your innovation framework.

The second role of the design-driven lab is to enable the development and renewal of relational assets. It acts as the main engine in building relationships with external interpreters (see figure 10-3). It scans the company for existing links with these interpreters and becomes a central hub that transforms into organizational assets the interesting relationships that people in your firm continuously develop. The lab enables cumulative investments in design-driven innovation by supporting these relationships over time. Especially if designed as an autonomous unit, the lab can identify an emerging network of interpreters that will be essential to future competition and will promote activities aimed at investigating this new network. In so doing, the lab may identify individuals to be hired, organizations to be acquired, and mediators to be involved.

The third role of the design-driven lab is to nurture the interpretation process—that is, to enable design-driven research projects. The lab becomes the focal point that gathers stimuli, insights, and explorations from within your firm and external interpreters. It also provides continuity of analysis when no major projects are running. In this way you always have the most comprehensive and updated knowledge of the evolution of meanings and product languages. Companies and interpreters are permanently immersed in the design discourse and

FIGURE 10-3

The design-driven lab and the creation of relational assets

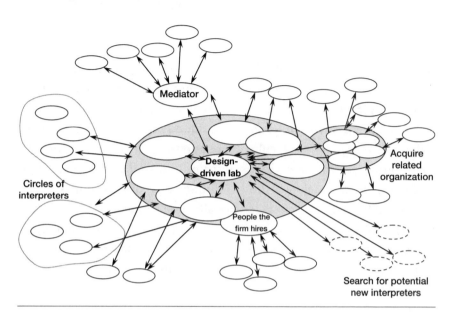

provide a continuous stream of insights: without a design-driven lab that can collect, connect, and interpret them, these insights are wasted. For example, I have often met with companies where the head of a functional unit has launched a workshop with students but other units are not aware of the wealth of ideas, stimuli, and relationships that have emerged from the workshop.

The design-driven lab also enables your firm to acquire and improve the methodologies and tools of design-driven innovation, such as learning how to conduct a Design Direction Workshop or how to select concepts to pursue. Such a lab is also in a privileged position to champion downstream product development, acting as an interface between interpreters who participated in the initial design research and engineers who will take care of implementation.

Finally, the design-driven lab helps your company address the design discourse. On the one hand, it communicates continuously with the design discourse to sustain your reputation as an innovative and forward-looking corporation, a practice that will allow you to attract key interpreters once you have identified them. On the other hand, the lab creates the cultural prototypes that you will diffuse among interpreters to leverage their seductive power.

An Enabling Lab

Note that the lab is not the locus where the capabilities of design-driven innovation are concentrated. It is not the team of creative (and lucky) people who are the only ones in your company to think about innovation. These capabilities are spread throughout your entire organization. All your people will cultivate relationships with interpreters and contribute ideas for new visions and interpretations. Participation in design-driven research will be multifunctional, and that makes the process effective because it leverages all your resources.

The design-driven lab is, rather, an enabler—a methodological repository whose role is to value all these companywide assets and direct, harness, focus, build, and transform them into real value. The lab is a low-quantity/high-quality unit. The number of people you need to run it is likely to be very small. Alessi relies on only three people: Alberto Alessi, his assistant Gloria Barcellini, and design manager Danilo Alliata, assisted by key external mediators such as Alessandro Mendini and Laura Polinoro (past director of Centro Studi Alessi, formerly the company's design-driven lab). Zucchi relies on three people. The Rino Snaidero Scientific Foundation has three employees and several collaborations.

Large corporations will enjoy the leverage this approach can provide, with a highly favorable ratio between the resources exploited (the entire organization) and the resources invested (the design-driven lab). Small firms will enjoy the accessibility of this approach to firms of limited size. For example, Filati Maclodio, a small yarn manufacturer, has created a design-driven lab to explore new applications of advanced technologies in fabric and to search for technology epiphanies. The firm leverages its small lab by relying on two people who interact with interpreters at schools, research centers, and universities.

In a design-driven lab, quality compensates for quantity. To fulfill its enabling role, the lab needs people who are both very well connected within the firm and immersed in the design discourse. Tools and applications can support them in this challenging task. For example, to strengthen its lab's enabling role, Zucchi Group has also created a Web-based knowledge repository to which functional units and external interpreters alike can submit contributions and insights. The central lab acts as a curator of this wealth of information: it finds connections among stimuli, analyzes their evolving nature, identifies weak signals and anomalies that could lead to more significant changes in technologies and the sociocultural environment, and feeds future design-driven research.

Extensions: Profiting from Design-Driven Capabilities

The value of a firm's design-driven capabilities is sometimes such that it can profit directly by delivering those capabilities as a service. Philips Design, for example, not only provides design-driven capabilities to the business units of the Dutch corporation but also acts as a design firm that delivers consulting services to external clients. Thus it not only provides a revenue stream that helps cover the company's investment in design research but also broadens the firm's interactions and provides additional insights for Philips's own products.

IBM has created a new design consulting service as a branch of its design unit. The idea is to bundle IBM's expertise in interaction design, usability, and brand design with its other core services: business, engineering, and technology support. This approach enables Big Blue to deliver complex systems to its corporate customers, including the design of products and services that incorporate IBM technologies. This has led, for example, to the development of a handheld wireless device for the New York Stock Exchange and to a complex project for the Swedish Road Administration to reduce traffic congestion, for which IBM's design team created the in-vehicle technology.

Alessi also profits directly from its relational assets based on the design discourse. Given the enormous value of its connections with more than two hundred designers, companies are coming to Alessi for help in pursuing their design-driven research and identifying key interpreters who fit their strategy. For example, Alessi has recently supported Henkel, a German manufacturer of laundry, cosmetic, and home care products, in developing a toilet-cleaning flushing soap. Alessi helped the company define the proper design language and meaning and then to identify the designer (in this case Miriam Mirri) who could best interpret that meaning and language. The resulting product, called FreshSurfer, is shaped in the form of a little windsurfer who surfs the waves of water whenever the toilet is flushed. Alessi has been involved in similar projects with corporations as diverse as FIAT, Siemens, Philips, Seiko, and Mitsubishi, which now supply almost 30 percent of Alessi's revenues and a significant profit stream.

Creating design-driven capabilities is a challenge because you cannot easily buy and replicate them. However, once you have built them, the competitive position you can achieve becomes an inimitable and sustainable source of profits—well beyond the scope you originally envisioned.

11

BUSINESS*PEOPLE*

[The Key Role of Top Executives and Their Culture]

These executives immerse themselves where mainstream competitors do not search. They purposely explore unexplored areas. Books on creativity love to talk about "thinking outside of the box." These executives, rather, immerse themselves "outside of the network."

I N 2000 TONY FADELL, a young computer engineer, was shopping around, searching for a company willing to invest in his innovative idea: to combine an MP3 player with an online music store. Fadell had been working as a hardware and software architect for General Magic, a start-up that spun off from Apple when the Cupertino firm was run by John Sculley. Fadell then became director of engineering at the Mobile Computing Group at Philips Electronic, which he left to promote his business idea in the MP3 music industry. He knocked on several doors but was ignored by many executives—except one. Steve Jobs, who had meanwhile rejoined Apple as interim CEO, was looking for just such a person. Apple hired Fadell to lead a one-year project that would overturn the music industry: to design the iPod.[1]

Since the development of the Macintosh and the iMac, Steve Jobs had had an intense devotion to radical innovation projects. The iPod was no exception. He set the direction and defined the requirements for a product for which there was no reference in the market. He insisted that the iPod work seamlessly with iTunes, the music application that Apple planned to release in January 2001. He supervised the development of the iPod's user interface, demanded that many functions be automated, and set the memory capacity at one thousand songs.[2] A former senior manager at PortalPlayer, a contractor whom Apple approached to help develop the iPod, reports, "The interesting thing about the iPod is that since it started, it had 100 percent of Steve Jobs' time . . . He was heavily involved in every single aspect of the project . . . Steve would be horribly offended he couldn't get to the song he wanted in less than three pushes of a button. We'd get orders: 'Steve doesn't think it's loud enough, the sharps aren't sharp enough, or the menu's not coming up fast enough.' Every day there were comments from Steve saying where it needed to be."[3]

Vision, pride, and the ability to scout talent. Other business leaders and entrepreneurs we have met in this book share these characteristics— from Giulio Castelli, founder of Kartell (the only company that dared to invest in Bookworm, the spiral bookshelf created by Ron Arad) to Aldo Romano, CEO of STMicroelectronics.

This book is about the *management* of innovation and design. I have not talked about how designers, inventors, engineers, and scientists come up with creative ideas. Rather, I have examined the process through which executives leverage external and internal resources and creativity to develop breakthrough innovations. I have not analyzed how Ron Arad conceived of Bookworm, but how Kartell's chairman spotted and attracted this talented artist, envisioned the business potential in his idea that competitors had overlooked, and transformed it into a blockbuster product.

There is no radical innovation without inspiring leaders. This chapter delves into their crucial role.

This Is a Job for Top Executives

Alberto Alessi is a lawyer by training, as is Luca Cordero di Montezemolo, chairman of Ferrari and of the holding company of furniture makers Cassina and Poltrona Frau. Ernesto Gismondi, chairman of Artemide, is an aerospace engineer. Giulio Castelli of Kartell, Matteo Zucchi, CEO of textile manufacturer Zucchi Group, and Edi Snaidero, chairman of Snaidero, are also engineers. Scott Cook, founder of the software firm Intuit, has a bachelor's degree in economics and mathematics and an MBA, as does Lee Kun Hee, chairman of Samsung Group. Claudio Luti, CEO of Kartell, has a background in economics. Satoru Iwata, president and CEO of Nintendo, was trained in computer science. Nicolas G. Hayek, chairman and CEO of The Swatch Group, studied mathematics, physics, and chemistry. Jorma Ollila, chairman of Nokia, studied political science, economics, and engineering physics.

If there is one sure thing in design-driven innovation, it is that one need not be artistic or have a degree in design to lead the process. Nor does one need to be vegetarian and be worshipped as a guru like Steve Jobs. Alberto Alessi is a peaceable man who does not like to keynote public events. Scott Cook is a genteel executive whose attentive and respectful attention to the thoughts of others does not match the cliché of the counterculture.

Design-driven innovation needs more than external and internal interpreters. It needs executives. It needs their leadership, which they can exert in various ways.

Some, for example, tend to be directly involved in managing innovation. Alberto Alessi is not only the CEO of the company but also directly leads the unit that is responsible for innovation and branding. Ernesto Gismondi unleashes his passion for lamps by creating some of Artemide's products. Claudio Luti attends every meeting with external designers. And Steve Jobs pays attention to every detail of a product. He wants to be sure that the people who develop it share and respect its meaning and vision—even down to the smallest features, such as the visual quality of the circuit wiring for Macintosh and iMac computers.

Other executives provide inspiration for design-driven innovation. Scott Cook, who in addition to being board chairman of Intuit retains the title chief design officer, created the vision that accounting applications should be quick and simple. He does not participate directly in designing products but rather sees himself as an amplifier of talent—a coach and a mentor whose role is to strengthen the company's capability to delight people through its software applications.

The Three Roles of Top Executives

Whatever their background, attitude, and intensity of presence, these managers share a few essential characteristics and assume roles that they cannot delegate to anyone else.

First, they set the direction and ignite the process of design-driven innovation. Outcomes depend strongly on how an innovation strategy is framed. And executives play a crucial role in framing the strategy by asking the right questions. In design-driven innovation, the questions that ignites the process are, "What is the deepest reason people will buy our products? What meaning could they be looking for? How can we gratify them and make them more content by providing products that suggest new meanings?" Employees, designers, and engineers at many companies may ask themselves those questions, but only firms whose top executives have also asked and seriously embraced them invest in the perilous search for answers. Thinking about meanings instead of features, searching for radical changes instead of improvements, proposing visions instead of satisfying existing needs—all these efforts require an organization mind-set that does not occur by chance. It can be nurtured only by top executives.

Second, design-driven leaders directly participate in creating relational assets. They are on the front line identifying key interpreters in the design discourse. This direct involvement has a simple, precise economic rationale: executives always focus their time and energies on the most crucial investment decisions, and in design-driven innovation the key investment concerns relational assets. As Claudio Luti says, Kartell invests in designers and not in solutions. The direct involvement of top executives is important both to attract talented interpreters (who, because they have an open door to the boardroom, see that the company values their contribution) and to select them.

I once asked Alberto Alessi which tasks, among those he handles directly, would be challenging to transfer to other people in his organization. He replied as follows:

> I see two separate problems. One is how to find the new designers who might be interesting for Alessi. The other is how to then manage the relationships and keep them alive. The latter is not a major concern . . . I do not believe I'm the only one who could manage these relationships. You need certain types of qualities. You need to express trust and show you intimately believe in what they show you, that you will do everything to realize their imagery, their dreams. Much more difficult is to find new talents. In our context, where the swarm of talented people is so huge and noisy, it's becoming very difficult. And also to understand, once you receive the ideas, whether they are good or not.

This passage clarifies that identifying and attracting key interpreters are more important than the daily management of that relationship, which executives can more easily assign to carefully trained and attentive managers.

It also clarifies that the third crucial role of top executives is to select the solution that eventually results from a design-driven research project. An executive is irreplaceable when it comes to choosing the vision—the radical new meaning—that will drive a company's future innovation.

Setting the direction, attracting and selecting key interpreters, and choosing the vision are the three key roles of top executives who want to promote design-driven innovation. They cannot delegate these roles, not only because they exert the most significant impact on return on investment but also because analytical tools cannot ensure safe and straightforward results. As I said in chapter 5 when introducing the example of the director of industrial design whose boss wanted to see an ROI on the design, you will get little help (if not, sometimes, wrong answers) from financial spreadsheets, market tests, and focus groups. There is only judgment and risk.

And when judgment and risk combine with significant investment, this is a job for top executives. They must personally dedicate the time and develop the skills required for attracting, selecting, and directing.

Everyone acknowledges that top executives are busy and their time is precious. For this reason I have distilled the three roles only they can provide. Indeed, when they do so, time becomes less of a concern. Although these three roles are always on duty, they tend to be more concentrated in only a few moments in time: when a firm launches a project to develop radical innovation of meanings, and when it concludes such a project. In a firm with a balanced innovation strategy, these crucial moments do not occur frequently. The challenge is to develop the skills to provide effective leadership during those times. So, to answer the question that Susan, the director of design, asked me on how to have her CEO appreciate the value of design, my suggestion was, "He needs to have the skills himself to *personally* gauge the value of design. You or other analytical tools cannot substitute for these skills. And for developing these skills, you need to help him *immerse* in the design discourse."

The Art Dealer: A Matter of Immersion

"My job resembles that of an art dealer who chooses the artists who are capable of rendering the spirit of our time," says Enrico Astori, the founder of Driade, an innovative Italian furniture manufacturer. "We are like editors."[4]

Indeed, executives make a business of innovation just as art dealers make a business of art. Executives do not need to be inventors, just as art dealers do not need to be artists. Both build their competitive advantage on their ability to identify, attract, and select key interpreters. The successful art dealer is one who is capable of finding the talents of the future and developing privileged relationships with them while competitors are still looking at acknowledged, mainstream artists. Examples are Betty Parsons, who discovered many American abstract expressionists, and Leo Castelli, the first to sell a Warhol painting of a Campbell's soup can. They had no formula. They had a radical vision.

How do art dealers create their skills? It is through immersion: they are immersed in the art scene and its social network. Betty Parsons was first exposed to art in 1913, at the age of thirteen, when she attended the New York Armory Show, meant to introduce Americans to modern art. Leo Castelli married an art dealer and befriended French surrealists when he was in his twenties and living in Paris, before moving to the United States because of World War II.

Immersion means that art dealers personally search for and meet talents through a web of relationships. It is the only way they can detect the subtle voices of unknown interpreters. Immersion allows them to be invited by emerging circles as trusted members and makes the quest for unidentified talent a cumulative process characterized by small but continuous personal investments in networking.[5]

Similarly, executives of firms that pursue design-driven innovation build their skills and fulfill their role through immersion—not in art but in the design discourse. Probably the most remarkable entrepreneur who spotted talents through immersion is Cesare Cassina, the founder of furniture manufacturer Cassina (from which other prominent firms I have mentioned, such as B&B Italia and Flos, have spun off). Cassina was among the first in Italy to develop a business model based on close collaboration with architects. He spent his Saturdays with Gio Ponti, the architect who designed the Pirelli Tower in Milan, discovered Gaetano Pesce when he was twenty-four and subsidized him with a monthly salary to pursue novel explorations, invited Afra and Tobia Scarpa to stay at his home for long periods before they were famous, attended avant-garde architectural exhibitions, and cooperated with Mario Bellini and Vico Magistretti in their early days.[6]

Alberto Alessi underlines the importance of being immersed in the right community: "In the 1970s I had infinitely less experience. But I spent time with architects. I turned to one side and had Sottsass, and on the other side had Mario Bellini, then Marco Zanuso, Achille Castiglioni, Gae Aulenti, all extraordinary people." I have seen Ernesto Gismondi, the founder of Artemide, participating in workshops and design seminars as well as sitting at tables with young design students and discussing their projects.[7]

Executives of large corporations can leverage the support of their entire organizations if they are open to becoming immersed in the design discourse. Says Brian Walker, CEO of Herman Miller, "When I was transitioning from chief financial officer to CEO, I used to sit in on every team meeting for launching a design review. I spent a lot of time listening to the details of what was going on, not as a boss critiquing their work but as an observer trying to understand where it was going. Even today, when one of our designers is in town, Don Goeman, the executive vice president of research, design, and development at Herman Miller, checks to see if I have an hour or two to meet. It's not about time to approve anything; sometimes it's to take me through the latest model and hear what they are thinking."[8]

Immersing Yourself "Outside of the Network"

Successful executives, like successful art dealers, have a dual strategy of immersion. On the one hand, they keep an eye on the institutionalized design discourse. They keep updated on what meanings are dominant and what is emerging, and that helps them understand whether a proposal or an interpreter is really innovative or is merely replicating what already exists. On the other hand, they immerse themselves in parts of the design discourse where mainstream competitors do not search. They explore unexplored areas. Books on creativity love to talk about "thinking outside of the box." These executives, rather, immerse themselves "outside of the network."

What Cesare Cassina did was to search for interpreters where no one in his industry had thought to look: among architects. Participating in big design events can acquaint you with the most acknowledged trends and respected designers. But it will not lead you to new visions and new talent. For example, everyone today is looking at Milan, San Francisco, London, and Copenhagen as major centers where the design discourse is intense and events must be attended. China, in contrast, is considered an interesting location only for manufacturing. In other words, China is outside the network. But Enrico Astori of Driade sees it differently: "Since 2000 I've been taking care of a project that sees Asia not only as a place where you manufacture, but also as a provider of creativity . . . China and other Asian countries express great vitality in the movie industry, and in other forms of creativity such as graphics and images. They still have not moved into the field of design, and indeed there are more artists than designers. However, economy, art, and creative capacity have often followed a parallel growth. Therefore I'm closely following the changes there."[9]

Managers Are People Before Being Managers

January 15, 2008. 10 a.m. Steve Jobs is at the zenith of his keynote address at the Macworld Conference & Expo in San Francisco. He moves close to the podium. Picks up an envelope. Pulls out of it a thin notebook, the Apple MacBook Air. The audience gasps. He explains in detail all the features of the new product and how the engineers squeezed them into this slice of hardware. Then he says, "No matter how hard you look, one thing you are not gonna find in a MacBook Air is an optical drive. If you really want one we have built one [he shows an external CD-DVD drive that one can plug in to the notebook] . . . But you know what? We do not think most users will miss the optical drive. We do not think they will need an optical drive. Because the MacBook Air was built to be a wireless machine."

Then he explains the user scenario Apple has designed, where people do things wirelessly: download movies from iTunes Stores, make backups to Apple's Time Machine and Time Capsule, install software through a new feature that gives them access to discs on other computers in the vicinity, and avoid burning music CDs because their movie collections are on their iPods. At the end of the keynote he leaves the stage while speakers blast the U2 song "Pride." It couldn't be a more appropriate soundtrack.

Pride

Steve Jobs's keynotes at the Macworld Conference are big events. Thousands of people in the audience and many more remotely connected are there to hear about Apple's latest visions for how we could listen to music, entertain ourselves with movies, live in our houses, offices, and cars. To many, these shows reveal Jobs's star quality. A more subtle side, however, creeps up—one that I have found common among executives who invest in design-driven innovation: they are proud of their products.

You may attest that many executives feel intense passion for their jobs. Pride about a product, however, is something different. It implies that you are proud of what you are offering to customers, to people. Passion is about what you do. Pride is about what you deliver. It assumes a consistency between the product and your vision as an executive, so that you are never ashamed of your proposal. It may even be that people will not like it—that you have taken too big a step. But you are nevertheless proud of it, and you are ready to learn and transform it into a success next time.

Sometimes I have the feeling that some executives are afraid of what they offer. If we asked them whether they would put their nametags on their products and services, they would probably decline, saying, "Our product reflects the merit of our design team." Or, "We start from what users want. Our product is molded on their needs." This implicitly also means that if the product fails, or if users are not completely delighted, it's the responsibility of the design team or the users themselves. But Steve Jobs is saying, "*We* do not think most users will miss the optical drive." And given that he is saying that, he is putting his nametag on the product.

Executives of design-driven firms are proud of what they propose, although not all put their nametags on the product in the same pyrotechnic way that Steve Jobs does. Alberto Alessi, more humbly, writes books and articles that explain his vision. His firm periodically produces a magazine that presents the company's new products. Whereas executives of other firms might write the introduction, Alberto Alessi personally writes the description of each product and explains the motivation behind it.

Culture

Executives in every industry and company should be proud of their products. Indeed, every product, as we know, has a meaning. Willy-nilly, through products we convey a vision—a set of values and norms. In other words, products embed culture. Game consoles are meant to entertain teenagers, and there is an entire culture of gaming.

As long as you are not innovating meanings, as long as you stick to the dominant concept in the industry and reinforce the existing culture in the market, you may feel comfortable: people asked for this. Design-driven innovation is much less comfortable. It challenges the dominant culture that surrounds a product. When an executive sets the direction and decides to invest in a radical new product, he has no handrail, no excuse, no place to hide: *he* is embracing a new meaning. He is proposing to people a vision of their context of life, which, inevitably, is his vision.

I'm not referring to corporate values, brand value, or organizational culture. All these are important. But in leading and managing breakthrough changes, the person who sets and selects the direction has the greatest influence. When it comes to radical innovation of meanings, a product's culture reflects the culture of the executive who has launched it.

This is a great challenge. And it is the reason executives of design-driven firms are often maniacal about details. Because these products convey their culture—their values, norms, beliefs, aspirations. The products have their nametag on them, and they want to be proud.

Business

An executive's personal culture is not something ethereal. It is, rather, a personal asset, built during years of immersion in the context of life. It includes values, norms, visions, and knowledge created, often unconsciously, through social explorations, experiments, relationships. It comes from a continuous stream of small, cumulative investments that started in school and goes well beyond the corporate setting. It is the result of a huge personal research endeavor.

Management theories, especially innovation theories, disregard the fact that businesspeople are people and that they therefore have a culture. These theories are "culturally neutral." Or they purposely try to ensure that cultural insight does not affect any decision. Their assumption is that culture does not lead to business and that culture can even be detrimental to it. The result is that this enormous asset remains unharnessed.

The research I have conducted shows that personal culture does lead to business. The companies I have examined have been thriving for decades. Maybe, as often happens, they will suffer in the future, as they sometimes did in the past. But meanwhile they have given us the chance to observe a very profitable and sustainable model for doing business. Many of these executives are entrepreneurs. They have invested their own money. They are therefore extremely interested in financial payback. And they have shown that management practices can be more financially effective when they are not culturally neutral.

The framework provided in this book has, in essence, shown how you can profit from people's personal culture—and conversely, that people are eager to tap in to their culture to create profit. The strategy and process of design-driven innovation nurture that culture, make it distinctive, and drive it toward business. Design-driven innovation values three precious assets, three treasures, which often remain untapped.

The first is the *personal culture of the interpreters* who surround every firm, a culture built through their own research on meanings in the contexts of life.

The second is the *personal culture of people in your organization*, a culture built through interaction with the design discourse that only awaits transformation into a corporate asset.

The third is *your personal culture as an executive,* a culture built through immersion. It is your vision of the world, painstakingly developed through years of research, which you are proud of, but which, as a business*person,* you do not know how to apply to business. You have often been taught that business and culture are two different things. The former concerns your profession, the second, your private life. The framework presented here shows that they can, and should, sustain each other. Why do you have to have a schizophrenic personality? After all, managers are people before being managers.

COMPANIES, INDUSTRIES, AND MARKETS DISCUSSED IN THIS BOOK

Company	Industry	Country	Product (P) Service (S)	Consumer (C) Business (B)	Niche market (N) Mass market (M)	Small firm (SM) Large firm (L)	Chapter
Alessi	Household objects	Italy	P	C	N	SM	1, 3, 6, 7, 8, 11
Apple	Information technology	U.S.	P, S	C	M	L	1, 3, 4, 7, 11
Aprilia	Motorcycles	Italy	P	C	M	L	7
Artemide	Lighting	Italy	P	C, B	N	SM	1, 2, 3, 6, 7, 8, 9
Arthur Bonnet	Kitchen furniture	France	P	C	M	SM	8
Barilla	Food	Italy	P	C	M	L	7, 8, 10
Bayer Material Science	Materials	Germany	P	B	M	L	4, 6
Bang & Olufsen	Consumer electronics	Denmark	P	C	N	L	3, 5, 7, 8
Brembo	Brakes	Italy	P	B	N	L	4
B&B Italia	Furniture	Italy	P	C	N	SM	6, 7

Company	Industry	Country	Product (P) Service (S)	Consumer (C) Business (B)	Niche market (N) Mass market (M)	Small firm (SM) Large firm (L)	Chapter
Casio	Consumer electronics	Japan	P	C	M	L	1, 4
Color Kinetics	LED lighting	U.S.	P	B	M	SM	10
Corning	Materials	U.S.	P	B	M	L	4, 7
Creative Technology	Multimedia	Singapore	P	C	M	L	4
Diamond Multimedia	Multimedia	U.S.	P	C, B	M	L	4
Driade	Furniture	Italy	P	C	N	SM	11
Dupont	Materials	U.S.	P	B	M	L	9
Endemol	Broadcasting	The Netherlands	S	B	M	L	3
Ferrari	Automotive	Italy	P	C	N	L	8, 10
FIAT	Automotive	Italy	P	C	M	L	5
Filati Maclodio	Textile	Italy	P	B	M	SM	10
Flos	Lighting	Italy	P	C	N	SM	6, 7
Henkel	Cosmetics, home care	Germany	P	C	M	L	10
Herman Miller	Furniture	U.S.	P	B	N	L	3, 7, 11
IBM	Information technology	U.S.	P, S	B	M	L	10
Indesit Co.	White goods	Italy	P	C	M	L	10
Intuit	Software	U.S.	P, S	C, B	M	L	2, 11
Kartell	Furniture	Italy	P	C, B	M	SM	2, 6, 7
LSI Corp.	Information technology	U.S.	P, S	B	M	L	4
Lucesco	Lighting	U.S.	P	C	N	S	7
McDonald's	Food services	U.S.	S	C	M	L	2
Material ConneXion	Materials	U.S.	S	B	M	SM	6, 7

Company	Industry	Country	Product (P) Service (S)	Consumer (C) Business (B)	Niche market (N) Mass market (M)	Small firm (SM) Large firm (L)	Chapter
Microsoft	Information technology	U.S.	P	C, B	M	L	4
Molteni	Furniture	Italy	P	C	N	SM	6, 7, 11
New Halls Wheelchairs	Wheelchairs	U.S.	P	C	N	SM	6
Nintendo	Game consoles	Japan	P	C	M	L	1, 3, 4
Nokia	Telecommunications	Finland	P	C, B	M	L	4, 6
Philips	Consumer electronics	The Netherlands	P	C, B	M	L	2, 6, 9, 10
Safaricom	Telecommunications	Kenya	S	C	M	L	2
Sahean Information Systems	Information technology	Korea	P, S	C, B	M	L	4
Samsung	Consumer electronics	Korea	P	C	M	L	6
Snaidero	Kitchen furniture	Italy	P	C	M	L	2, 7
Sony	Consumer electronics	Japan	P	C	M	L	4
Starbucks	Food services	U.S.	S	C	M	L	2
STMicro-electronics	Semi-conductors	France, Italy	P	B	M	L	4, 7
Swatch Group	Watches	Switzerland	P	C	M	L	1, 4
Texas Instruments	Information technology	U.S.	P	C, B	M	L	3
Whole Foods Market	Retailing	U.S.	S	C	M	L	1
Xerox	Imaging	U.S.	P	C, B	M	L	7
Zucchi Group	Textiles	Italy	P	C	M	L	10

IMPLICATIONS FOR EDUCATION AND DESIGN POLICIES

Many governments have launched policies to support greater use of design in diverse arenas, acknowledging its value and its impact on a country's economic growth. One of the earliest was the United Kingdom, which created a Design Council in 1944 and has since promoted pioneering policies, including a recent strong focus on applying design to service industries and even public services. (For example, the Design Council has launched a new program called Public Services by Design, which has tackled problems such as reducing crime levels in hospital emergency rooms and improving government-owned postal services.)

Other countries have joined the United Kingdom in recent years, beginning with the Scandinavian countries of Denmark, Norway, and especially Finland. The latter developed its first National Design Strategy in 2000, which then became a key element of its National Innovation Strategy in 2008. Although European countries are in the forefront in this field, design policies have taken root all over the world, from Hong Kong to Brazil, from South Korea to India, from Thailand to New Zealand.

TABLE A-1

The typical approach to design policies (left) and the different perspective called for by design-driven innovation (right)

Design policies supporting incremental innovation of meanings	Design policies supporting radical innovation of meanings
Center on collaborations—the more the better	Center on *how* to collaborate and *with whom*
Encourage local collaborations	Encourage global collaborations
Focus on collaborations between firms and designers	Focus on collaborations between firms and multiple interpreters
Educate designers on business	Educate business leaders on design

Most design policies are still in their infancy, with governments experimenting in different directions. Yet these policies usually share four common traits (see the left side of table A-1).

First, design policies often promote collaboration between manufacturers and designers. The underlying hypothesis is that several skilled designers reside in any given local territory and that governments simply need to facilitate local manufacturers' access to this wealth of talent, and innovation will occur. Several government officials have told me that they would like to replicate the miracle of Italian design, where collaboration between manufacturers and designers is amazingly strong. This, however, is an incomplete interpretation of what happens in Italy and of the dynamics of design-driven innovation.

As chapter 7 shows, successful as well as unsuccessful Italian firms have intense collaborations with designers. What differentiates the former from the latter is not whether they collaborate but with *whom* they collaborate and *how*. Collaborating with a generic designer does not make any difference. Or, even worse, collaboration with a generic designer may even be detrimental for a firm, because not all designers are likely to be talented (as in any profession, such as management or engineering). Public policies should instead focus on helping firms develop the capabilities to spot, meet, select, and attract the unidentified, talented designers that best fit their needs.

The Norwegian Design Council is experimenting with interesting measures in this regard. When approaching a manufacturer, the council identifies challenges and opportunities for innovation and introduces the manufacturer to a selection of designers that fit its profile. The designers then illustrate how they would address those challenges and opportunities, and the manufacturer selects the most promising among them.

Second, most public design policies have a narrow, local scope. Governments promote collaborations only among local firms and local designers. The design discourse, however, is global. Talent is internationally distributed, and the best interpreter for a firm is not likely to live a hundred miles from its headquarters. You have seen that 46 percent of the collaborations of innovative Italian furniture manufacturers occur with foreign designers, versus 16 percent of those of unsuccessful manufacturers. What's more, local designers can better profit from selling their services and their insights on the local culture and market to international firms rather than to local ones. Policies should therefore aim to strengthen local participation in global design networks. That approach would strengthen both local manufacturers and the local design industry, regardless of the extent of local links.

Third, public policies often focus on encouraging firms to collaborate only with designers. However, although designers play an important role in design-driven innovation, firms should not have to trust a single designer, no matter how talented she is. You have seen that a firm envisions new scenarios and radical new meanings by combining insights from several interpreters from a variety of categories (designers, firms in other industries, suppliers, retailers, artists, sociologists, and so on).

To support that process, my team at PROject Science and I have helped governments create programs that foster deeper and multifaceted insights into innovation. These programs bring together local firms that offer complementary products and services in a given context, such as nutrition, mobility, or domestic lifestyle. Those firms—which do not compete with each other—collaborate with multiple international interpreters to build common scenarios that each company, individually, could not create because of a lack of contacts or resources. Each single firm then leverages this scenario to create its own radical products.

Finally, many design policies aim to increase the business skills of designers through educational programs. The assumption is that designers who are more business aware can better interact with managers and propose concepts with sound business value. Design schools have targeted this assumption in two ways: by including a variety of courses on business administration in their core programs on industrial design, and by creating new programs that focus specifically on design management, targeted to designers who want to become more business literate. This education strategy closes the gap between designers and managers by bringing the former closer to the latter and by making designers more pragmatic. However, this approach also has a downside: it makes designers more aware of the constraints of business dynamics and less prone to explore radical patterns not yet demanded by markets.

Again, my research (see chapter 7) shows that design-driven innovation follows the opposite path. It often comes from forward-looking researchers who may be business unaware and who have been tapped by business leaders who are significantly design aware. The gap is therefore closed by bringing *managers closer to designers*. These managers said, "Feel free to explore radical new scenarios of how people give meaning to things. Do not worry about the business implications—I'll take care of them. Just think about possible new meanings for users."

Design-driven innovation therefore has profound implications for the education of designers and managers. On the one hand, it requires the support of circles of radical researchers who can perform experiments still not requested by users. On the other hand, as a balancing mechanism, it asks managers to become more design literate. Unfortunately, business schools still neglect the importance of design, apart from a few exceptions, such as the Rotman Business School at the University of Toronto, Copenhagen Business School, and the School of Management at the Politecnico di Milano.

Design-driven innovation, therefore, requires unique policies that move in an opposite although complementary direction compared with traditional design policies. The latter—with their focus on generic collaborations between local firms and local designers who are business aware—tend to promote the diffused use of design, resulting mainly in incremental innovation. Such policies can suit countries where the use of design is still in its infancy, and they can spur an industry to upgrade. But as these traditional policies take effect and countries become more design literate, they are hardly a source of differentiation.

Policies targeted to design-driven innovation then become more interesting and effective. These policies—which could coexist with more-traditional approaches—increase the design awareness of business leaders and encourage them to participate in elite global networks of interpreters. The radical innovations of meaning promoted by these policies increase the chances that local manufacturers and designers—along with their regions and even entire nations—will reap sustainable competitive advantage.

[Notes]

Letter to the Reader

1. Klaus Krippendorff, "On the Essential Contexts of Artifacts, or on the Proposition That 'Design Is Making Sense (of Things),'" *Design Issues* 5, no. 2 (Spring 1989): 9–38.

2. Jeffrey S. Young and William L. Simon, *Icon: Steve Jobs—The Greatest Second Act in the History of Business* (Hoboken, NJ: Wiley, 2005).

3. Richard Florida, *The Rise of the Creative Class—and How It's Transforming Work, Leisure, Community, and Everyday Life* (New York: Perseus, 2002).

4. Michael P. Farrell, *Collaborative Circles: Friendship Dynamics and Creative Work* (Chicago: University of Chicago Press, 2003).

Chapter 1

1. Funded by the Italian Ministry of University and Scientific and Technological Research with a 1.5 million budget, Sistema Design Italia involved seventeen research teams all over Italy. The project's unit of analysis was not products or designers but innovation processes, manufacturers, and economic systems. The project yielded seventy-four in-depth case studies and received the 2001 Compasso d'Oro, the most prestigious design award in Italy—the first time a research project won the prize.

2. Where possible I pursued the approach of case immersion and close contact with the senior executives who led the innovation process. Otherwise, especially for firms that limit the amount of information they disclose (Apple is a well-known example), I relied on secondary sources, in which case I provide the references.

3. Steve Jobs, keynote speech at the Macworld Conference & Expo, San Francisco, January 15, 2008, emphasis added.

4. For a deeper analysis of differences between open and closed modes of collaboration with external parties see Gary P. Pisano and Roberto Verganti, "Which Kind of

Collaboration Is Right for You? The new leaders in innovation will be those who figure out the best way to leverage a network of outsiders," *Harvard Business Review* 86, no. 12 (December 2008): 78–86.

Chapter 2

1. Peter Butenschøn, "Worlds Apart: An International Agenda for Design" (keynote speech at the Design Research Society, Common Ground International Conference, Brunel University, UK, September 5, 2002).

2. The book that Manzini suggested was Renato De Fusco, *Storia del Design* [History of Design] (Bari, Italy: Laterza, 1985), a comprehensive analysis of the evolution of design, in Italian. For books in English, see John Heskett, *Industrial Design* (London: Thames and Hudson, 1985), and Penny Sparke, *An Introduction to Design and Culture: 1900 to the Present,* 2nd edition (London: Routledge, 2004).

3. The robust scientific debate on the definition of design rests on a rich array of contributions. For a glimpse into this debate, see Victor Margolin, ed., *Design Discourse: History, Theory and Criticism* (Chicago: University of Chicago Press, 1989), and Victor Margolin and Richard Buchanan, eds., *The Idea of Design* (Cambridge, MA: MIT Press, 1996). For an epistemological discussion, see Terence Love, "Philosophy of Design: A Metatheoretical Structure for Design Theory," *Design Studies* 21 (2000): 293–313; and Per Galle, "Philosophy of Design: An Editorial Introduction," *Design Studies* 23 (2002): 211–218. An introduction to design targeted to MBA students is Robert D. Austin, Silje Kamille Friis, and Erin E. Sullivan, "Design: More Than a Cool Chair," Note 9-607-026 (Boston: Harvard Business School Press, 2007).

4. Ted Koppel, *Nightline*, ABC News, July 13, 1999.

5. For an interesting investigation of the struggle between beauty and cultural progress, see Umberto Eco, ed., *History of Beauty* (Milano: Rizzoli, 2004).

6. Vivien Walsh, Robin Roy, Margaret Bruce, and Stephen Potter, *Winning by Design: Technology, Product Design and International Competitiveness* (Cambridge, MA: Blackwell Business, 1992).

7. International Council of Societies of Industrial Design, http://www.icsid.org/about/about/main/articles33.htm.

8. International Council of Societies of Industrial Design, http://www.icsid.org/about/about/articles31.htm.

9. On branding, see Design Management Institute, "18 Views on the Definition of Design Management," *Design Management Journal* (summer 1998): 14–19. On understanding user needs, see Karel Vredenburg, Scott Isensee, and Carol Righi, *User-Centered Design: An Integrated Approach* (Upper Saddle River, NJ: Prentice Hall, 2002); and Robert W. Veryzer and Brigitte Borja de Mozota, "The Impact of User-Oriented Design on New Product Development: An Examination of Fundamental Relationships," *Journal of Product Innovation Management* 22 (2005): 128–143. On business strategy and organizational design, see Roger Martin, "The Design of Business," *Rotman Management* (Winter 2004): 9. On market design, see Alvin E. Roth, "The Art of Designing Markets," *Harvard Business Review* (October 2007).

10. Herbert Simon, *The Sciences of the Artificial*, 2nd ed. (Cambridge, MA: MIT Press, 1982), 129.

11. Herbert Simon, *The Sciences of the Artificial*, 3rd ed. (Cambridge, MA: MIT Press, 1996), xii.

12. Tim Brown, "Design Thinking," *Harvard Business Review* (June 2008): 84–92.

13. Richard Boland and Fred Collopy have edited a book on this debate: *Managing as Designing* (Palo Alto, CA: Stanford Business Books, 2004). In their introduction, they point to a weakness of management education: "We portray the manager as facing a set of alternatives from which a choice must be made. This decision attitude assumes it is easy to come up with alternatives to consider, but difficult to choose among them. The design attitude towards problem solving, in contrast, assumes that it is difficult to design a good alternative, but once you have developed a truly good one, the decision about which alternative to select is trivial. The design attitude appreciates that the cost of not conceiving a better alternative is often much higher than making the wrong choice among existing alternatives. In a clearly defined and stable situation, when the feasible alternatives are well known, the decision attitude may be the best approach. But in the current context a design attitude is required. In our focus on teaching students advanced analytical techniques for choosing among alternatives, our attention to strengthening their design skills for shaping new alternatives has withered."

14. We discuss the implications for business and design education that emerge from this study in appendix B.

15. Designers themselves tend to stretch the boundaries of their discipline. However, as Thomas Maldonado has noted, this undermines the field: "[There is] a progressive desemanticization of the word *design*. As it is applied to respond to the programmatic (and promotional) needs of all kinds of activities—the architect, the engineer, the designer, the fashion stylist, the scientist, the philosopher, the manager, the politician, the programmer, the administrator—the word winds up losing its specific meaning . . . In some languages people are trying to avoid the use of the word *design* . . . This indeterminacy appears today as the main obstacle to a definition of design as a discipline" (opening lecture, Design + Research Conference, Milano, May 18, 2000).

16. For a complete case study of the development of Metamorfosi, see Giuliano Simonelli and Francesco Zurlo, "Metamorfosi di Artemide: la luce che cambia la luce" ["Metamorfosi by Artemide: The Light That Changes the Light"], in Francesco Zurlo, Raffaella Cagliano, Giuliano Simonelli, and Roberto Verganti, *Innovare con il Design. Il caso del settore dell'illuminazione in Italia* [Innovating Through Design: The Case of the Lighting Industry in Italy] (Milano: Il Sole 24 Ore, 2002).

17. Ibid., 55.

18. Ibid., 56.

19. The system consists of a patented electronic control system that can create and memorize several combinations of monochromatic lights and haloes generated by three parabolic reflectors equipped with dichroic filters.

20. Philips has recently launched a product, LivingColors, with exactly the same meaning, and even the same product language as Metamorfosi, although based on more recent LCD technologies. Many other imitations of the Metamorfosi concept have followed, such as the light cube by Viteo. The fact that ten years later, Metamorfosi still sells for eight times the price of these imitations is proof of the value of the Artemide vision, and the prize for having been first on the market.

21. Klaus Krippendorff, "On the Essential Contexts of Artifacts or on the Proposition That 'Design Is Making Sense (of Things),'" *Design Issues* 5, no. 2 (Spring 1989): 9–38. See also Klaus Krippendorff, *The Semantic Turn: A New Foundation for Design* (Boca Raton, FL: CRC Press, 2006). This proposition is perfectly in line with the archaic definition of design. See, for example, Merriam-Webster: Design – 1: to create, fashion, execute, or construct according to plan: devise, contrive. 2 a: to conceive and plan out in the mind. b: to have as a purpose. c: to devise for a specific function or end. 3 *archaic:* to *indicate* with a distinctive mark, sign, or name [italics added]. 4 a: to make a drawing, pattern, or sketch of. b: to draw the plans for. Merriam Webster Online, http://mw1.merriam-webster.com/dictionary/design.

22. See, for example, John Heskett, *Toothpicks and Logos: Design in Everyday Life* (Oxford: Oxford University Press, 2002): "Design, stripped to its essence, can be defined as the human capacity to make our environment in ways without precedent in nature, to serve our needs, and give us meaning in our lives." For other discussions of design and meaning, see Rachel Cooper and Mike Press, *The Design Agenda* (Chicester, UK: Wiley, 1995); Nigan Bayazit, "Investigating Design: A Review of Forty Years of Design Research," *Design Issues* 20 (Winter 2004): 1; and Donald A. Norman, *Emotional Design: Why We Love (or Hate) Everyday Things* (New York: Basic Books, 2004).

23. Margolin and Buchanan, *The Idea of Design: A Design Issues Reader,* xix.

24. Mihalyi Csikszentmihalyi and Eugenie Rochberg-Halton, *The Meaning of Things: Domestic Symbols and the Self* (Cambridge: Cambridge University Press, 1981).

25. Among sociologists, see, for example, the postmodern and post-structuralist Jean Baudrillard, *The System of Objects,* trans. James Benedict (London and New York: Verso Books, 1968). On the anthropology of consumption, see, for example, Mary Douglas and Baron Isherwood, *The World of Goods: Towards an Anthropology of Consumption* (Harmondsworth, UK: Penguin, 1980).

26. Andries Van Onck, "Semiotics in Design Practice" (Design + Research Conference, Milano, May 18–20, 2000); and Giampaolo Proni, "Outlines for a Semiotic Analysis of Objects," *Versus* 91/92 (January–August 2002): 37–59.

27. Sidney J. Levy, "Symbols for Sale," *Harvard Business Review* 37 (July–August 1959): 118. For consequent studies see, for example, Robert A. Peterson, Wayne D. Hoyer, and William R. Wilson, *The Role of Affect in Consumer Behaviour: Emerging Theories and Applications* (Lexington, MA: Lexington Books, 1986); Elizabeth C. Hirschman, "The Creation of Product Symbolism," *Advances in Consumer Research* 13 (1986): 327–331; Robert E. Kleine III, Susan Schultz Kleine, and Jerome B. Kernan, "Mundane Consumption and the Self: A Social-Identity Perspective," *Journal of Consumer Psychology* 2, no. 3 (1993): 209–235; Susan Fournier, "A Meaning-Based Framework for the Study of Consumer/Object Relations," *Advances in Consumer Research* 18 (1991): 736–742; Jagdish N. Sheth, Bruce I. Newman, and Barbara L. Gross, "Why We Buy What We Buy: A Theory of Consumption Values," *Journal of Business Research* 22 (1991): 159–170; and Gerald Zaltman, *How Customers Think: Essential Insights into the Mind of the Market* (Boston: Harvard Business School Press, 2003). For a recent review, see Susan Boztepe, "User Value: Competing Theories and Models," *International Journal of Design* 1, no. 2 (2007): 57–65.

28. Joseph B. Pine and James H. Gilmore, *The Experience Economy: Work Is Theatre and Every Business a Stage* (Boston: Harvard Business School Press, 1999); Berndt

Schmitt, *Experiential Marketing: How to Get Customers to Sense, Feel, Think, ACT, and Relate to Your Company and Brands* (New York: Free Press, 1999).

29. Clayton M. Christensen, Scott Cook, and Taddy Hall, "Marketing Malpractice: The Cause and the Cure," *Harvard Business Review* 83, no. 12 (December 2005): 74–83; Clayton M. Christensen, Scott D. Anthony, Gerald N. Berstell, and Denise Nitterhouse, "Finding the Right Job for Your Product," *MIT Sloan Management Review* 48, no. 3 (Spring 2007): 38–47.

30. Heskett, *Toothpicks and Logos: Design in Everyday Life.*

31. "The increasingly appealing suggestion that *form* may not follow *function* but *meaning*, brings the *user* back into the picture and strongly suggests that designers need to discuss not only the contexts in which their forms are used, but also how these forms are made sense of or what they mean to someone other than themselves." Krippendorff, "On the Essential Contexts of Artifacts or on the Proposition That 'Design Is Making Sense (of Things).'"

32. Stephen Brown, *Postmodern Marketing* (London: Routledge, 1995).

33. Bernhard Wild, "Invisible Advantage: How Intangibles Are Driving Business Performance" (7th European Design Management Conference, Design Management Institute, Cologne, Germany, March 16–18, 2003).

34. Managers in design-intensive firms are aware of the profound difference between luxury and design, even when they are positioned in the high end of the market. Flemming Møller Pedersen, director of design and concepts at Bang & Olufsen, once told me, "We constantly strive to do our best. Eventually it might happen that it costs a lot. But we do not target luxury. A Vertu phone is luxury, they target luxury." Piero Gandini, CEO of Flos, another iconic Italian lamp manufacturer, shares this philosophy: "We are not a luxury firm. We have products from 50 to 5,000 euros. Luxury separates. Our aim is to unite, not to separate."

35. See, for example, Massimo Montanari, *Food Is Culture (Arts and Traditions of the Table: Perspectives on Culinary History)* (New York: Columbia University Press, 2006), and Franco La Cecla, *Pasta and Pizza* (Chicago: Prickly Paradigm Press, 2007).

36. The theory of product languages is fairly well developed both within design (see, for example, Toni-Matti Karjalainen, "Strategic Design Language: Transforming Brand Identity into Product Design Elements," 10th EIASM International Product Development Management Conference, Brussels, June 10–11, 2003) and within semiotics. See, for example, Proni, "Outlines for a Semiotic Analysis of Objects." For an analysis of the link between product languages and innovation, see Claudio Dell'Era and Roberto Verganti, "Strategies of Innovation and Imitation of Product Languages," *Journal of Product Innovation Management* 24 (2007): 580–599.

Chapter 3

1. This is an excerpt from a master's thesis by Elisabeth Glickfeld, a student at Swinburne University, sent to Alberto Alessi by eighty-seven-year-old British psychoanalyst Harold Bridger (who had worked for many years with Donald Winnicott). Cited in Alberto Alessi, *La storia della Alessi dal 1921 al 2005 e il fenomeno delle Fabbriche del design italiano* [The History of Alessi from 1921 to 2005 and the Phenomenon of the Italian Design Factories], unpublished.

2. Donald W. Winnicott, "Transitional Objects and Transitional Phenomena," *International Journal of Psychoanalysis* 34 (1953): 89–97.

3. The paternal code relates to the functional-institutional side of things, the maternal code to gratification, the childish code to playfulness, the erotic codes to the survival of the species, and the code of birth and death to personal survival and the contrast between growth and regression. Franco Fornari, *La vita affettiva originaria del bambino* [The primordial affective life of the child] (Milano: Feltrinelli, 1963).

4. Alessi, *La storia della Alessi dal 1921 al 2005 e il fenomeno delle Fabbriche del design italiano.* Note that Alessi calls his research projects "meta-projects," because they occur before product development. Chapter 8 describes Tea and Coffee Piazza, a research metaproject that eventually led to Michael Graves's kettle with a whistling bird.

5. Jacob Jensen (keynote speech, 12th EIASM International Product Development Management Conference, Copenhagen Business School, Copenhagen, June 11–12, 2005). Curiously, eventually some competitors understood that audio systems should speak the language of apartments more than laboratories. They did not change their design approach, however. They kept the same meaning of their instruments and simply added wooden covers around the racks to superficially make them more like furniture, as if it were simply a matter of body material. Indeed, the audio systems of Bang & Olufsen stand apart as unique, often in flat, thin forms, with a user interface designed to facilitate interaction, often with some touch of magic (such as the front cover of the CD players that opens automatically as the user approaches). Bang & Olufsen used very little wood in its audio system but rather used polished aluminum, and that helped to convey a sense of contemporary lifestyle in houses.

6. Giuliano Simonelli and Francesco Zurlo, "Metamorfosi di Artemide: la luce che cambia la luce" [Metamorfosi by Artemide: The Light That Changes the Light], in Francesco Zurlo, Raffaella Cagliano, Giuliano Simonelli, and Roberto Verganti, *Innovare con il Design. Il caso del settore dell'illuminazione in Italia* [Innovating Through Design: The Case of the Lighting Industry in Italy] (Milano: Il Sole 24 Ore, 2002), 55.

7. Alessi, *La storia della Alessi dal 1921 al 2005 e il fenomeno delle Fabbriche del design italiano*, 15.

8. Alberto Alessi, *The Design Factory* (London: Academy Editions, 1994), 105, italics added.

9. Alberto Alessi, interview by author, tape recording, Omegna (VB), October 12, 2006.

10. Flemming Møller Pedersen (speech, Copenhagen Business School, Design Management course, June 20, 2007), italics added.

11. Gene M. Franz and Richard H. Wiggins, "Design Case History: Speak & Spell Learns to Talk," *IEEE Spectrum* (February 1982): 45–49.

12. Kenji Hall, "The Big Ideas Behind Nintendo's Wii," *BusinessWeek*, November 16, 2006.

13. Jeffrey S. Young and William L. Simon, *iCon: Steve Jobs: The Greatest Second Act in the History of Business* (Hoboken, NJ: Wiley, 2005), 264.

14. Ibid., 262.

15. Clayton M. Christensen, *The Innovator's Dilemma: When New Technologies Cause Great Firms to Fail* (Boston: Harvard Business School Press, 1997).

16. According to Clifford Geertz, "Culture denotes an historically transmitted pattern of meanings embodied in symbolic forms by means of which men communicate, perpetuate and develop their knowledge about and attitudes toward life." *The Interpretation of Cultures* (New York: Basic Books, 1973), 69. For further references to studies of products, meanings, and sociocultural models, see chapter 2.

17. For more on the concept of technological regimes, see Richard R. Nelson and Sidney G. Winter, "In Search of a Useful Theory of Innovation," *Research Policy* 6 (1977): 36–67. Giovanni Dosi introduced the concept of technological paradigms in "Technological Paradigms and Technological Trajectories: A Suggested Interpretation of the Determinants and Directions of Technical Change," *Research Policy* 11 (1982): 147–162. For more on sociocultural regimes, see Frank W. Geels, "From Sectoral Systems of Innovation to Socio-technical Systems: Insights About Dynamics and Change from Sociology and Institutional Theory," *Research Policy* 33 (2004): 897–920.

18. An intense debate in the 1970s on technology push versus market pull culminated in Giovanni Dosi's milestone contribution (Dosi, "Technological Paradigms and Technological Trajectories: A Suggested Interpretation of the Determinants and Directions of Technical Change"). Dosi suggested that any innovation implies an understanding of technologies as well as markets. However, breakthrough changes in technology (what he calls new technological paradigms) are mainly technology push, whereas incremental innovations within existing technological paradigms are mainly market pull. More recent research on the relationship between disruptive innovations and user needs shares this approach. See, for example, Clayton M. Christensen and Richard S. Rosenbloom, "Explaining the Attacker's Advantage: Technological Paradigms, Organizational Dynamics, and the Value Network," *Research Policy* 24 (1995): 233–257; Clayton M. Christensen and Joseph L. Bower, "Customer Power, Strategic Investment, and the Failure of Leading Firms," *Strategic Management Journal* 17 (1996): 197–218; and Clayton M. Christensen, *The Innovator's Dilemma: When New Technologies Cause Great Firms to Fail.*

19. Summarizing years of research in this field would be a Herculean endeavor. In addition to the studies cited earlier, see also William J. Abernathy and Kim B. Clark, "Innovation: Mapping the Winds of Creative Destruction," *Research Policy* 14 (1985): 3–22; Michael L. Tushman and Philip Anderson, "Technological Discontinuities and Organizational Environments," *Administrative Science Quarterly* 31, no. 3 (1986): 439–465; James M. Utterback, *Mastering the Dynamics of Innovation* (Boston: Harvard Business School Press, 1994); Henry Chesbrough, "Assembling the Elephant: A Review of Empirical Studies on the Impact of Technical Change upon Incumbent Firms," in *Comparative Studies of Technological Evolution*, ed. Robert A. Burgleman and Henry Chesbrough (Oxford: Elsevier, 2001), 1–36; and Kristina B. Dahlin and Dean M. Behrens, "When Is an Invention Really Radical? Defining and Measuring Technological Radicalness," *Research Policy* 34 (2005): 717–737.

20. "Herman Miller's Brian Walker on Design," *@issue* 12, no. 1 (2007): 2–7.

Chapter 4

1. A. D., "Game Watch, " *Sports Illustrated*, July 2, 2007, 26.

2. People often claim that Microsoft has used market dominance to survive several transitions in technologies and meanings over three decades. However, this is not

completely correct. As Alan MacCormack and Marco Iansiti show in "Intellectual Property, Architecture, and the Management of Technological Transitions: Evidence from Microsoft Corporation" (forthcoming in *Journal of Product Innovation Management*), the company has survived thanks to its superior ability to define the architecture of its products and components. The resulting market dominance, in turn, has allowed Microsoft to passively survive transitions in meanings, such as the way people love to use icons and graphical user interfaces to interact with a PC and to access the Internet through browsers. Indeed, one of Microsoft's greatest weaknesses seems to be its inability to lead in design-driven innovation.

3. Sociologists of technology have focused especially on how technological breakthroughs spur cultural transitions (think of how the Internet has changed our lives). Bruno Latour's actor-network theory, in particular, links technological evolution to the network of human and nonhuman actors that can support or prevent its development. See Bruno Latour, *Science in Action: How to Follow Scientists and Engineers Through Society* (Cambridge, MA: Harvard University Press, 1987); Wiebe E. Bijker and John Law, eds., *Shaping Technology/Building Society: Studies in Sociotechnical Change* (Cambridge, MA: MIT Press, 1994); and, more recently, Frank W. Geels, "From Sectoral Systems of Innovation to Socio-technical Systems: Insights About Dynamics and Change from Sociology and Institutional Theory," *Research Policy* 33 (2004): 897–920. On the coevolution of technology and society, see also Dorothy Leonard-Barton, "Implementation as Mutual Adaptation of Technology and Organization," *Research Policy* 17 (1988): 251–267.

4. This discussion of the Nintendo Wii comes from several sources, in particular Kenji Hall, "The Big Ideas Behind Nintendo's Wii," *BusinessWeek*, November 16, 2006; Kris Graft, "iSuppli: 60GB PS3 Costs $840 to Produce," *Next Generation*, November 16, 2006; James Griffiths, "The Name of the Game," *Environmental Engineering* (Winter 2006/2007): 30–34; Kenji Hall, "Nintendo Scores Ever Higher," *BusinessWeek Online*, June 27, 2007; A. D., "Game Watch," *Sports Illustrated*, July 2, 2007, 26; Matt Richtel and Eric A. Taub, "In Battle of Consoles, Nintendo Gains Allies," *New York Times*, July 17, 2007; Christopher Megerian, "A Wii Workout," *BusinessWeek Online*, August 3, 2007; Beth Snyder Bulik, "Chips, Dip and Nintendo Wii," *Advertising Age* (Midwest region edition) 78, no. 34 (August 27, 2007): 4; Ann Steffora Mutschler, "Nintendo Wii Trumps Xbox 360 in Sales," *Electronic News* 52, no. 35 (August 27, 2007); "Sony's Plan to Cut PS3 Costs," *BusinessWeek Online*, September 20, 2007; Mariko Sanchanta, "Nintendo's Wii Takes Console Lead," *Financial Times*, September 12, 2007; and Devin Henry, "Nintendo's Wii Finds Use in Physical Therapy," *Minnesota Daily*, October 12, 2007.

5. The Xbox 360 has a high-speed IBM 3.2GHz Xenon CPU, up to a 120GB hard drive, and superior multimedia functionality, and it is associated with blockbuster titles such as Halo3, which offer advanced and detailed graphics. The PlayStation 3 has a 3.2GHz multicore Cell chip and a high-definition Blu-Ray DVD player.

6. Hall, "The Big Ideas Behind Nintendo's Wii."

7. Quoted in Henry, "Nintendo's Wii Finds Use in Physical Therapy."

8. Quoted in William Taylor, "Message and Muscle: An Interview with Swatch Titan Nicolas Hayek," *Harvard Business Review* (March–April 1993): 99–110.

9. This discussion of the Swatch comes from several sources, in particular Amy Glasmeier, "Technological Discontinuities and Flexible Production Networks: The Case of Switzerland and the World Watch Industry," *Research Policy* 20

(1991): 469–485; Taylor, "Message and Muscle: An Interview with Swatch Titan Nicolas Hayek"; Dominik E. D. Zehnder and John J. Gabarro, "Nicolas G. Hayek," Case 9-495-005 (Boston: Harvard Business School, 1994); Cyril Bouquet and Allen Morrison, "Swatch and the Global Watch Industry," Case 9A99M023 (London, Ontario: Richard Ivey School of Business, University of Western Ontario, 1999); Cate Reavis, Carin-Isabel Knoop, and Luc Wathieu, "The Swatch Group: On Internet Time," Case 9-500-014 (Boston: Harvard Business School, 2000); Daniel B. Radov and Michael L. Tushman, "Rebirth of the Swiss Watch Industry, 1980–1992 (A)," Case 9-400-087 (Boston: Harvard Business School, 2000); Daniel B. Radov and Michael L. Tushman, "Rebirth of the Swiss Watch Industry, 1980–1992 (B): Hayek and Thomke at SMH," Case 9-400-088 (Boston: Harvard Business School, 2000); Youngme Moon, "The Birth of the Swatch," Case 9-504-096 (Boston: Harvard Business School, 2004).

10. Quoted in Taylor, "Message and Muscle: An Interview with Swatch Titan Nicolas Hayek."

11. Zehnder and Gabarro, "Nicolas G. Hayek."

12. Quoted in Taylor, "Message and Muscle: An Interview with Swatch Titan Nicolas Hayek."

13. Ibid.

14. http://www.systemshootouts.org/ipod_sales.html.

15. Marco Polo, *The Travels*, trans. Ronald Latham (London: Penguin Books, 1958), 48.

16. See, for example, James M. Utterback, *Mastering the Dynamics of Innovation* (Boston: Harvard Business School Press, 1994).

17. Giampaolo Proni, interview by author, Bologna, November 15, 2007.

18. Etimologically, *epiphany* means a "manifestation" that "stands in a superior position," Merriam Webster Online, http://mw1.merriam-webster.com/dictionary/epiphany. Hence the use of the term to describe the revelation of a technology's more competitively powerful meaning.

19. The stream of studies on "lead users" shows that innovation sometimes emerges through users outside the market mainstream (i.e., extreme users) who have the ability to play with the new technology. This occurs especially when no companies are actively searching for the quiescent meanings of new technologies. See, for example, Eric Von Hippel, *Democratized Innovation* (Cambridge, MA: MIT Press, 2005).

20. Stefan Thomke and Eric Von Hippel, "Customers as Innovators: A New Way to Create Value," *Harvard Business Review* 80, no. 4 (April 2002): 74–81.

21. All quotations for this STMicroelectronics case come from author interviews with executives of the firm conducted in December 2007 and January 2008.

22. Eckard Foltin, "Develop Today What Will Be Needed Tomorrow," *VisionWorks* 5 (2007): 37.

23. Curiously, Corning could envision sociocultural changes by pursuing privileged interactions with designers and artists. That's because in 1918 Corning acquired Steuben, a maker of art glass that, thanks to Corning's innovations, soon became famous for its purity and clarity. Corning's president at the time, Alanson B. Houghton, had expected a resulting fruitful exchange between the arts and industry. Michael Graves and Richard Meier, for example, have designed for Steuben. However, despite Houghton's hopes, the firm has not seized on this strategic connection between

technology-push and design-driven innovation. According to one Corning scientist, the company regularly interacts with Steuben, but its scientists focus on keeping the quality of the glass and its other properties as consistent as possible. Situations sometimes arise in which Corning scientists alter the composition of the glass, but such changes typically meet with protest, because they interfere with the production of standard products. It was only recently that Steuben approached Corning for the first time in many decades about developing colored glass.

Chapter 5

1. http://www.jacobjensen.com/#/int/heritage/jacob_jensen/technology/pages/page1.

2. The gift market may be a key source of high volumes. When people want to give a present, delightful and unique products typically win over anonymous, functional ones (as Alberto Alessi says, "We have double sales: one for yourself, and one for a friend"). And gift revenues are significant in many markets. For example, the number of iPods sold during the Christmas season is about the same as the number sold during the remaining part of the year.

3. For further insights on compatibility in product languages, see Rossella Cappetta, Paola Cillo, and Anna Ponti, "Convergent Designs in Fine Fashion: An Evolutionary Model for Stylistic Innovation," *Research Policy* 35 (2006): 1273–1290.

4. A leaf spring suspension is a simple form of spring, based on several layers of slender arc-shaped lengths of steel, historically used in carriages and then in old automobiles, and now used only in heavy vehicles.

5. Vijay Vaitheeswaran, "Revving Up," *Economist*, October 11, 2007.

6. Susan Sanderson and Yi-Nung Peng, "Business Classics: The Role of Outstanding Design in the Survival and Success of Apple Computer" (Rensselaer, NY: Lally School of Management, Rensselaer Polytechnic Institute, 2003).

7. This analysis of business classics in the automotive industry draws significantly on investigations conducted with Susan Sanderson and Alessio Marchesi. See Alessio Marchesi, Roberto Verganti, and Susan Sanderson, "Design Driven Innovation and the Development of Business Classics in the Automobile Industry" (paper presented at the 10th International Product Development Management Conference, EIASM, Brussels, Belgium, June 2003); and Alessio Marchesi, "Business Classics: Managing Innovation through Product Longevity" (PhD dissertation, Politecnico di Milano, 2005). I am indebted to their stimulating insights.

8. Interview with Giorgietto Giugiaro in Paolo Malagodi, "Un amore chiamato Panda" (A Love Called Panda), *IlSole24Ore*, August 31, 2003, 14.

9. Ibid.

10. Kim B. Clark and Takahiro Fujimoto, *Product Development Performance* (Cambridge, MA: Harvard Business School Press, 1991).

11. Susan Sanderson and Mustafa Uzumeri, *Managing Product Families* (New York: Irwin/McGraw Hill, 1997).

12. Alberto Alessi, *La storia della Alessi dal 1921 al 2005 e il fenomeno delle Fabbriche del design italiano* ("The History of Alessi from 1921 to 2005 and the Phenomenon of the Italian Design Factories"), unpublished.

13. Clayton M. Christensen, *The Innovator's Dilemma: When New Technologies Cause Great Firms to Fail* (Boston: Harvard Business School Press, 1997).

14. Jennifer Fishbein, "Bang & Olufsen's Sorensen Out," *BusinessWeek Online,* January 10, 2008.

Chapter 6

1. I talk in this regard of the "seductive power" of the interpreters. This notion mirrors the concept of semiotic power proposed by theories on the sociology of technology. This concept indicates the power of an actor, especially in relevant social groups, to influence and elaborate the meaning of artifacts. See Wiebe E. Bijker and John Law, eds., *Shaping Technology/Building Society: Studies in Sociotechnical Change* (Cambridge, MA: MIT Press, 1994).

2. Note that the term *design discourse* has been used in different contexts with different acceptations—for example, to indicate the debate on the definition of design and its scope (see Victor Margolin, ed., *Design Discourse: History, Theory and Criticism,* Chicago: University of Chicago Press, 1989). In this book I use this term to address the research process on the meaning of things, a process that always occurs in society through the interaction of a network of interpreters. In fact, as you will see in chapter 7, these interactions in society have the form of a debate—a continuous discourse— about making sense of things, that is, about design.

3. A branch of sociology, usually referred to as production of culture, has thoroughly investigated the process through which actors in creative industries help shape the symbolic elements of culture. See, for example, Howard S. Becker, "Art as Collective Action," *American Sociological Review* 39, no. 6 (1974): 767–776; Howard S. Becker, *Art Worlds* (Berkeley: University of California Press, 1982); Paul Du Gay, ed., *Production of Culture/Cultures of Production,* (London: Sage, 1997); David Hesmondhalgh, *The Cultural Industries* (London: Sage, 2002); and Richard A. Peterson and Narasimhan Anand, "The Production of Culture Perspective," *Annual Review of Sociology* 30 (2004): 311–334.

4. Investigations in the field of the sociology of art have shown that artists are not lone creators but are immersed in a web of social influences and interactions. See, for example, Pierre Bourdieu, *Distinction: A Social Critique of the Judgment of Taste* (Cambridge, MA: Harvard University Press, 1984); and Vera L. Zolberg, *Constructing a Sociology of the Arts* (New York: Cambridge University, 1990). For an application of these theories to design, see Jeffrey F. Durgee, "Freedom for Superstar Designers? Lessons from Art History," *Design Management Review* 17, no. 3 (Summer 2006): 29–34.

5. Hesmondhalgh, *The Cultural Industries.*

6. Scholars in the field of production of culture see the mass media as gatekeepers that act as "institutional regulators of innovations"— that is, they may promote or filter changes in culture, meanings, and languages. See, for example, Paul M. Hirsch, "Processing Fads and Fashions: An Organization-Set Analysis of Cultural Industry Systems," *American Journal of Sociology* 77 (January 1972): 639–659.

7. Sociologists of technology, particularly proponents of the actor-network theory, have deeply investigated the process through which novel technology challenges the dominant sociocultural paradigms. These theories illustrate the process through which

different social actors provide their own interpretations of the technology and negotiate a common meaning until they reach an agreement. See Bruno Latour, *Science in Action: How to Follow Scientists and Engineers Through Society* (Cambridge, MA: Harvard University Press, 1987); and Bijker and Law, *Shaping Technology/Building Society*.

8. http://www.materialconnexion.com/PB2.asp.

9. For other examples of Artemide's participation in special architectural projects, see www.artemide.com.

10. John A. Quelch and Carin-Isabel Knoop, "Marketing the $100 PC (A)," Case N2-508-024 (Boston: Harvard Business School, August 2007).

11. Stefano Marzano, "People as a Source of Breakthrough Innovation," *Design Management Review* 16, no. 2 (Spring 2005): 23–29.

12. Karen J. Freeze and Kyung-won Chung, "Design Strategy at Samsung Electronics: Becoming a Top Tier Company," (Boston: The Design Management Institute, 2008).

13. Eric Von Hippel has long investigated the role of lead users in innovation. His major contributions include *The Sources of Innovation* (New York: Oxford University Press, 1988) and *Democratized Innovation* (Cambridge, MA: MIT Press, 2005). For an interesting account of innovation of meanings in the wheelchair industry, see Jim Utterback, Bengt-Arne Vedin, Eduardo Alvarez, Sten Ekman, Susan Sanderson, Bruce Tether, and Roberto Verganti, *Design-Inspired Innovation* (Singapore: World Scientific, 2006).

14. Recent studies on technological innovation have shown that similar dynamics also occur in science- and engineering-driven industries. Theories of collaborative innovation show how firms—aware of the growing complexity of technologies and the enormous stock of knowledge developed outside their boundaries—are increasingly cooperating with external labs, ventures, and universities. See, for example, Henry W. Chesbrough, *Open Innovation: The New Imperative for Creating and Profiting from Technology* (Boston: Harvard Business School Press, 2003); and Larry Huston and Nabil Sakkab, "Connect and Develop: Inside Procter & Gamble's New Model for Innovation," *Harvard Business Review* 84, no. 3 (March 2006): 58–66. In this perspective, design-intensive firms can be seen as precursors of open innovation models. Scholars and practitioners engaged in understanding collaborative innovation can consider these practices an interesting arena for investigation. For a comprehensive model of collaborative innovation, embracing both technology and design, see Gary P. Pisano and Roberto Verganti, "Which Kind of Collaboration Is Right for You? The new leaders in innovation will be those who figure out the best way to leverage a network of outsiders," *Harvard Business Review* 86, no. 12 (December 2008): 78–86.

15. Indeed, design-intensive Italian manufacturers seldom have processes and methods to formally conduct trend analyses. If they need these studies, they usually outsource them to external consultants. This does not impair their innovative capabilities, given that these studies are only one of the multiple insights these manufacturers absorb from the design discourse and then integrate in a unique fashion.

Chapter 7

1. Regarding media, see Jay Greene, "Where Designers Rule: Electronics Maker Bang & Olufsen Doesn't Ask Shoppers What They Want; Its Faith Is in Its Design Gurus," *BusinessWeek*, November 5, 2007; Jeffrey F. Durgee, "Freedom for Superstar

Designers? Lessons from Art History," *Design Management Review* 17, no. 3 (Summer 2006): 29–34. An example of the superstar stereotype is Van den Puup, a fictional superstar designer invented by IKEA to challenge high-end furniture manufacturers. Van den Puup, who appeared in IKEA advertisements in the United Kingdom, is the quintessential personification of the capricious and elitist design guru. A flamboyant figure, physically halfway between Philippe Starck and Marcel Wanders, he dictates the latest rules of luxury lifestyle and throws fits when he sees that IKEA can manufacture similar things at a low price. See his fictional Web site at http://www.elitedesigners.org/.

2. Steve Hamm, "Richard Sapper: Fifty Years at the Drawing Board," *Business Week*, January 10, 2008, http://www.businessweek.com/magazine/content/08_03/b4067038197222.htm.

3. See Claudio Dell'Era and Roberto Verganti, "Strategies to Leverage on Creative Networks in Design-Intensive Industries" (paper presented at the 14th International EurOMA conference, Ankara, Turkey, June 17–20, 2007). The analysis focused on a sample of 658 collaborations between 98 companies and their designers. Innovators (25 percent of the sample) are companies that have been awarded the Compasso d'Oro, the most prestigious design award in Italy. Data on the collaborations comes from Webmobili (www.webmobili.it), the most comprehensive database on the Italian furniture industry.

4. Peter Lawrence, "Herman Miller's Brian Walker on Design," *@issue* 12, no. 1 (Winter 2007): 2–7.

5. Note that when we search for interpreters, we are not looking for a generic institution (such as a white goods manufacturer) or a category (e.g., a journalist). We are looking for specific people—for *that* manager of Snaidero and for *that* journalist from *Stern*.

6. Roberto Verganti and Claudio Dell'Era, *I Distretti del Design: Modello e quadro comparato delle politiche di sviluppo* [The Design Districts: A Model and a Comparative Framework of Development Policies] (Milano: Finlombarda, 2003).

7. For a discussion of effective policies to support design-driven innovation see appendix B.

8. In the past few years, several studies have promoted open approaches to innovation, implying that firms may create and develop innovation by sourcing from crowds of anonymous external contributors, including users, scientists, inventors, and so forth. However, my recent studies with Gary Pisano have shown that open innovation, albeit an interesting option, is neither the sole nor the best way to leverage outsiders. The choice between "open" or "closed" modes (such as the one described in this book, which is based on collaboration with a selected, unique, and privileged circle of key external parties), strictly depends on the innovation problem at hand. In particular, design-driven innovation consists of solving innovation problems that are ambiguous (based on intangible features, such as meaning and product language, rather than codified performance and functionality), integral (they cannot be decomposed in smaller and modular problems that can be solved independently), complex, and hard to test by external contributors. In this case, we show that closed modes of collaboration are way more effective. For an extensive framework that leads managers in the choice for the most appropriate collaboration mode according to the problem to be faced, see

Gary P. Pisano and Roberto Verganti, "Which Kind of Collaboration Is Right for You? The new leaders in innovation will be those who figure out the best way to leverage a network of outsiders," *Harvard Business Review* 86, no. 12 (December 2008): 78–86.

9. Giulio Castelli, Paola Antonelli, and Francesca Picchi, *La Fabbrica del Design: Conversazioni con i Protagonisti del Design Italiano* [The Design Factory: Conversations with the Protagonists of Italian Design] (Milano: Skira Editore, 2007).

10. Politecnico di Milano started Italy's first graduate program of industrial design in 1995, and the first students entered the job market in 2000. Milan had had some design schools earlier, but not at the graduate level.

11. Tom Wolfe, *From Bauhaus to Our House* (New York: Farrar, Straus and Giroux, 1981).

12. Pallavi Gogoi, "Michael Graves: Beyond Kettles," *BusinessWeek*, August 18, 2005, http://www.businessweek.com/innovate/content/aug2005/id20050818_669685.htm.

13. Claudio Dell'Era and Roberto Verganti, "Strategies to Leverage on Creative Networks in Design-Intensive Industries."

14. Quoted in Alessio Marchesi, "Business Classics: Managing Innovation through Product Longevity" (PhD diss., Politecnico di Milano, 2005).

15. Studies on technological forecasting call these *vertical* technological transfers, to distinguish them from horizontal transfers between industries. See, for example, Eric Jantsch, *Technological Forecasting in Perspective* (Paris: Organisation for Economic Co-operation and Development, 1967).

16. "Memphis Remembered," *Designboom*, http://www.designboom.com/eng/funclub/memphisremember.html.

17. To further highlight the principle that debates about new meanings move along complex chains of interactions in the design discourse, often spanning several years, I should point out that Memphis was not the first and only collective exploring post-modernist languages. In Italy, groups such as Archizoom, Superstudio, and Alchimia in Milan, and the antidesign movement in Tuscany, conducted embryonic experiments. Artists such as Picasso, Mondrian, and Kandinsky also influenced Ettore Sottsass.

18. "Ettore Sottsass: Designer Who Helped to Make Office Equipment Fashionable and Challenged the Standard Notion of Tasteful Interiors," *Timesonline*, January 8, 2008, http://www.timesonline.co.uk/tol/comment/obituaries/article3118052.ece.

19. "Memphis Remembered."

20. Alessi's Family Follows Fiction project, illustrated in chapter 3, is an example of how Memphis's emotional and symbolic work influenced consumer products. Chapter 8 discusses another example: Alessi's Tea and Coffee Piazza.

21. "Memphis Remembered."

22. Italian entrepreneurs carefully nurture the design discourse. Examples abound in which they have sponsored talented designers when they were still unknown, enabling them to conduct research and explore new visions. Cesare Cassina, founder and chairman of leading furniture manufacturer Cassina, has long provided a monthly check to Gaetano Pesce. Olivetti has been the host of prominent designers such as Sottsass and De Lucchi. Marco Iansiti and Roy Levien investigated a similar phenomenon in high-tech industries, showing that effective corporations are those that understand and sustain the health of an industry ecosystem, in *The Keystone Advantage* (Boston: Harvard Business School Press, 2004).

23. This perspective can be traced to studies by Joseph A. Schumpeter; see Schumpeter, *Theory of Economic Development* (Cambridge, MA: Harvard University Press, 1934). For more recent developments, see Rebecca M. Henderson and Kim B. Clark, "Architectural Innovation: The Reconfiguration of Existing Product Technologies and the Failure of Established Firms," *Administrative Science Quarterly* 35 (1990): 9–30; and Bruce Kogut and Udo Zander, "Knowledge of the Firm, Combinative Capabilities and the Replication of Technology," *Organization Science* 3, no. 3 (1992): 383–397.

24. See Tom J. Allen, *Managing the Flow of Technology* (Cambridge, MA: MIT Press, 1977); Andrew Hargadon, *How Breakthroughs Happen: The Surprising Truth About How Companies Innovate* (Boston: Harvard Business School Press, 2003); Andrew Hargadon and Robert I. Sutton, "Building an Innovation Factory," *Harvard Business Review* (May–June 2000): 157–166; and Lee Fleming and Matt Marx, "Managing Creativity in Small Worlds," *California Management Review* 48, no. 4 (Summer 2006): 6–27.

25. Andrew Hargadon and Robert I. Sutton, "Technology Brokering and Innovation in a Product Development Firm," *Administrative Science Quarterly* 42, no. 4 (December 1997): 716–749. See also Paola Bertola and Carlos J. Texeira, "Design as a Knowledge Agent: How Design as a Knowledge Process Is Embedded into Organizations to Foster Innovation," *Design Studies* 24 (2003): 181–194.

26. Examples are many Kartell plastic furniture products (such as Mobil, designed in 1994 by Antonio Citterio), Alessi's Family Follows Fiction kitchenware of 1991, Flos's Miss Sissi lamp, designed in 1991 by Philippe Starck, and even electronic appliances such as Rowenta's irons.

27. Analysts of technological innovation have also investigated the distinction between brokers who provide knowledge and mediators who provide contacts with other interpreters. The former tend to keep unconnected worlds separate and exploit their profitable network position to generate innovation; see Roland S. Burt, "Structural Holes and Good Ideas," *American Journal of Sociology* 110 (2004): 349–399. The latter have a more socially constructive role, because they introduce disconnected individuals and facilitate coordination among them. See David Obstfeld, "Social Networks: The *Tertius Iungens* Orientation, and Involvement in Innovation," *Administrative Science Quarterly* 50 (2005): 100–130.

28. See, for example, Ikujiro Nonaka and Hirotaka Takeuchi, *The Knowledge-Creating Company: How Japanese Companies Create the Dynamics of Innovation* (New York: Oxford University Press, 1995). For more on the importance of tacit knowledge in innovation, see Eugene S. Ferguson, "The Mind's Eye: Nonverbal Thought in Technology," *Science* 197, no. 26 (1977): 827–836.

29. The book is an invaluable account of the Italian design discourse narrated directly by the protagonists (mainly entrepreneurs, but also designers) through more than fifty interviews. Unfortunately, at the moment it is available only in Italian. Castelli, Antonelli, and Picchi, *La Fabbrica del Design: Conversazioni con i Protagonisti del Design Italiano* [The Design Factory: Conversations with the Protagonists of Italian Design].

30. This section shows how firms can deal with the geography of the design discourse. However, the analysis also has significant implications for policy makers who want to nurture a more radical approach to design and innovation in their region. See appendix B for the implications of this analysis for design and innovation policies.

31. Richard Florida, *The Rise of the Creative Class: And How It's Transforming Work, Leisure, Community, and Everyday Life* (New York: Perseus Books Group, 2002). According to a joint study by the Progressive Policy Institute and Case Western Reserve University, an average of 2.33 utility patents per 1,000 Rochester workers were issued over the three years 1996–1998; the U.S. average is 0.40.

32. Verganti and Dell'Era, *I Distretti del Design: Modello e quadro comparato delle politiche di sviluppo* [The Design Districts: A Model and a Comparative Framework of Development Policies].

33. As chapter 6 notes, the itinerant Centro Studi Alessi organizes workshops at major design schools around the globe, sometimes asking participants for a subscription fee. Note that scholars have also investigated the dynamics of incentives in scientific jobs. These analysts have shown that scientists do pay to be scientists, if one considers the opportunity cost of lost income. Scott Stern, "Do Scientists Pay to Be Scientists?" *Management Science* 50, no. 6 (June 2004): 835–853.

34. For the importance of flexibility in radical innovation processes, see Alan MacCormack, Roberto Verganti, and Marco Iansiti, "Developing Products on 'Internet Time': The Anatomy of a Flexible Development Process," *Management Science* 47, no. 1 (January 2001): 133–150; and Alan MacCormack and Roberto Verganti, "Managing the Sources of Uncertainty: Matching Process and Context in Software Development," *Journal of Product Innovation Management* 20, no. 3 (May 2003): 217–232.

35. Robert D. Austin and Daniela Beyersdorfer, "Bang & Olufsen: Design-Driven Innovation," Case 9-607-016 (Boston: Harvard Business School Press, September 2007).

36. Roberto Pellizzoni, *Kartell SpA*, Report of the European Value Network Project IPS-2001-42062.

37. Quoted in Lawrence, "Herman Miller's Brian Walker on Design."

38. Austin and Beyersdorfer, "Bang & Olufsen: Design-Driven Innovation,"

39. Michael P. Farrell, *Collaborative Circles: Friendship Dynamics and Creative Work* (Chicago: University of Chicago Press, 2003). See also Charles Kadushin, "Networks and Circles in the Production of Culture," *American Behavioural Science* 19 (1976): 769–785.

40. Claudio Dell'Era and Roberto Verganti, "Strategies of Innovation and Imitation of Product Languages," *Journal of Product Innovation Management* 24 (2007): 580–599.

41. Kadushin emphasizes that circles, with their particular and sometimes "unfair" nature, may be a source of both innovation (especially in their early stages) and blockage (in their mature stages). See Charles Kadushin, "Social Circles and the Organization Environment" (paper presented at the 20th Sunbelt Social Network Conference, Vancouver, April 13–17, 2000). This observation mirrors findings in the investigation of the invisible college in science, where cohesive clusters of researchers tend, once established, to remain insulated from new information and to be less prone to radical changes. See Fleming and Marx, "Managing Creativity in Small Worlds."

42. Farrell, *Collaborative Circles: Friendship Dynamics and Creative Work*.

43. This last instance is more unusual. Even though designers are not bound by exclusivity agreements with Italian manufacturers, they almost never cooperate with direct competitors. Reputation—a powerful force within creative circles and communities—prevents this opportunistic behavior. Yet especially when the circle

gets closer to its descending slope, the temptation to exploit fame and position pushes members to work for competitors. This potential threat is therefore another major incentive for innovative firms to keep searching for new interpreters.

44. Austin and Beyersdorfer, "Bang & Olufsen: Design-Driven Innovation,"

45. Antonio Capaldo provides a more detailed analysis of this dual network structure and its dynamics in Italian furniture in "Network Structure and Innovation: The Leveraging of a Dual Network as a Distinctive Relational Capability," *Strategic Management Journal* 28 (2007): 585–608.

Chapter 8

1. Pallavi Gogoi, "Michael Graves: Beyond Kettles," *BusinessWeek*, August 18, 2005.

2. For an account of the Tea and Coffee Piazza project, see also Roberto Verganti, "Innovating Through Design," *Harvard Business Review* 84, no. 12 (December 2006): 114–122.

3. Indeed, studies of scientific and technological research show that teamwork is not always the most effective approach, especially when it comes to radical innovation. Lee Fleming, in particular, has explored the role of lone inventors in creating breakthroughs. See Lee Fleming, "Lone Inventors as the Source of Technological Breakthroughs: Myth or Reality?" working paper, Harvard Business School, Boston, October 2006.

4. The design discourse about food is intense in Parma, where Barilla's headquarters are located, and indeed throughout Italy. Parma has a long tradition in the industry, not only in pasta but also in cold cuts (think of prosciutto di Parma) and dairy products (think of the world-renowned "Parmesan"). Parma is also the headquarters of the European Food Safety Authority.

5. For more on the characteristics of this process, which is much more structured and articulated than shown here, see Francois Jegou, Roberto Verganti, Alessio Marchesi, Giuliano Simonelli, and Claudio Dell'Era, *Design Driven Toolbox: A Handbook to Support Companies in Radical Product Innovation* (Brussels: EU Research Project EVAN European Value Network, IPS-2001-42062, 2006).

6. In other words, the Bang & Olufsen process sequences the three main product requirements that Kano identifies in his model of innovation: attractive, monodimensional, and must-be. See Noriaki Kano, "Attractive Quality and Must-Be Quality," *Journal of the Japanese Society for Quality Control* (April 1984): 39–48.

7. See, for example, Kim B. Clark and Takahiro Fujimoto, *Product Development Performance* (Cambridge, MA: Harvard Business School Press, 1991); Mitzi M. Montoya-Wiess and Roger Calantone, "Determinants of New Product Performance: A Review and Meta-Analysis," *Journal of Product Innovation Management* 11 (1994): 397–417; Shona L. Brown and Kathleen M. Eisenhardt, "Product Development: Past Research, Present Findings, and Future Directions," *Academy of Management Review* 20, no. 2 (1995): 343–378; and Karl Ulrich and Steven Eppinger, *Product Design and Development*, 4th ed. (New York: McGraw-Hill, 2008).

8. Jeanne M. Liedtka and Henry Mintzberg, "Time for Design," *Design Management Review* 17, no. 2 (Spring 2006): 10–18.

Chapter 9

1. Sociologists have thoroughly reported on how social negotiation of meanings has affected the diffusion of major technological innovations. This negotiation occurs among not only users but also institutions, firms, and engineers—some of whom have a more powerful influence (called *semiotic power*) on the final interpretation than others. See Bruno Latour, *Science in Action: How to Follow Scientists and Engineers Through Society* (Cambridge, MA: Harvard University Press, 1987); and Wiebe E. Bijker and John Law, eds., *Shaping Technology/Building Society: Studies in Sociotechnical Change* (Cambridge, MA: MIT Press, 1994).

2. Stefano Marzano, "People as a Source of Breakthrough Innovation," *Design Management Review* 16, no. 2 (Spring 2005): 23–29.

3. For more on strategies for profiting from innovation, see David J. Teece, "Profiting from Technological Innovation," *Research Policy* 15, no. 6 (1986): 285–305; and Gary G. Pisano and David J. Teece, "How to Capture Value from Innovation: Shaping Intellectual Property and Industry Architecture," *California Management Review* 50, no. 1 (Fall 2007): 278–296.

4. Claudio Dell'Era and Roberto Verganti, "Strategies of Innovation and Imitation of Product Languages," *Journal of Product Innovation Management* 24 (2007): 580–599; and Claudio Dell'Era and Roberto Verganti, "Diffusion of Product Signs in Industrial Networks: The Advantage of the Trend Setter" (paper presented at the 14th EIASM International Product Development Management Conference, Porto, Portugal, June 10–12, 2007, 311–324. A compendium of these studies is provided in Julia Hanna, "Radical Design, Radical Results," interview with Roberto Verganti, in *Working Knowledge for Leaders*, Harvard Business School, February 19, 2008, http://hbswk.hbs.edu/item/5850.html.

Chapter 10

1. Artemide is a unique case. Although the company does not have a design unit, President Ernesto Gismondi and his wife, Carlotta de Bevilacqua, who sits on the board, sometimes design the firm's products.

2. Giulio Castelli, Paola Antonelli, and Francesca Picchi, *La Fabbrica del Design: Conversazioni con i Protagonisti del Design Italiano* [The Design Factory: Conversations with the Protagonists of Italian Design] (Milano: Skira Editore, 2007).

3. Building relational assets poses a second major challenge when disruptive changes in the strategic environment, such as breakthrough shifts in technologies or sociocultural models, make the current network obsolete. In fact, the need to build relational assets invites companies to make small additional investments in interpreters they already know. However, they risk remaining locked on an evolutionary path and being unable to radically redesign their network of relationships when a new environment calls for a novel set of interpreters. Chapters 5 and 7 address this challenge. For further insights on the development and renewal of dynamic capabilities for addressing rapidly changing environments, see David J. Teece, Gary Pisano, and Amy Shuen, "Dynamic Capabilities and Strategic Management," *Strategic Management Journal* 18, no. 7 (1997): 509–533.

4. Politecnico di Milano has more than one thousand adjunct professors, most of whom are professional engineers, managers, and designers. Lecturers at Politecnico include the founders of design firms such as Giorgietto Giugiaro and Sergio Pininfarina, executives such as Alberto Alessi, Luca Cordero di Montezemolo, and Giorgio Armani, artists such as Arnaldo Pomodoro, and journalists such as Federica Olivares, who publishes catalogs for exhibitions at the Museum of Modern Art in New York.

Chapter 11

1. Fadell eventually became senior vice president of the iPod division. Leander Kahney, "Straight Dope on the iPod's Birth," *Wired*, October 17, 2006, http://www.wired.com/gadgets/mac/commentary/cultofmac/2006/10/71956?currentPage=all.

2. Ibid.

3. Leander Kahney, "Inside Look at Birth of the iPod," *Wired*, July 21, 2004, http://www.wired.com/gadgets/mac/news/2004/07/64286?currentPage=all.

4. Giulio Castelli, Paola Antonelli, and Francesca Picchi, *La Fabbrica del Design: Conversazioni con i Protagonisti del Design Italiano* [The Design Factory: Conversations with the Protagonists of Italian Design] (Milano: Skira Editore, 2007).

5. For further insights into the role of art dealers in creative industries, see Charles Kadushin, "Networks and Circles in the Production of Culture," *American Behavioral Science* 19 (1976): 769–785; and David Hesmondhalgh, *The Cultural Industries* (London: Sage, 2002).

6. Castelli, Antonelli, and Picchi, *La Fabbrica del Design: Conversazioni con i Protagonisti del Design Italiano.*

7. Note that the structure of many Italian firms—which are often family businesses—creates a favorable environment for developing relational assets. When the top executive is also the owner of the company, she retains leadership of innovation for long time spans, often decades, something that guarantees that investments in personal relationships are cumulative and makes immersion easier. Family businesses can also transfer relational assets across generations more easily. In this regard, Claudio Molteni, chairman of furniture manufacturer Molteni, says, "I was lucky. When I was a child I hung around with the great architects with my father."

8. Peter Lawrence, "Herman Miller's Brian Walker on Design," *@issue* 12, no. 1 (Winter 2007): 2–7.

9. Castelli, Antonelli, and Picchi, *La Fabbrica del Design: Conversazioni con i Protagonisti del Design Italiano.*

[Index]

[About the Author]

ROBERTO VERGANTI is Professor of Management of Innovation at Politecnico di Milano, where he teaches in the School of Management and the School of Design, and where he directs MaDe In Lab, the laboratory for executive education on the management of design and innovation. He is also a Visiting Professor of Design Management at the Copenhagen Business School and serves on the editorial board of the *Journal of Product Innovation Management* and on the advisory board of the Design Management Institute.

Through more than twenty years of research, Professor Verganti has investigated the challenges and processes of innovation in more than a hundred companies, ranging from dominant players such as Microsoft and Vodafone to small and dynamic firms such as Alessi and Nintendo. His studies, which lie at the intersection of strategy, design, and technology management, have appeared in a number of scholarly and applied journals, including *Management Science* and the *Harvard Business Review*. They have shed new light on how executives can envision breakthrough strategies, collaborate with external innovators, deploy flexible development processes, and foster creativity and learning in their teams. His research on management of design in Italy has been awarded the Compasso d'Oro (the most prestigious design award in Italy).

Professor Verganti is founder and chairman of PROject Science (www.pro-jectscience.com), a consulting institute dedicated to helping companies achieve strategic innovation. He has served as an advisor to senior managers at a wide variety of *Fortune* 500 firms and has helped national and regional governments around the world to conceive design and innovation policies. He can be reached at roberto. verganti@polimi.it.